Slí na Fírinne

The Traditional Catholic Proofs of God's Existence

Corstown – MMXI

Paperback ISBN: 978-0-9556812-8-8
© Brian Nugent, Corstown, Oldcastle, Co. Meath, 2011.

CONTENTS

PREFACE..4

CHAPTER 1
Historical Accuracy and Authenticity of the Bible.....................5

CHAPTER 2
The Five Proofs, or 'ways', of St Thomas Aquinas...................18
    Proof from Motion..18
    Proof from Causation...22
    Proof from the Necessary Being...25
    Proof from Degrees of Perfection...28
    Proof from Final Causes,..36
    Analysis of the Proofs..48
    Promissory Materialism...51

CHAPTER 3
Evidence of the Supernatural in general....................................64

CHAPTER 4
Importance of Christianity to a Nation......................................89

Footnotes...93

APPENDIX A
Frequently Asked Questions..101

APPENDIX B
The Proofs by Philosophers and Scientists through history.......158
    Greek Language Philosophers...159
    Latin Language Philosophers..188
    17th Century...201
    18th Century...236
    19th Century...260
    20th Century...278

PREFACE

This book attempts to explain in modern terms the traditional proofs of God's existence, as outlined by St Thomas Aquinas and others through history.

It seems to this observer quite extraordinary the degree to which this question has exploded onto the Irish scence, in a country where, over so many millenia, the existence of God was hardly ever questioned. No doubt thesists and atheists go around in circles in these arguments, the substance of which have been debated for millenia, as can be seen in the Appendix B to this book. Nonetheless they are interesting debates which bring in passionately so many fields like history, physics, genetics, and even psychology, if you believe that explains the reports of supernatural activity.

It strikes this observer though that many modern commentators are very naive in thinking that somehow Christianity or religion in general will die out in the near future, never to be heard from again! That prospect has faced the citizens of many countries, such as Ireland when its Catholic religious leaders were all either killed or exiled in the mid 17th century to Russia where the same thing could be said of Christianity in the 20th century. But of course those religions came back, maybe because quite simply there is a God and you cannot expect a civilization to long prosper without acknowledging him? That at any rate was the verdict of Plutarch in the first century AD and nobody has proved him wrong since.

Slí na Fírinne means "the path of truth", a path that the Irish always felt you had to travel after death.

I would like to thank the many people that have contributed to the numerous discussions of this topic on Irish internet fora in recent times, for helping to clarify the author's arguments, and I would particularly like to thank all on politics.ie who contributed comments for a related thread on this topic. Many thanks also to my parents and extended family.

Brian Nugent, Co. Meath, 17th Sept 2011.

CHAPTER 1
Historical Accuracy and Authenticity of the Bible

Maybe one simple enough way of approaching this is to say that the Bible tells us the story of God and his relationship to us and the world. So if we can, as scientifically as possible, show that the Bible is an authentic, genuinely old, and, as far as can be shown, truthful document then it will bolster the idea that there is a God.

An example of this is that many Biblical references have been corroborated by archaeological evidence in the Holy Land.[1] One interesting example of this kind of archaeology corroborating the Bible is the Moabite stone, or the Mesha Stele, now in the Louvre in Paris but originally found in Dhiban in Jordan in 1868. It is dated to c.840 BC with an inscription on it that inter alia describes a war between the Moabites and the Israelites, a war that is also mentioned in the Bible at 2 Kings 3. Here is part of the inscription on the stone, with some of the biblical references that correspond to it in brackets:

> "I am Mesha, son of Kemosh[-yat], the king of Moab, ["Now Mesa, king of Moab," (2 Kings 3:4)] the Dibonite. My father was king of Moab thirty years, and I reigned after my father. And I built this high-place for Kemosh ["and Chamos, the god of Moab" (1 Kings 11:33), "Woe to thee Moab: thou art undone, O people of Chamos." (Numbers 21:30)] in QRH ("the citadel"), a high place of [sal]vation because he saved me from all the kings [or "all the attackers"], and because let me be victorious over all my adversaries. Omri was king of Israel ["all Israel made Amri their king" (1 Kings 16:16)] and he oppressed Moab for many days because Kemosh was angry with his land.
>
> ...
>
> So I [re]built Baal Meon ["And Nabo, and Baalmeon (their names being changed)" (Numbers 32:38), "Dibon also, and Bamothbaal, and the

town of Baalmaon," (Joshua 13:17)], and I the water reservoir in it. And I bu[ilt] Qiryaten. The man of Gad had dwelt in Ataroth from of old; and the king of Israel built Ataroth for him. ["And the sons of Gad built Dibon, and Ataroth, and Aroer," (Numbers 32:34)]

...

And Kemosh said to me, "Go! Seize Nebo ["unto mount Nebo, which is in the land of Moab over against Jericho" (Deuteronomy 32:49)] against Israel." So I proceeded by night and fought with it from the crack of dawn to midday, and I took it and I slew all of them: seven thousand men and boys, and women and gi- and maidens because I had dedicated it to Ashtar Kemosh I took [the ves]sels of Yahweh [obviously this is the Jewish word for God mentioned in the Bible], and I dragged them before Kemosh.

...

I built Aroer, and I made the highway in the Arnon. ["From Aroer, which is situate upon the bank of the torrent Arnon, unto mount Sion, which is also called Hermon," (Deuteronomy 4:48)]

...

and Horonain, in it dwelt the house of [D]VD [many modern scholars now state that this reads 'House of David', which obviously again corroborates the Bible.]" [2]

This is truly an amazing amount of corroboration of events and places in the Bible of some 2,850 years ago.

Very old fragments and whole parts of the Gospels exist, and these fragments show that the copies that come down to us are authentic good quality copies of what was written down at the time of the Evangelists. So for example we have a small portion of the Gospel of St John dated to about 125 AD – known as P52 –, not long at all after he would have written it, and we have a full copy of the Book of Isaiah from c.100 BC – among the Dead Sea Scrolls –, again a tremendous age for any document. Indeed the degree of similarity between the Dead Sea Scroll text of Isaiah and the previously known texts can almost be described as miraculous, as described by the Bible scholar Gleason Archer:

> "Even though the two copies of Isaiah discovered in Qumran Cave 1 near the Dead Sea in 1947 were a thousand years earlier than the oldest dated manuscript previously known (A.D. 980), they proved to be word for word identical with our standard Hebrew Bible in more than 95 percent of the text. The 5 percent of variation consisted chiefly of obvious slips on the pen and variations in spelling...They do not affect the message of revelation in the slightest." [3]

So our Bible can be, and has been, corroborated with exceptionally old copies of it and found to be authentically and not corruptly copied from an incredibly ancient date. Hence people like Sir Frederic G. Kenyon, former director and principal librarian of the British Museum, have concluded, in this case with respect to the New Testament:

> "The interval, then, between the dates of original composition and the earliest extant evidence becomes so small as to be in fact negligible, and the last foundation for any doubt that the Scriptures have come down to us substantially as they were written has now been removed. Both the authenticity and the general integrity of the books of the New Testament may be regarded as finally established." [4]

Then there are original, contemporary or nearly contemporary, accounts, from Roman and other writers, that partly corroborate the Bible story. Since these are quite interesting it might help to quote a few here.

Firstly we have the Jewish writer Philo (c.20BC-40AD) of Alexandria, who in writing about his Embassy to Gaius in c.39/40 AD relates this anecdote about Pilate, which captures a little bit of the tense atmosphere between Pilate and the Jews around the time of the crucifixion:

> "Pilate was one of the emperor's lieutenants,

having been appointed governor of Judaea. He, not more with the object of doing honor to Tiberius than with that of vexing the multitude, dedicated some gilt shields in the palace of Herod, in the holy city; which had no form nor any other forbidden thing represented on them except some necessary inscription, which mentioned these two facts, the name of the person who had placed them there, and the person in whose honor they were so placed there.

But when the multitude heard what had been done, and when the circumstance became notorious, then the people, putting forward the four sons of the king, who were in no respect inferior to the kings themselves, in fortune or in rank, and his other descendants, and those magistrates who were among them at the time, entreated him to alter and to rectify the innovation which he had committed in respect of the shields; and not to make any alteration in their national customs, which had hitherto been preserved without any interruption, without being in the least degree changed by any king of emperor.

But when he steadfastly refused this petition (for he was a man of a very inflexible disposition, and very merciless as well as very obstinate), they cried out: 'Do not cause a sedition; do not make war upon us; do not destroy the peace which exists. The honour of the emperor is not identical with dishonour to the ancient laws; let it not be to you a pretence for heaping insult on our nation. Tiberius is not desirous that any of our laws or customs shall be destroyed. And if you yourself say that he is, show us either some command from him, or some letter, or something of the kind, that we, who have been sent to you as ambassadors, may cease to trouble you, and may address our supplications to your master.'

But this last sentence exasperated him in the greatest possible degree, as he feared least they might in reality go on an embassy to the emperor, and might impeach him with respect to other particulars of his government, in respect of his corruption, and his acts of insolence, and his rapine, and his habit of insulting people, and his cruelty, and his continual murders of people untried and uncondemned, and his never ending, and gratuitous, and most grievous inhumanity.

Therefore, being exceedingly angry, and being at all times a man of most ferocious passions, he was in great perplexity, neither venturing to take down what he had once set up, nor wishing to do any thing which could be acceptable to his subjects, and at the same time being sufficiently acquainted with the firmness of Tiberius on these points. And those who were in power in our nation, seeing this, and perceiving that he was inclined to change his mind as to what he had done, but that he was not willing to be thought to do so, wrote a most supplicatory letter to Tiberius.

And he, when he had read it, what did he say of Pilate, and what threats did he utter against him! But it is beside our purpose at present to relate to you how very angry he was, although he was not very liable to sudden anger; since the facts speak for themselves; for immediately, without putting any thing off till the next day, he wrote a letter, reproaching and reviling him in the most bitter manner for his act of unprecedented audacity and wickedness, and commanding him immediately to take down the shields and to convey them away from the metropolis of Judaea to Caesarea, on the sea which had been named Caesarea Augusta, after his grandfather, in order that they might be set up in the temple of Augustus. And accordingly, they were set up in that edifice. And in this way he

> provided for two matters: both for the honour due to the emperor, and for the preservation of the ancient customs of the city." [5]

So while this non-Christian source does not mention Our Lord or the Apostles directly, nonetheless it clearly does corroborate for us the general atmosphere between the Jews and Pilate that the Bible claims existed in Jerusalem at that time.

Meanwhile another ancient Jewish writer, Flavius Josephus (37 - 100 AD), an advisor to successive Roman Emperors, some of whose writings come to us from Arabic and some from Greek, does indeed corroborate the basic facts of the New Testament:

> "At this time there was a wise man who was called Jesus. And his conduct was good, and he was known to be virtuous. And many people from among the Jews and other nations became his disciples. Pilate condemned him to be crucified and to die. And those who had become his disciples did not abandon his discipleship. They reported that he had appeared to them three days after his crucifixion and that he was alive; accordingly, he was perhaps the Messiah concerning whom the prophets have recounted wonders.
>
> ...
>
> After the death of the procurator Festus, when Albinus was about to succeed him, the high-priest Ananius considered it a favorable opportunity to assemble the Sanhedrin. He therefore caused James the brother of Jesus, who was called Christ, and several others, to appear before this hastily assembled council, and pronounced upon them the sentence of death by stoning. All the wise men and strict observers of the law who were at Jerusalem expressed their disapprobation of this act...Some even went to Albinus himself, who had departed to Alexandria, to bring this breach of the law under his observation, and to inform him that Ananius had acted illegally in assembling the Sanhedrin

without the Roman authority.

...

Now some of the Jews thought that the destruction of Herod's army came from God, and that very justly, as a punishment of what he did against John, that was called the Baptist: for Herod slew him, who was a good man, and commanded the Jews to exercise virtue, both as to righteousness towards one another, and piety towards God, and so to come to baptism; for that the washing [with water] would be acceptable to him, if they made use of it, not in order to the putting away [or the remission] of some sins [only], but for the purification of the body; supposing still that the soul was thoroughly purified beforehand by righteousness." [6]

Turning now to Roman sources, Suetonius, an important Roman historian who lived from 69-75 to c.130 AD wrote this reference to the riot of Rome of c.49 AD during the reign of Emperor Claudius 41-54 AD: "As the Jews were making constant disturbances at the instigation of Chrestus, he expelled them from Rome," and referring to the great fire in Rome in 64 AD he wrote: "Punishment by Nero was inflicted on the Christians, a class of men given to a new and mischievous superstition." [7]

Here we have a reference by another major influential Roman historian, Cornelius Tacitus (c.55-120 AD), describing the year 64 AD:

"Consequently, to get rid of the report, Nero fastened the guilt and inflicted the most exquisite tortures on a class hated for their abominations, called Christians by the populace. Christus, from whom the name had its origin, suffered the extreme penalty during the reign of Tiberius at the hands of one of our procurators, Pontius Pilatus, and a most mischievous superstition, thus checked for the moment, again broke out not only in Judaea, the first source of the evil, but even in

Rome, where all things hideous and shameful from every part of the world find their centre and become popular." [8]

These two Roman historians, Tacitus and Suetonius, are among the really great historians of Rome whose writings are usually held as a gold standard with respect to whether or not various events really happened. This it seems is partly because of their diligent and honest research and writing and partly because they seemed to have access to a good quantity of written government records existing at that time in Rome. With respect to Suetonius it is accepted by all that he was 'director of Imperial archives' [9] and he explicitly mentions reading letters from the early Emperors.[10] Also Tacitus mentions a few times archives like this, for example: "There was in the Senate one Junius Rusticus, who having been appointed by the emperor to register its debates was therefore supposed to have an insight into his secret purposes," [11] and "I find in the registers of the Senate that Cerialis Anicius, consul-elect, proposed a motion that a temple should as soon as possible be built at the public expense to the Divine Nero." [12] That these archives must have been extensive we can see from the fact that the Romans normally did preserve copies of important documents, as Suetonius himself relates:

"Vespasian undertook to restore the 3,000 bronze tablets which were destroyed with the [Capitoline] temple, making a thorough search for copies: priceless and most ancient records of the empire, containing the decrees of the Senate and the acts of the commons almost from the foundation of the city, regarding alliances, treaties, and special privileges granted to individuals." [13]

Bearing in mind then the correct dates these two historians usually have for events many years before their time, and the high political position and prestige both of those held in Rome, Tacitus was a Senator and Consul and Suetonius was the Emperor Hadrian's secretary and also (too!) close to the Empress, and their many years diligent research into historical matters, leads us to safely assume that they consulted the very many written records that existed in the Imperial archives in Rome at that time.

Which brings us to the next point, did they consult written Roman records from or to Pilate which helped them in writing the historical references listed above? I would say that it is very likely they did, especially when you consider what Philo said about an incident when the Jews wrote to the Emperor in a way that got Pilate into trouble. The chances are then, of course, that Pilate would make sure to get in his version of events this time with an early letter to the Emperor. The interesting thing is that there exists three ancient references to a written document from Pilate on these biblical events – and this is exclusive of an old forged letter supposed to be from him – that existed in the Roman archives at the time that Tacitus and Suetonius were writing their histories.[14] Naturally any idea that these two historians were relying on authentic contemporary written records increases not a little their credibility, and hence the credibility of their references to Our Lord.

In any case here is another example of the early Christians being mentioned by Roman writers, in this case not by an historian as such but by Pliny the Younger (c.62-c.113 AD) who was a lawyer and administrator with a flair for poetry and letter writing, including this one which he wrote in 112 or 113 AD to the Emperor Trajan:

> "It is a rule, Sir, which I inviolably observe, to refer myself to you in all my doubts; for who is more capable of guiding my uncertainty or informing my ignorance? Having never been present at any trials of the Christians, I am unacquainted with the method and limits to be observed either in examining or punishing them. Whether any difference is to be allowed between the youngest and the adult; whether repentance admits to a pardon, or if a man has been once a Christian it avails him nothing to recant; whether the mere profession of Christianity, albeit without crimes, or only the crimes associated therewith are punishable -- in all these points I am greatly doubtful.
>
> In the meanwhile, the method I have observed

towards those who have denounced to me as Christians is this: I interrogated them whether they were Christians; if they confessed it I repeated the question twice again, adding the threat of capital punishment; if they still persevered, I ordered them to be executed. For whatever the nature of their creed might be, I could at least feel not doubt that contumacy and inflexible obstinacy deserved chastisement. There were others also possessed with the same infatuation, but being citizens of Rome, I directed them to be carried thither.

These accusations spread (as is usually the case) from the mere fact of the matter being investigated and several forms of the mischief came to light. A placard was put up, without any signature, accusing a large number of persons by name. Those who denied they were, or had ever been, Christians, who repeated after me an invocation to the gods, and offered adoration, with wine and frankincense, to your image, which I had ordered to be brought for that purpose, together with those of the gods, and who finally cursed Christ – none of which acts, it is into performing – these I thought it proper to discharge. Others who were named by that informer at first confessed themselves Christians, and then denied it; true, they had been of that persuasion but they had quitted it, some three years, others many years, and a few as much as twenty-five years ago. They all worshipped your statue and the images of the gods, and cursed Christ.

They affirmed, however, the whole of their guilt, or their error, was, that they were in the habit of meeting on a certain fixed day before it was light, when they sang in alternate verses a hymn to Christ, as to a god, and bound themselves by a solemn oath, not to any wicked deeds, but never to commit any fraud, theft, or adultery, never to falsify their word, nor deny a trust when they should be called upon to deliver it up; after which it was their custom to separate, and then reassemble to partake of food – but food of an ordinary and innocent kind. Even this practice, however, they had abandoned after the publication of my edict, by which, according to your orders, I had forbidden political associations. I judged it so much the more necessary to extract the real truth, with the assistance of torture, from two female slaves, who were styled deaconesses: but I could discover nothing more than depraved and excessive superstition.

I therefore adjourned the proceedings, and betook myself at once to your counsel. For the matter seemed to me well worth referring to you, especially considering the numbers endangered. Persons of all ranks and ages, and of both sexes are, and will be, involved in the prosecution. For this contagious superstition is not confined to the cities only, but has spread through the villages and rural districts; it seems possible, however, to check and cure it." [15]

So the basic facts of the Bible can be quite well corroborated by a number of sources, as one writer who has examined this concluded:

"In addition to the nine New Testament authors who wrote about Jesus in separate accounts, I found at least twenty additional early Christian authors, four heretical writings, and seven non-Christian sources that make explicit mention of Jesus in their writings within 150 years of his life. This amounts to a minimum of 40 authors, all of whom explicitly mention Jesus and the expansion of a spiritual movement in his name. More authors mention Jesus Christ within 150 years of his life than mention the Roman Emperor who reigned during His lifetime. Scholars are only aware of ten sources that mention Emperor Tiberius within 150 years of his life, including Luke, Tacitus, Suetonius, and Paterculus. Thus, within this short time frame, the number of ancient writers who mention Jesus outnumber those who mention the leader of the entire Roman Empire (effectively, the ancient world of the time) by a ratio of 4:1!" [16]

It seems to this observer then that you have to take the Bible seriously, it isn't really very scientific to dismiss it as just a 'third hand fairytale' as some try to describe it. Consider for example this passage from the First Letter to the Corinthians (15:3-8):

"For I delivered unto you first of all, which I also received: how that Christ died for our sins, according to the scriptures: And that he was buried: and that he rose again according to the scriptures: And that he was seen by Cephas, and after that by the eleven. Then was he seen by more than five hundred brethren at once: of whom many remain until this present, and some are fallen asleep. After that, he was seen by James: then by all the apostles. And last of all, he was seen also by me."

We know who wrote this letter, St Paul, where it was written, in Ephesus on the western coast of Turkey, in what language, Greek, who it was written to, the Corinthians, the inhabitants of the well known city of Corinth obviously, and we know the date it was written at least to within a narrow 4 or 5 year period, between 53 and 57 AD. And as you can also see it is a clear explicit statement of facts about the Resurrection written by, as you have just read, an eye witness to it. Hence we have here in the Bible a first hand eye witness account of the Resurrection from a text dated approximately 20 years after the event described.

From which we can conclude that the Bible should be taken seriously as an authentic, important document outlining facts, which in not a few respects, have been verified as true from other sources. Hence if we are to take the Bible seriously like this then it should be considered as a proof of the existence of God, who is obviously described at length in it.

CHAPTER 2
The Five Proofs, or 'ways', of St Thomas Aquinas

Between 1265 and 1274 an Italian Dominican friar by the name of St Thomas Aquinas wrote his great work on Christian theology called the 'Summa Theologica' and he began the work by explaining how the existence of God can be proven through human reason. He then listed five 'ways' by which this could be done, and these are the basic methods that you see numbered I-V below. Because of the great standing of that book in the pantheon of Christian theology – to be frank its really only exceeded by the Bible as a source of theology – these five 'way's then became the standard 'proofs' used in Christian theology to prove the existence of God. They are surprisingly relevant to the present day and even where later more modern proofs have been developed – such as the fine tuned universe argument and the proof from conscience – they are really just adaptations of these basic categories drawn up by Aquinas: [17]

I. Proof from Motion (sometimes called 'change'), or the Kinetological Argument

The ancient Greeks actually thought that everything had, at least in some sense, motion or energy. How they knew that about such obvious non-candidates as a lump of rock is a mystery to this observer, but they did, and, furthermore, they were right! Clearly everything that exists has molecules with atoms who in turn have electrons spinning around inside etc, in short everything has motion and a type of energy. And everything seems to be the result of motion or energy. If you like you could take anything in front of you and try to put it into a long sequence of moved and movers, or things that accepted and then imparted energy. So you have an iron lamp in from of you, for example, and we can say that it is there as a result of the energy or motion you imparted in bringing it to that spot at some point. It is also the result of motion and energy that were imparted to it in the foundry and in the foundry it was made from an iron bar which in turn was worked on .i.e. had energy and motion imparted to it etc etc.

If you take an interest in physics you will realise that this exercise is simply using the 'law of conservation of energy,' i.e. the idea that the energy cannot be created out of nothing, energy derives from some source which gets it from some other source etc. So in this proof that is all you are doing, you move up along the sequence of something that was hit by the energy or motion of something else, and that something else got its energy or motion from something else etc etc.

Lets imagine that sequence and think about it for a while. Is it the case that this is a circular type of motion or energy chain? Or are you moving backwards in time to a discreet point, to some original source of this energy or motion? Could there be at some point back in time an original 'first mover', from which we get all this motion and energy originally, or is it, as I say, a circular type of motion? Well to answer this question it might help to go back to the original source of this proof.

St Thomas Aquinas when he drew up these proofs was influenced by the works of some of the great thinkers in philosophy and science, one of which was Aristotle, a famous Greek philosopher, who, in fact, could justifiably be called the greatest philosopher in history. Furthermore this idea of a first mover was indeed Aristotle's, and it might be helpful to read at this point what Aristotle says about it:

> "Motion, then, being eternal, the first movent [i.e. the thing that moves], if there is but one, will be eternal also: if there are more than one, there will be a plurality of such eternal movents. We ought, however, to suppose that there is one rather than many, and a finite rather than an infinite number. When the consequences of either assumption are the same, we should always assume that things are finite rather than infinite in number, since in things constituted by nature that which is finite and that which is better ought, if possible, to be present rather than the reverse: and here it is sufficient to assume only one movent, the

first of unmoved things, which being eternal will be the principle of motion to everything else.

The following argument also makes it evident that the first movent must be something that is one and eternal. We have shown that there must always be motion. That being so, motion must also be continuous, because what is always is continuous, whereas what is merely in succession is not continuous. But further, if motion is continuous, it is one: and it is one only if the movent and the moved that constitute it are each of them one, since in the event of a thing's being moved now by one thing and now by another the whole motion will not be continuous but successive." [18]

Aristotle in fact stated that there are a number of reasons why we say that there has to be an original discreet 'first mover,' and not that that the sequence of moved and movers can go on ad infinitum i.e. in a kind of circle of continuous motion, like some kind of perpetual movement machine.

a) The first point he makes is that if you had some kind of machine like that then the type of motion would have to be 'continuous' as opposed to 'consecutive' (and I am simplifying his categories here). Imagine if you had a machine like that, a continuous motion machine, that would maybe look like the cogs and dials of a watch which goes on nearly forever. You see such a machine has a particular type of motion, it is all the one motion, if you like, and it is continuing over a finite space of time. Think about it for a minute, in that machine the cog wheel hits each gear which in turn hits something else which, in a very exact way, returns the motion to the beginning and starts the sequence again.

But what Aristotle reasoned was that the motion that you actually see in the universe today is 'consecutive motion.' He gave the example of a torch relay – which we see now in the Olympics, copying the ancient Greeks – to explain this idea of 'consecutive motion.' Another modern example could be the player hitting the balls on a billiard table, he hits one ball which hits another etc. But notice what happens to the motion in this latter example. The motion starts powerful in the beginning with the striking of the first ball and then it kind of 'dribbles out' after hitting all the other balls, that's what we mean by 'consecutive' as opposed to the earlier 'continuous' type.

Now look around you as you examine the mover sequence in the universe. Say you are walking through a field and you look at a rock, of igneous type we will say. So you use the rock in this sequence of movers: we know that the rock is there because it was moved, it got its motion and energy from, a volcanic eruption, and the volcano got its motion from various chemical reactions etc deep under the crust of the earth. But look what happened to this motion when it threw up this rock, doesn't it look like a kind of scattered 'dribbling out' type of motion, like the billiard balls? You see the rock is just thrown onto the ground beside you and then does nothing with its motion, the same as the billiard balls coming to rest. If it was some type of continuous motion machine, like the cogs of a watch, then we would expect the rock to rest on some kind of lever which would be attached to some gear which would return the motion, so to speak, to the volcano so that it could start this motion over again. But it just isn't like that, the motion in the universe is not of that type. It seems rather to be a type of motion that points to a discreet beginning, like an inverted tree structure with some original motion that is dissipating itself around us.

b) The second point he makes is that even if you constructed a perfect circular motion machine, or if the sequence of moved and movers went on literally to infinity, you still need an original source of motion. Imagine if you did make that machine, the perpetual motion machine, the problem would be that you would need to start it somehow! It would just sit there until someone actually began motion to begin it, you still need a first mover. And as regards a huge infinite series of moved and movers you face the same problem, at some point you need to actually 'create motion'. No matter how long the sequence is it needs to have a beginning where somebody actually starts the motion off, the long sequence of moved and movers would be just like the billiard balls hitting into one another, that only happens because the player started the sequence off by giving motion via his arm.

So Aristotle concluded that the universe needed some original outside source of motion or energy, this sequence of moved and movers couldn't continue ad infinitum. Hence he said there must be an original being out there from whom we get this 'first movement' in the sequence of motion or energy that you see around you in the universe. He thought there must be something out there, some 'X' being that started all this motion and energy. Aristotle, although obviously not a Christian, in fact came to the explicit conclusion that this original source of movement must be God.

Notice too that we are referring here, as we are to the 'beings' thrown up by the two subsequent proofs, to some entity that exists before the universe existed. If you like then, this X is out there when nothing else is out there, naturally enough because we are talking about something that starts the whole energy or motion sequence of the universe in the first place. Consequently it isn't limited in the area it occupies, it expands into infinity. Various complicated deductions have been made then that this X is a spirit, rather than a body as such, which I think is pretty intuitive, but also that it would occupy, in a way, all space that we can imagine, since it cannot have been limited in the space it occupies before the universe was created. I appreciate that sounds very complicated but it is well established in philosophy that a being in that type of environment must occupy a space that we would call infinity, it is then an infinite being.

We will analyse these 'beings', or 'X's, at the end of the proofs but hopefully at this stage you can see that there must be a 'being' like that out there, or at least must have been one at the beginning of the universe, and that it would be infinite.

II. Proof from Causation, or the Aetiological Argument

This proof is based on some deductions that arise from considering the 'cause and effect' sequence of everything that exists in the universe. To begin, consider that table standing beside you. It doesn't exist on its own strength as it were, it didn't come out of nothing, it had a cause. Basically it was made by a carpenter, but he in turn used wood from a forest to create the table, then the forest comes about because of seeds being planted etc etc. In otherwords everything we see around us seems to have a place in this 'cause and effect' sequence, nothing seems to be there because it was always there, it seems to have been made by something which was made by something else etc. And yes, if you find yourself suffering from deja vu here it is true that there are similarities in the way that these first two proofs are explained, although they are quite different in their basic premise, 'cause and effect' is a different concept to 'motion' or 'energy'.

Again the important thing about this sequence is that we cannot continue going back up along doing this cause and effect deduction forever, we have to arrive at some point where the first thing is 'created,' an event that was not just another notch in the cause and effect chain.

Why we cannot go back ad infinitum in this series of causes and effects is outlined here by Aristotle in his book on Metaphysics:

> "But evidently there is a first principle, and the causes of things are neither an infinite series nor infinitely various in kind. For neither can one thing proceed from another, as from matter, ad infinitum (e.g. flesh from earth, earth from air, air from fire, and so on without stopping), nor can the sources of movement form an endless series (man for instance being acted on by air, air by the sun, the sun by Strife, and so on without limit). Similarly the final causes cannot go on ad infinitum, – walking being for the sake of health, this for the sake of happiness, happiness for the sake of something else, and so one thing always for the sake of another. And the case of the essence is similar. For in the case of intermediates, which have a last term and a term prior to them, the prior must be the cause of the later terms. For if we had to say which of the three is the cause, we should say the first; surely not the last, for the final term is

the cause of none; nor even the intermediate, for it is the cause only of one. (It makes no difference whether there is one intermediate or more, nor whether they are infinite or finite in number.) But of series which are infinite in this way, and of the infinite in general, all the parts down to that now present are alike intermediates; so that if there is no first there is no cause at all." [19]

This might seem somewhat complicated so hopefully an analogy might help. Imagine if you were in some closed environment, like at a summer camp we will say, and somebody hands you a dollar and you decide to trace the history of that dollar. So you find out that Frank is giving it to you for an apple, he got it from Joseph for a bar of chocolate, Joseph found it in the playing ground and doesn't know where it came from to there. So you investigate that and you discover it fell out of Pat's pockets etc etc. I know that scenario means nothing just at the minute but bear with us!

We are saying that you and the universe's existence now is a bit like holding onto that dollar you have in your hand, and tracing back through the causes and effects is very like tracing the history of that dollar. So the same way you trace back the cause and effect of anything, e.g. you have a car, and the car was made from X components, which came out of the ground in such and such place etc etc, works like chasing the origin of that dollar. But if you sit back and think about it, although you can indeed see numerous intermediate steps in chasing the origin of the dollar (Joe had it for a while, Frank had it for a while etc) but nonetheless you can see that somehow you need to arrive at a point where the dollar is actually created. It doesn't matter how many Joes and Franks etc that are in the middle here, the point is that there must come an end to the sequence, an end where you arrive at a point of creation. This was Aristotle's great deduction and if you consider it you may well find yourself in agreement.

As Aristotle says, the intermediate steps can go on to infinity, or close to it, and it still doesn't matter, you know, to go back to the dollar analogy, that somewhere the dollar had to have been created, now that you are looking at the dollar in your hand, and the number of intermediate people who are passing on the dollar is irrelevant to that certainty. Another way of viewing this is that sometimes this chain of cause and effects is looked upon as exactly that, links in a giant chain, but a chain that then needs to be anchored somewhere, we need to ground the first cause on some solid earth, some creation.

So by these means we arrive at our conclusion that there was some original cause out there that created the universe, the cause and effect sequence needs to start at some discreet beginning, which we call 'the first cause.' The truth is, of course, that this idea that the universe had just one beginning was not really popular in scientific circles, as opposed to philosophical and theological ones, until the advent of the Big Bang theory for the origin of the universe in the mid 20th century. Before that scientists had forgotten all about the clever reasoning of Aristotle, and the conclusions from that made by St Thomas Aquinas, but this is not the case now with most people accepting that, at least in some sense, Aristotle was right, we do have a 'first cause' to the universe.

Now we sit back and think about what that being actually looks like, what nature of 'being' could it be that caused the universe to come into existence? Well we will just park that discussion for a minute by again just calling this being 'X', and content ourselves with the simple deduction that it must be an infinite being. It must be infinite because we are referring to a being that was in existence before anything else that we see around us in the universe was in existence. Because of that this being had nothing to limit its extent, just like storing gas in a container or water in a bucket, you need something to hold in a 'being' to create 'finiteness' in it, otherwise we say that it simply occupies everywhere.

III. Proof from the Necessary Being, or the Argument from Contingency
(This and the previous two proofs are known collectively as the Cosmological Argument)

Aristotle [20] talked a lot in his writings about a 'necessary being' in the Universe but the coherent finished proof for God's existence that derives from this originated with Al-Farabi (c.872 - c.951) a Persian philosopher who lived in Baghdad, his idea was then copied by Avicenna, a Persian thinker who was born in modern day Uzbekistan, and was brought to the West by a Jewish writer who lived in Spain called Maimonides. From there it came to the attention of St Thomas Aquinas and having been accepted by him (bear in mind that Aquinas was not happy with many of the proofs floating around in his time, he only accepted five and rejected thirteen, one of which, at least, was quite popular in some circles) it became number three in these famous proofs or 'ways' by which the existence of God can be demonstrated.

The proof goes something like this:

– Everything we see around us in the universe is not necessary to exist, there is no particular reason why Mt Etna or you or me *has* to exist, you could conceive of a time when these things, or people, did not exist. Technically the philosophers called this a contingent being, i.e. a being dependent on something else and not necessary to exist.

– Now if everything around us is like that, if everything *doesn't have to* exist, then presumably there could come a time when everything went blank, so to speak, when actually nothing at all existed?

What you have to do is imagine that everything around us in the universe are like the lights in the windows going on and off on a skyscraper that you are looking at at night. So you are looking at room 13 on the 19th floor as the lights go on and you see the light at room 57 on the 13th floor go off etc etc, and this is analogous to everything around us going into or out of existence in the universe. Just like things coming and going in the universe you are looking at the skyscraper and watching the lights go on and off randomly all over the building. But now consider that presumably there will come a time when all the lights will be off at the same time, why not if you give it enough time and if all the lights can just go on and off randomly like this? Doubtless its not going to be like that most of the time but you can envisage it happening at some stage maybe? But getting back to our universe what we are then saying is that maybe there will come a time when everything doesn't exist? Why not, if everything we see might or might not exist then all the lights could go off like this in the universe?

– But if that was ever to happen in the universe, i.e. if there was to be a time when absolutely nothing existed, then the universe would stop at that point because of course there would be nothing to carry it forward, because you can get nothing out of nothing. If everything goes blank, universally speaking!, then our existence, here and now, could never have come about because the universe would have just stopped at the time when nothing was in existence. And, the philosophers tell us, there is no reason, under this scenario, not to believe that such a time could not happen, why not if everything we see around us 'might' or 'might not' exist?

– Hence what the philosophers say is that there must be some being out there that is 'necessary to exist', some being that keeps the home fires burning in the universe, as it were, some being that seems to be always there so that a complete blank slate never seems to happen to the universe. (Again, we know this, that that blank vacuum state never happened to the universe, because we have the universe now, and the universe wouldn't be here now if at any previous time it was ever hit with this real vacuum state.)

– So we have a being that is 'necessary' somehow, it has some permanence if you like, and also must be eternal because it seems to be always there to ensure the survival of the Universe. John Duns Scotus, c.1270-1308 ('Scotus', by the way, means 'Irishman' in Medieval Latin and when the Franciscan librarians at Assisi in Italy in 1381 were drawing up their book catalogue they referred to his works as "magistri fratris Johannis Scoti de Ordine Minorum, qui et Doctor Subtilis nuncupatur, de provincia Hiberniæ," which means "the work of master John Scotus of the

Franciscan Order known as the subtle doctor, from the province of Ireland"), a famous scholastic from the Middle Ages, remarked that: "nothing however is more perfect than a being having necessary existence of itself." [21]

We can chalk up another X being that seems to be out here then, which is eternal and 'perfect' and there is only one of them, since you cannot have two or more perfect beings. It is also infinite, for the same reason given under the first two proofs.

IV. Proof from Degrees of Perfection, or the Henological Argument
(It is also known as the Proof by Gradation, or the Superlative Principle, because if gradation exists then a standard by which the others are measured exists i.e. 'the Superlative Principle.' This general area is also sometimes known as the Proof from Morality.)

This proof is in part derived from the views of Plato, as articulated by a later exponent of his called Plotinus. Here is a paraphrase of the views of Plotinus which describes this:

> "Plotinus argues instead that the multiple cannot exist without the simple. The "less perfect" must, of necessity, "emanate", or issue forth, from the "perfect" or "more perfect"." [22]

According then to these ancient Greek and Roman philosophers, at least with respect to some things, once we have the ability to grade anything we then accept that a perfect (or 100% grade) of that thing exists.

A confusing concept I know, but consider this analogy: Picture what happens when an exam is marked in a history test say. Obviously the examiner can come to the conclusion that Mr Joe Blogs has a 65% knowledge of history and Mr John Smith has a 35% knowledge because he has a list of the correct answers to the exam questions. If the examiner did not himself have at least a near perfect knowledge of history, or that list of the perfect answers, then he just couldn't grade those students, he can only grade them because a perfect 100% knowledge of history – or that course of history anyway – exists. So the fact that you are able to see grades, or degrees, of knowledge of history means ipso facto that a perfect 100% knowledge of that history exists somewhere.

This also works if you discard the outside objective standard we have in an exam setting. Say we have an ordinary person, with a poor or no knowledge of history, meeting two people who describe themselves as historians. Because he has a poor grasp of history himself he won't jump to some conclusion as to how good an historian each is, or who is better. You will find that this person will just not offer an opinion as to which of the historians is the best. Now consider if these two historians meet a person who happens to have studied the history of this particular place for the last thirty years or so. This new person will probably act differently, he will probably ask a few questions, testing out the real knowledge of history of the two historians. And if his own knowledge of this history is good enough, he will come to some strong opinions as to which of his two companions really knows his stuff. So we can see in fact that the ancient Greeks were right, if you are enthusiastically or confidently grading something, then you are accessing somehow a perfect knowledge of that thing, a perfect state that genuinely exists.

At this stage that crafty Angelic Doctor, St Thomas Aquinas, would like to ask you a question. Do you feel that you can grade in your own mind nobleness, truthfulness or goodness in people? In fact do you sometimes get enthusiastic about your grading of those qualities in people, do you bang the table and declare that such and such a thing is 'not right', not 'good, true, or noble' ? If so aren't you reacting a little like our second person above, the person with a perfect knowledge of history grading those two historians? Aren't you reacting more like him than the person who doesn't know any history, and aren't these three qualities somewhat analogous to our example of history knowledge? In short then are you somehow acknowledging, or tapping into, a perfect knowledge of goodness, truth and nobleness? Are we saying then that a perfect state (or being) of goodness, truth and nobleness exists? Well surely that is close to our understanding then of a Christian God, a being that incorporates a perfect state of goodness, truthfulness and nobleness, so are we saying then that he exists?

You might not like this piece of Greek sophistry but the fact is that many great thinkers over the years have also arrived at the opinion that our human sense of conscience and morality is remarkable, must have come from somewhere, and is not easily explained away by evolution, for example, or what you would expect in the reasoned actions of a mechanically engineered mind. Its hard to see how it could come from evolution because, if you think about examples of how conscience hits people, it frequently conflicts with a notion of the 'survival of the fittest', the idea that its the person who lives who gets to pass down their genes. For example conscience often hits murderers many decades after they have committed their crime, and it frequently causes ex-soldiers to wake up at night in a sweat thinking of the persons who may have been killed by them.

This is hard to put into a context of evolution and actually its equally hard to see how this can be the product of a purely mechanical mind. Remember, according to the atheist theory, our minds, like all the rest of us, are just a bunch of atoms and molecules working together exactly like a machine. But in the 21st century world we know exactly what a machine with the thinking power of the human mind looks like, as we have computers that can play chess and otherwise reach the heights that the scientists could hitherto only imagine in science fiction. And no, none of those machines show any tendencies to act like the human conscience. No computer is known to have burst a fuse because it has programmed in the deaths of thousands of humans, in military computers say, and that sat nav that freezed up did not do so because it has a guilty conscience having led you astray! Computers, mechanically structured 'brains', do not act like that at all, not even a little! And that, let us not forget, is indeed the model to use when trying to understand the human brain, if you don't believe in the supernatural.

So where does this 'morality' or 'conscience' element come from? Well the obvious objection atheists might raise is that possibly it arrives in people as a result of being educated in

Christian principles .i.e. that people learned all this as they grew up, that it isn't inherent, built into, the human mind. But in fact many reputable thinkers (like the Belfast writer turned Oxford don, C. S. Lewis,[23] and John Henry Newman, who wrote about this proof of God's existence in the Dublin Review in 1870 [24]) have looked at the pattern of human societies across the world, including pagan and primitive races, and they can see traces of that same morality working there too. Theists have concluded then that this conscience in people is a kind of mark of your maker, that it indicates the presence of a God who cares for people and who is unhappy at injustice being inflicted on his creatures or creation.

So what kind of being is our 'X' here? Where does this conscience thing come from, how did we get it? To take an analogy here, imagine if we all woke up tomorrow morning all with the same knowledge of horse racing, and also we now react very badly whenever we see a jockey make a mistake in a race. Maybe then we could conclude that whatever being had implanted this in us, during the night, must be some kind of horse racing fanatic, with an encyclopedic knowledge of form and results going back centuries, a being that must be very passionate about horse racing? Following this analogy then can we conclude that our 'X' here, from whence conscience and morality comes from, must have a huge, perfect knowledge of 'goodness'? It must be a being that is very passionate about seeing humans obey this morality?

The ancient Greeks would also say that a being perfect in 'goodness' is a perfect being in general, it would then be 'the' perfect being. It was felt that 'goodness' and existence itself, in a way, were in some senses the same thing. At any rate we can say that our X being here is a perfect entity.

A consciousness of the divine in humans

A related argument to the above is the idea that humans seem to have within them a sense of the divine, as it were, some part of them that seems to aspire towards God or towards some supernatural existence. How could we explain that except again that it must be the 'mark of your maker'?

This has certainly been well discussed over the millennia. We might as well start with Socrates, of course a great Greek philosopher:

> "Nor did it satisfy the gods to take care of the body merely, but, what is most important of all, they implanted in him the soul, his most excellent part. For what other animal has a soul to understand, first of all, that the gods, who have arranged such a vast and noble order of things, exist? What other species of animal, besides man, offers worship to the gods?" [25]

Another example of a philosopher trying to reason with the existence of a kind of divine consciousness in humans is Seneca, an important Roman philosopher:

> "For instance, we infer that the gods exist, for this reason, among others – that there is implanted in everyone an idea concerning deity, and there is no people so far beyond the reach of laws and customs that it does not believe at least in gods of some sort." [26]

This next quote is by the great French philosopher Rene Descartes (1596-1650). I appreciate that these thoughts go on for some length but you might be more indulgent if you understand just how important Descartes is. His philosophy, captured in his immortal phrase 'cogito ergo sum,' 'I think therefore I am,' and which has given him the title "The Father of Modern Philosophy," gets to the heart of what we are referring to here. He could see that only humans have this 'will' or special 'consciousness' in their minds and that's what really distinguishes the human being. Incidentally he also invented the x, y, and z Cartesian planes, which are called after him obviously, and was the first to use superscript numbers to denote the powers or exponents in mathematics. Hence he was a really great thinker and it might be worthwhile to follow his complex thoughts on this in some depth:

> "So there remains only the idea of God: is there anything in that which couldn't have originated in myself? By the word 'God' I understand a substance that is infinite, eternal, unchangeable,

independent, supremely intelligent, supremely powerful, which created myself and anything else that may exist. The more carefully I concentrate on these attributes, the less possible it seems that any of them could have originated from me alone. So this whole discussion implies that God necessarily exists.

It is true that my being a substance explains my having the idea of substance; but it does not explain my having the idea of an infinite substance. That must come from some substance that is itself infinite. I am finite.

It might be thought that this is wrong, because my notion of the infinite is arrived at merely by negating the finite, just as my conceptions of rest and darkness are arrived at by negating movement and light. That would be a mistake, however. I clearly understand that there is more reality in an infinite substance than in a finite one, and hence that my perception of the infinite, i.e. God, is in some way prior to my perception of the finite, i.e. myself. Whenever I know that I doubt something or want something, I understand that I lack something and am therefore not wholly perfect. How could I grasp this unless I had an idea of a more perfect being that enabled me to recognize my own defects by comparison?

...

Given the failure of every other candidacy for the role of *cause of me and of my idea of a most perfect being*, I infer that the only successful candidacy is God's. Thus, I conclude that the mere fact that I exist and have within me an idea of a most perfect being—that is, God—provides a clear proof that God does indeed exist.

It remains for me only to ask how I received this idea from God. I didn't get it from the senses: it has never come to me unexpectedly, as do most of the ideas that occur when I seem to see and touch and hear things. And it's not something that I invented, either; for clearly I can't take anything away from it or to add anything to it. When an idea is sheerly invented, the inventor is free to fiddle with it—add a bit here, subtract a bit there—whereas my idea of God is a natural unit that doesn't invite or even permit such interference. The only remaining alternative is that my idea of God is innate in me, just as the idea of myself is innate in me.

It is no surprise that God in creating me should have placed this idea in me, to serve as a mark of the craftsman stamped on his work. The mark need not be anything distinct from the work itself. But the mere fact that God created me makes it very believable that I am somehow made in his image and likeness, and that I perceive that likeness in the same way that I perceive myself. That is, when I turn my mind's eye upon myself, I understand that I am a thing that is incomplete and dependent on something else, and that aspires without limit to ever greater and better things; but I also understand at the same time that he on whom I depend has within him all those greater things—not just indefinitely but infinitely, not just potentially but actually—and hence that he is God. The core of the argument is this: I couldn't exist with the nature that I have—that is, containing within me the idea of God—if God didn't really exist. By 'God' I mean the very being the idea of whom is within me—the one that has no defects and has all those perfections that I can't grasp but can somehow touch with my thought. This shows clearly that it is not possible for him to be a deceiver, since the natural light makes it clear that all fraud and deception depend on some defect.

But before examining this point more carefully

and investigating other truths that may be derived from it, I want to pause here and spend some time contemplating God; to reflect on his attributes and to gaze with wonder and adoration on the beauty of this immense light, so far as the eye of my darkened intellect can bear it. For just as we believe through faith that the supreme happiness of the next life consists in contemplating the divine majesty, so experience tells us that this same contemplation, though much less perfect, provides the greatest joy we can have in this life." [27]

There is also another interesting twist to this. C S Lewis, when he wrote his book 'Mere Christianity', looked back on the time when he was an atheist and he felt that in retrospect he had a kind of a rage within him, or a sense of justice/injustice, which was incompatible with the theory that his mind and body were only the products of mechanical processes. It was like if God really didn't exist then he should be calm and carefree about the issue but wasn't. A number of other modern commentators have also noted this illogical rage in some atheists, like the Australian TV journalist Mike Willesee speaking here: http://www.youtube.com/watch?v=r6gig45spWI . In passing we might note that Sir Francis Bacon, the English philosopher who was the originator of the scientific method, had observed this phenomenon, and contradiction, among atheists many centuries ago:

> "It appeareth in nothing more, that atheism is rather in the lip, than in the heart of man, than by this; that atheists will ever be talking of that their opinion, as if they fainted in it, within themselves, and would be glad to be strengthened, by the consent of others. Nay more, you shall have atheists strive to get disciples, as it fareth with other sects. And, which is most of all, you shall have of them, that will suffer for atheism, and not recant; whereas if they did truly think, that there were no such thing as God, why should they

trouble themselves?" [28]

In any case its interesting to read C S Lewis' somewhat more gentle and sympathetic thoughts on this:

> "My argument against God was that the universe seemed so cruel and unjust. But how had I got this idea of just and unjust? A man does not call a line crooked unless he has some idea of a straight line. What was I comparing this universe with when I called it unjust? If the whole show was bad and senseless from A to Z, so to speak, why did I, who was supposed to be part of the show, find myself in such a violent reaction against it?... Of course I could have given up my idea of justice by saying it was nothing but a private idea of my own. But if I did that, then my argument against God collapsed too – for the argument depended on saying the world was really unjust, not simply that it did not happen to please my fancies. Thus, in the very act of trying to prove that God did not exist – in other words, that the whole of reality was senseless – I found I was forced to assume that one part of reality – namely my idea of justice – was full of sense. If the whole universe has no meaning, we should never have found out that it has no meaning: just as, if there were no light in the universe and therefore no creatures with eyes, we should never have known it was dark. Dark would be without meaning." [29]

V. Proof from Final Causes, or the Teleological Argument, often known as Intelligent Design

Not a few of the highly respected philosophers and scientists of history and the present day felt, and feel, that the world as we know it, nature as it were, shows signs of a strange order or purposefulness, as opposed to randomness or pure chance, and this, it is felt, proves the existence of some being responsible for arranging this order. Predictably enough (!) I will try to explain this using an analogy but, mercifully, I will spare you any reference to watches or clocks! It is in fact one of the most peculiar aspects of the historiography of this question that virtually all the great thinkers start talking about watches and clocks when seeking to explain this proof. It really is very remarkable, it starts all the way from Cicero, and he was only talking about sundials!, to Robert Boyle, who talked about the Strasbourg town clock, to Voltaire, to William Paley – a Church of England rector who wrote one of the most influential books in history on this subject: 'Natural Theology,' published in 1802 – who famously talked about a watch found on a heath etc etc. Instead, by way of something different, I will begin with our hero marooned on a romantic desert island, trudging through the forest on his lonely atoll and suddenly coming across a trap, an elaborate Indiana-Jones-type large animal trap:

Naturally you move to examine it and find that it has a rope net which is designed to capture any large animal that falls into the corresponding hole that the trap maker has dug. The hole is just a large rectangular job and the rope, which is wide and sturdy, is just made from slashing together vines that abound in this forest. Of course you look at this trap and you immediately say "there is somebody out there, we are not alone!", and no, you are not referring to aliens! This then is the basic idea of this proof, we see the same type of organised purposeful design in nature and we conclude that we are not alone, there must be a designer behind this design.

To get back to our Robinson Crusoe hero here, obviously he reached the natural conclusion anybody would reach having seen that elaborately designed trap. But why, exactly? How do you know there is somebody else on the island now that you have seen this trap? There are other holes in the forest of course, made randomly around the place by rabbits and other animals and by trees falling over etc, maybe the hole you were looking at arose that way? Sometimes the vines that you see hanging down from the trees intertwine a bit, so is that how the rope was made?

We will say that you pause and consider this question, was this trap created by random forces like rabbits and the wind creating the rope by winding the vines together like that? And therefore there might not be anybody out there, it could be just natural forces and not the result of an intelligent designer, because what you had thought at first was that there must be some intelligent resourceful guy on this island, seeing as somebody like that had to have built such a crafty trap. But could it have come about then by these natural sources? Well, as you think about it, indeed the parts used in the trap were all natural, they were all around each other in the forest, so yes in theory the wind and rabbits etc could have created the trap.

But no, now that you give it more thought it couldn't have happened like that because the trap was too structured or ordered. For example you are looking at the hole and you see it has four pretty sharp sides, as in a rectangle, and how could you have rabbits creating a large perfect rectangular hole like that? In theory they could have of course, you could have ten rabbits lined up together who start digging in unison etc etc, I mean it could happen, in theory? There is no law states that rabbits cannot form a line? But in reality we know that didn't happen, and the reason is that we know that things cannot form that ordered or structured pattern by chance or randomness alone. What you could do is calculate the odds in your mind. You could picture the day you watched a few rabbits eating in a field and you could guess the odds of two rabbits lined up in perfect unison and then calculate the odds of 10 rabbits lined up like that. As you calculate the odds you rapidly realise that it just couldn't happen and what you are doing in your head is the classic, and indeed only, way of distinguishing the two states of randomness and design. Basically you have design, i.e. somebody, a human or some being with intelligence, deliberately bringing about this state, taking over from randomness and chance, i.e. the outcome of natural undirected forces in nature, like wind or rain or something, as the only possible explanation when you find these huge odds stacking up, like the odds of rabbits coming together like that. Remember you never find that there is zero odds, there is always some chance that ten rabbits could line up in unison like that, because as I said there is no law against it, but when the odds start to get astronomical then you know it was design.

I will come back to that question of probabilities in a minute but lets look at some other aspects of the trap. You see you also have to consider that the wind would have to have arranged the vines in a rope or net structure at just the right time and place to coincide with the hole, and what are the odds of that? The point then is that when we see a kind of purposeful interlocking structure – I say purposeful because obviously the designer had put the hole in front of the net like that 'on purpose,' and you can note with interest that purposefulness – then the probabilities of it happening by chance, again, rise astronomically.

The other thing to remark on about the trap is that it doesn't have to be perfect to show intelligent design. Say for the sake of argument that in one corner of the rectangular hole there is a small collapse in the earthwork. Hence it isn't actually a perfect rectangular chasm, but still we can see that enough of the design of the whole remains that will show us that it couldn't have come about by chance. So, in short, even though it isn't actually a perfect rectangle nonetheless its close enough to rule out the rabbit theory. This is an important point because when we come to talking about DNA etc in a minute you will hear some people say that the intelligent design in nature is actually not perfectly designed – because after all we have cancer cells that use the DNA structure for example – to support life, but I would say it doesn't have to be, as long as enough of it remains that does show the design.

In any case hopefully at this stage you get the general idea, the way to distinguish design from chance, that is two competing possibilities if you like, opposed to one another, is to check the probabilities. If the probabilities become astronomically high – but they never hit zero remember, when we are trying to distinguish randomness from design – then it is design, and that is what our hero did instinctively when he first saw the trap, he knew that some intelligent being had to have designed it.

You see this is what any intelligent person does on an ongoing basis. Say you were playing cards and your opponent got three aces dealt into him. Well it happens and you will congratulate him on his luck. Then it happens again on the next hand. That is certainly a talking point and everybody will be remarking on how lucky the guy was but I guess these things happen. But by the time it happens on the third hand you are going to react differently. Now you know it isn't luck and you will be quietly fixing an eagle eye on your opponent's sleeve! So what is happening here? You are calculating the odds of it happening by chance in your head. It could happen once, sure, happen twice, yes but very rare, but happen three times in a row? Now you have calculated that last probability in your head and you can see that those odds are ridiculous and you move to the design option, you know somebody has done that deliberately, you know that because the odds of it happening by chance have become astronomical. Remember the odds of it happening three times in a row are not zero, they never are under this type of analysis, but once they hit very big numbers then you know it is design – your opponent somehow did this deliberately, purposefully – and not by chance – it was not the mere random shuffling of the cards.

Another scenario could be if you were walking along a street and you seemed to feel that the person behind you is walking in step with you, as if you are being followed. So you look at him and scratch you head and think probably not, how can I be sure anyway?, but you note his face just in case. Then twenty minutes later you have walked to a different part of the city and look behind you and lo and behold, there he is again! Its a bit of a concern now, how could he be here just behind me now? Was he walking around the city randomly like me and he just happened to walk into this street, having earlier being beside me on the other street? What are the odds of that happening by chance? As you consider it though you might feel that it is just possible. These are two large streets with lots of people on them, maybe he is just going to the same shops you are? Now you walk through a huge thoroughfare with thousands of people jostling around each other as they go to work maybe, and you peel off into some insignificant side street where you know hardly anybody goes and look behind you and there he is again! So again, an intelligent person will now calculate the odds of this person being in the same three streets at the same time you were, and you will conclude that because the odds are too high then it had to be deliberate, it has to be 'by design' that he is following you.

So hopefully you begin to get the general picture here, once the odds start getting astronomical then you lift the possibility out of the realm of chance, or luck or randomness or undirected natural causes, and into the realm of design, or order or purposefulness. In fact right from the beginning this was held to be one of the great advantages of the science of probability, it was seen as a great new tool to help people identify the difference between design and chance. Here, for example, is a quote from the introduction to only the second book ever published on probability, 'The Doctrine of Chances' by Abraham de Moivre, a French Huguenot writing in early 18th century London:

> "Further, the same Arguments which explode the Notion of Luck, may on the other side, be useful in some Cases to establish a due comparison between Chance and Design: We may imagine Chance and Design to be, as it were, in Competition with each other, for the production of some sorts of Events, and may calculate what Probability there is, that those Events should be rather owing to one than to the other. To give a Familiar Instance of this. Let us suppose that two Packs of Piquet-Cards being sent for, it should be perceived that there is, from Top to Bottom, the same Disposition of the Cards in both Packs; let us likewise suppose that, some doubt arising about this Disposition of the Cards, it should be questioned whether it ought to be attributed to Chance, or to the Maker's Design: In this Case the Doctrine of Combinations decides the question; since it may be proved by its Rules, that there are the Odds of above 263 130830000 Millions of Millions of Millions of Millions to One, that the Cards were designedly set in the Order in which they were found.
>
> From this last Consideration we may learn, in ma[n]y Cases, how to distinguish the Events which are the effects of Chance, from those which are produced by Design: The very Doctrine that finds

Chance where it really is, being able to prove by a gradual Increase of Probability, till it arrive at Demonstration, that where Uniformity, Order and Constancy reside, there also reside Choice and Design." [30]

Why dwell so much on the theory of probability, I hear you ask? What has that got to do with the existence of God anyway? Because this actually is the great battle ground between theists and atheists over this question of intelligent design. In practice its accepted by all, or nearly all, that there are indeed aspects of nature and the universe which do show events, or 'laws', that have huge improbabilities against saying that they happened, or exist, as a blind result of randomness or chance. In these instances many atheists continue to say that they came about by undirected natural forces whereas theists are saying that they must be the result of design, because of the huge probabilities against these being caused by chance. Theists talk about three areas in particular:

a) Various constants – i.e. precise mathematical figures that are revealed by physics – that have to be very exact to allow life to exist at all on earth. Meaning that if there was the slightest difference in figures like the cosmological constant then we wouldn't be alive here on earth at all, and what are the odds of those figures magically arising so exactly like this by accident? Because there is this huge improbability that those figures could have arisen just by chance, then, just like in the examples given above, does it not mean that earth was 'designed' so that life could happen here on earth? So we have some 'designer' for earth and who could that be if not God? This is sometimes known as the Fine Tuned Universe Argument – i.e. fine tuned to a precise point to allow life to exist – for God's existence and in fact is becoming increasingly popular as these strange constants keep getting discovered. [31]

b) The Laws of Physics, are called 'laws' because they show a precise order and structure to the universe, but again if we are into order and structure then we have to ask are we not in the 'design,' as opposed to 'chance,' bracket? Then if so, the natural question that follows is who designed them? [32] Even Euclid (c.325 BC - c.265 BC), the great Greek mathematician who lived a lot of his life in Alexandria, and is the 'father of geometry', said that "The laws of nature are but the mathematical thoughts of God." [33]

c) But DNA, and lifeforms themselves, form the really great battleground in this argument between atheists and theists. This is because it has been shown that life, and in particular the structure of DNA and the cell, is built on enormously complex structures which, it is felt, couldn't possibly have arisen by chance. To give you a flavour of these odds here is a quote on the state of our knowledge of these probabilities:

> "In the last 30 years a number of prominent scientists have attempted to calculate the odds that a free-living, single-celled organism, such as a bacterium, might result by the chance combining of pre-existent building blocks. Harold Morowitz calculated the odds as one chance in 10 to the power of 100,000,000,000. Sir Fred Hoyle calculated the odds of only the proteins of an amoebae arising by chance as one chance in 10 to the power of 40,000.
>
> ...the odds calculated by Morowitz and Hoyle are staggering. The odds led Fred Hoyle to state that the probability of spontaneous generation 'is about the same as the probability that a tornado sweeping through a junk yard could assemble a Boeing 747 from the contents therein.' Mathematicians tell us that any event with an improbability greater than one chance in 10 to the power of 50 is in the realm of metaphysics – i.e. a miracle." [34]

The aforementioned Professor Harold Morowitz (1927-), a PhD from Yale in 1951, Professor of Biophysics at Yale 1960-86 and Director of the Krasnow Institute (1993-), wrote:

> "The probability for the chance of formation of the smallest, simplest form of living organism known is 1 to 10-340,000,000. This number is 1 to 10 to the 340 millionth power! The size of this

figure is truly staggering, since there is only supposed to be approximately 10-80 (10 to the 80th power) electrons in the whole universe!" [35]

These odds were also calculated by Sir Francis Crick (1916-2004), Nobel Laureate in 1962, and of course the joint discoverer of the double helix form of the DNA molecule:

"To produce this miracle of molecular construction all the cell need do is to string together the amino acids (which make up the polypeptide chain) *in the correct order.* This is a complicated biochemical process, a molecular assembly line, using instructions in the form of a nucleic acid tape (the so-called messenger RNA) ... Here we need only ask, how many possible proteins are there? If a particular amino acid sequence was selected by chance, how rare an event would that be?

This is an easy exercise in combinatorials. Suppose the chain is about two hundred amino acids long; that is, if anything, rather less than the average length of proteins of all types. Since we have just twenty possibilities at each place, the number of possibilities is twenty multiplied by itself some two hundred times. This is conveniently written 20 [to the power of] 200 and is approximately equal to 10 [to the power of] 260, that is, a one followed by 260 zeros!

This number is quite beyond our everyday comprehension. For comparison, consider the number of fundamental particles (atoms, speaking loosely) in the entire visible universe, not just in our own galaxy with its 10 [to the power of] 11 stars, but in all the billions of galaxies, out to the limits of observable space. This number, which is estimated to be 10 [to the power of] 80, is quite paltry by comparison to 10 [to the power of] 260. Moreover we have only considered a polypeptide chain of a rather modest length. Had we considered longer ones as well, the figure would have been even more immense. It is possible to show that ever since life started on earth, the number of different polypeptide chains which could have been synthesized during all this long time is only a minute fraction of the number of imaginable ones. The great majority of sequences can never have been synthesized at all, at any time." [36]

So I invite you then to slot those figures into your new found insight into how probabilities work in helping us to distinguish between chance as opposed to design. We are just like that card player when he sees the three aces arise in the three consecutive hands. We can now solidly rule out chance, luck, randomness, accident, etc, in the creation of DNA, now that we see the very high probabilities, exactly as the card player did. Hence the DNA was created deliberately by some being, we know it couldn't have arisen by luck or randomly or by accident, we have lifted this event out of the realm of chance or randomness or undirected natural forces and slotted it comfortably into the bracket of design and purpose etc. And that's basically then the theory of Intelligent Design, we can see the hand of some designer at work in the creation of DNA and the many other areas that seem to be able to rule out chance or natural forces acting alone without a directing intelligence.

Sometimes atheists try to claim that over huge lengths of time these events, like the creation of DNA, could somehow come about but that is really a distortion of the doctrine of probability. To back up that last point consider here the words of Dr Émile Borel (1871-1956). This brilliant French mathematician, who authored more than 50 papers on the calculus of probability and "created the first effective theory of the measure of sets of points", a Professor at Lille University in 1893, Professor of Mathematics at Paris 1909-1941, in 1925 Minister of Marine in the French government, and finally President of the Science Committee of UNESCO in 1948, sets out here the reality behind events with huge negative probabilities:

> "The occurrence of any event where the chances are beyond one in ten followed by 50 zeros is an event which we can state with certainty will never happen, no matter how much time is allotted and no matter how many conceivable opportunities could exist for the event to take place." [37]

Viscount Ilya Prigogine (1917-2003), who inter alia in 1977 won the Nobel prize in Chemistry, sets out the reality behind these high probabilities when he said that:

> "The statistical probability that organic structures, and the most precisely harmonized reactions that typify living organisms would be generated by accident, is zero." [38]

Actually long before probability became a precise field of mathematics – the main figure here would be Pascal in early 17th century France – the issue of chance versus design was well known to philosophers and those that developed the field of Logic. For them it was a terrible logical fallacy to ever suppose that you could get order, structure or purposeful design from mere chance alone, and how right they were was proven once the science of probability took off. In any case its interesting to see how this chance versus design – or art, the ancients would call it – issue, and also the insight that design – and hence a designer – was the proper explanation for the Universe, was discussed by the great philosophers. Aristotle considered it and concluded that "as in intelligent action, so in nature," Xenophon (Memorabilia IV 3) and Plato mention it (Phaedo 96 ff), and ascribe it to Socrates – who describes it at length –, and it was also a favourite of Cicero's (De Natura Deorum II.5). Its mentioned by most of the big Christian philosophers, like St Augustine and St Boethius, and particularly by St John of Damascus (676-749). Cicero actually went into considerable detail on the subject, finding it absurd not to accept the presence of a divine hand in the universe, as he describes here:

> "But if the structure of the world in all its parts is such that it could not have been better whether

in point of utility or beauty, let us consider whether this is the result of chance, or whether on the contrary the parts of the world are in such a condition that they could not possibly have cohered together if they were not controlled by intelligence and by divine providence. If then the products of nature are better than those of art, and if art produces nothing without reason, nature too cannot be deemed to be without reason. When you see a statue or a painting, you recognize the exercise of art; when you observe from a distance the course of a ship, you do not hesitate to assume that its motion is guided by reason and by art; when you look at a sun-dial or a water-clock, you infer that it tells the time by art and not by chance; how then can it be consistent to suppose that the world, which includes both the works of art in question, the craftsmen who made them, and everything else besides, can be devoid of purpose and of reason? Suppose a traveller to carry into Scythia or Britain the orrery recently constructed by our friend Posidonius, which at each revolution reproduces the same motions of the sun, the moon and the five planets that take place in the heavens every twenty-four hours, would any single native doubt that this orrery was the work of a rational being? These thinkers however raise doubts about the world itself from which all things arise and have their being, and debate whether it is the product of chance or necessity of some sort, or of divine reason and intelligence; they think more highly of the achievement of Archimedes in making a model of the revolutions of the firmament than of that of nature in creating them, although the perfection of the original shows a craftsmanship many times as great as does the counterfeit." [39]

I will leave the last word on this to Professor Antony Flew, a philosopher who was the Richard Dawkins of his day until he was persuaded by the theist arguments, including with respect to DNA. When asked does he, Antony Flew, think that the new work on the origin of life points to a creative intelligence, he said at a public debate in New York in 2004:

> "Yes, I now think it does...almost entirely because of the DNA investigations. What I think the DNA material has done is that it has shown, by the almost unbelievable complexity of the arrangements which are needed to produce (life), that intelligence must have been involved in getting these extraordinarily diverse elements to work together. It's the enormous complexity of the number of elements and the enormous subtlety of the ways they work together. The meeting of these two parts at the right time by chance is simply minute. It is all a matter of the enormous complexity by which the results were achieved, which looked to me like the work of intelligence."
> [40]

Hence we have arrived at some X being here that seems to have intelligently designed life, and fine tuned the universe and earth to accommodate it, and the laws of physics. It certainly looks then that it must be an omniscient and omnipotent being, seeing as how it created such hugely complex structures like that?

Analysis of the Proofs

We can now sit on our philosopher's stone and think about these 'X's, these entities or 'beings' that we feel are out there somehow. The first thing to note is that each of them, if you remember, are either 'perfect' or 'infinite' or 'omnipotent', or some combination of those three. This is important because if you consider it you will have to agree that only one being can be either infinite, perfect or omnipotent.

If you don't believe this consider a hypothetical scenario

where you had two perfect beings, we will say X and Y. So X is perfect at playing the piano, no being or entity is better than it, perfect at the harp, perfect at the trombone, actually perfect at everything. So now we consider the Y being, it too is perfect at the piano, no being is better than it, which is what we mean by the perfect being, etc etc. So now if you think about it you can see that you could never come up with some quality that was different in Y as opposed to X, hence there is nothing to distinguish these beings in your mind, so you have to accept that they are the same being. There is no X and Y, just one being with two different names. You can do the same analysis for the omnipotent being and you will end up with the same conclusion, there can only be one omnipotent being.

The question of whether or not there can be two infinite beings works much the same way. Say we want to picture where X infinite being is, as opposed to Y infinite being. Well obviously they occupy the same space, infinity, so you could never distinguish between them. An infinite being is obviously a complicated being for the mind to imagine but its often felt that it would be easier if you use the word 'all' to indicate an infinite being. So lets use that word in our analysis. Imagine if you were just doling out sweets to five people, as a simple hypothetical to explain this. You give 10 sweets to Mary, 5 sweets to John, you give 'all' sweets to Joseph, 15 sweets to Valerie – if there is any left, bear with us here! – and you give 'all' sweets to James. As you can see, whatever figure 'all' – our infinity – actually is, there is certainly only one such figure, James and Joseph get the same number of sweets, whatever number that may be. There is only one 'all', you cannot imagine two entities, each having 'all', hence again you cannot distinguish between these entities. So you must conclude that your X and Y infinite being here is actually the one being with two different names.

Long winded philosophy as that might seem it nonetheless has got us to the point, satisfactorily I think, where we can see that our five beings, or Xs, listed above are actually the one entity, with just five different names. We cannot say they are five separate beings because then we would be talking about multiple infinite, perfect or omnipotent beings. So consequently we combine our analysis above, we look upon each of the proofs as giving us some of the qualities of the one being or entity that we now think is out there.

Well what have we got? So far we have a being – and we have just seen that there can only be one of them – that is infinite, eternal, omnipotent, omniscient, and containing a sense of perfect goodness, truthfulness, and nobleness. Finally we can speculate as to why the first mover and first causer actually did what they did. Why did that being in the first mover and first cause proof actually decide to set the universe going, in our proof we provide no necessity as to why it has to bring the universe, and hence us, into existence at all? Well Aristotle pondered this for a while and what he came up with was:

> "For the final cause ['the final cause' here is the same as our 'first cause', he calls it 'final' because it is the last cause if you are working backwards up the chain of cause and effect] is (a) some being for whose good an action is done, and (b) something at which the action aims; and of these the latter exists among unchangeable entities though the former does not. The final cause [i.e. the original act of cause], then, produces motion as being loved, but all other things move by being moved." [41]

So he felt that love for the world and its humans etc was why the first mover and causer did what it did, and also at this point it would be likely to love its creation, that it decided, through its own will, to create. Aristotle went on to wax lyrical at this comforting deduction:

> "Therefore the possession rather than the receptivity is the divine element which thought seems to contain, and the act of contemplation is what is most pleasant and best. If, then, God is always in that good state in which we sometimes are, this compels our wonder; and if in a better this compels it yet more. And God is in a better state. And life also belongs to God; for the actuality of thought is life, and God is that actuality; and God's self-dependent actuality is life most good and

eternal. We say therefore that God is a living being, eternal, most good, so that life and duration continuous and eternal belong to God; for this is God." [42]

And that sums up some of the essential qualities of the Christian God which can be derived using our natural reason, by which Aristotle had stumbled on them some three and half centuries before Christianity had come about at all.

Promissory Materialism

There is one interesting aspect to the way that atheists argue against these proofs. Generally speaking, it seems at any rate to this observer, they accept that science has at this time not disproved any of those theories, e.g. it doesn't know what happened before the Big bang and it doesn't know how life could have started on earth if it wasn't via Intelligent Design. However what you come across repeatedly is that they claim that science *will* soon enough be able to prove all these outstanding issues and *when* it does, so they say, it will use proper proofs and scientific reason and not any of this religion mumbo jumbo etc etc. In otherwords they are taking a bet on future developments in science and then claiming to believe in those scientific proofs and evidences which actually haven't been discovered yet! Sir John Eccles, a Nobel prize winning Australian scientist, called this phenomenon of atheists 'promissory materialism' and it does seem strange to reject a belief in God because they claim there is no scientific evidence for it, only to replace it with a belief in future scientific discoveries which at this point there certainly isn't evidence for. But nonetheless it might help to look at the current trend in scientific developments to see is their 'bet' on the shape of future discoveries a good one. So therefore we will try and see if science in modern times is moving closer to the atheist or to the theist position, particularly on the familiar battlegrounds of the origin of the Universe and the beginning of lifeforms on earth:

Modern Scientific Trends on the Origin of the Universe

To better understand where we are on the question of seeking a first cause and a first mover for the universe it might help to outline the history of the Big bang theory, the accepted scientific theory on the origin of the universe.

From about 1905 on, but especially in the next decade or so, Albert Einstein formulated some very important equations which explained gravity and how this effects space and time. Then in 1917 he turned his attention to the structure of the universe as a whole and produced a paper speculating as to how this would fit in to his theory of relativity (Einstein, Albert (1917), "Kosmologische Betrachtungen zur allgemeinen Relativitätstheorie [Cosmological Considerations in the General Theory of Relativity]", Königlich Preussische Akademie der Wissenschaften). Unfortunately in this he blundered because he found that in practice his theory of relativity could not be matched with a stable universe and so introduced a constant in order to artificially create the impression that the universe was static, a step he later regretted.

The first person to seriously question Einstein's stable universe was the Russian Alexander Friedmann in his paper "Über die Möglichkeit einer Welt mit konstanter negativer Krümmung des Raumes" ['About the possibility of a world with constant negative curvature'] published in Berlin in 1924. Unfortunately he was to die in Russia the following year.

Then in 1927, independently of Friedmann, a Belgian priest – and later President of the Pontifical Academy of Sciences – called Fr Georges Lemaitre SJ published a paper in Louvain called 'Un Univers homoge`ne de masse constante et de rayon croissant rendant compte de la vitesse radiale des ne'buleuses extragalactiques' ['A homogeneous Universe of constant mass and growing radius accounting for the radial velocity of extragalactic nebulae']. This really kick started the whole idea of a beginning to the universe – and a universe constantly expanding, unlike Einstein's stable one – and he was to become known as the 'Father of the Big Bang Theory'. He went on to try and persuade scientists from around the world that the universe was created in one big explosion, 'the Cosmic Egg exploding at the moment of the creation', as he called it. The truth was of course that many scientists were sceptical of taking this theory from a Jesuit priest because they suspected it was motivated to fit in with Genesis and the idea of a moment of creation. But as time went on his idea gained traction and probably the seminal moment – at least among the scientific community, its acceptance among the wider populace had to wait another few decades – was when Einstein, after hearing him outline the Big Bang theory at a meeting on the 10th of January 1933 at the Athenaeum, attached to Caltech in Pasadena, said: "This is the most beautiful and satisfactory explanation of creation to which I have ever listened." [43]

Such anyway is the short and sweet history of where we are now in terms of our modern understanding of how the universe came about. The interesting thing is that this new consensus surrounding the Big Bang theory is in fact bad news for atheists. (As indeed Einstein seems to recognise in the above quote.) You see the reality is that traditionally atheism held that the universe was 'a brute fact' or simply infinity. In otherwords they told theists to just accept that the universe is there and has always been there, as opposed to Aristotle's theories. The universe, after all, is obviously huge and has been there for millennia, in practice its near infinity in size and very ancient, so it wasn't really all that counter intuitive to just accept its existence as a fact.

That is until the Big Bang theory came along, clearly that has changed one's perspective on the universe. Now that we can see its beginning, and make serious guesses as to its age and size, we naturally feel more of an urgency and curiosity as to what caused it. Then we are thrown back on Aristotle and Aquinas and maybe find ourselves agreeing with them that no natural being could have originated it. Some atheists have recognised that the Big Bang theory raises disturbing questions for their side of the argument, as described here by Professor Antony Flew:

> "In fact, my two antitheological books were both written long before either the development of the big-bang cosmology or the introduction of the fine-tuning argument from physical constants. But since the early 1980s, I had begun to reconsider. I

confessed at that point that atheists have to be embarrassed by the contemporary cosmological consensus, for it seemed that the cosmologists were providing a scientific proof of what St Thomas Aquinas contended could not be proved philosophically; namely, that the universe had a beginning.

When I first met the big-bang theory as an atheist, it seemed to me the theory made a big difference because it suggested that the universe had a beginning and that the first sentence in Genesis ("In the beginning, God created the heavens and the earth") was related to an event in the universe. As long as the universe could be comfortably thought to be not only without end but also without beginning, it remained easy to see its existence (and its most fundamental features) as brute facts. And if there had been no reason to think the universe had a beginning, there would be no need to postulate something else that produced the whole thing.

But the big-bang theory changed all that. If the universe had a beginning, it became entirely sensible, almost inevitable, to ask what produced this beginning. This radically altered the situation."
44

This indeed is only common sense and it shows how the modern scientific consensus is quietly moving us away from the atheist position, although you would never think that reading the popular media! The fact that the popular perception is quite the opposite was also raised in this quote by Dr Arno Allan Penzias (1933-). He was awarded a PhD at Columbia in 1962, received the Nobel prize in 1978 "for the discovery of cosmic microwave background radiation," and wrote in 1992 in a paper entitled *Creation is supported by all the data so far*:

"Today's dogma holds that matter is eternal. The dogma comes from the intuitive belief of people (including the majority of physicists) who don't want to accept the observational evidence that the universe was created – despite the fact that the creation of the universe is supported by all the observable data astronomy has produced so far. As a result, the people who reject the data can arguably be described as having a 'religious' belief that matter must be eternal. These people regard themselves as objective scientists.

...

Astronomy leads us to a unique event, a universe which was created out of nothing, one with the very delicate balance needed to provide exactly the conditions required to permit life, and one which has an underlying (one might say 'supernatural') plan. Thus the observations of modern science seem to lead to the same conclusions as centuries-old intuition. At the same time, most of our modern scientific intuition seems to be more comfortable with the world as described by the science of yesterday. Kind of interesting, isn't it?" [45]

It is indeed interesting but in any case I think if people consider this they will find themselves agreeing with Dr Penzias, the modern scientific developments are trending towards the position of Genesis rather than away from it.

Modern Scientific Trends on the Origin of Life and DNA

While the question of the fine tuned universe, and the laws of physics, remain lively battlegrounds in the teleological argument the reality of course is that Darwin's theory of evolution, first put forward in the mid 19th century, is the great modern counter argument to Intelligent Design in biology. Obviously Darwinism – as modified by his later adherents – claims that random mutations which will occur by chance in species can create new types of lifeforms, and sometimes more complex ones, which in turn can takeover a species and progress up the 'tree of life' through Natural selection, i.e. the idea that the 'fittest' will supplant the weaker ones. In any case the basic theory is well known, and there is no real need to explore it in too much depth here, but the point is that this theory is held up as giving us a natural – and hence not supernatural – explanation as to why this apparent 'design' seems to exist in biology.

But for the theory of evolution to stand as a complete counterpart to teleology it has to show how lifeforms could have come about at all in the first instance. This is quite a vexed subject with a long history. Dr George Wald (1906-1997), who won the Nobel prize for physiology in 1967, describes here the scientific history of this question of the origin of life:

> "Throughout our history we have entertained two kinds of views of the origin of life: one that life was created supernaturally, the other that it arose "spontaneously" from nonliving material. In the 17th to 19th centuries those opinions provided the ground of a great and bitter controversy. There came a curious point, toward the end of the 18th century, when each side of the controversy was represented by a Roman Catholic priest. The principle opponent of the theory of the spontaneous generation was then the Abbe Lazzaro Spallanzani, an Italian priest; and its principal champion was John Turberville Needham, an English Jesuit.
>
> Since the only alternative to some form of spontaneous generation is a belief in supernatural creation, and since the latter view seems firmly implanted in the Judeo-Christian theology, I wondered for a time how a priest could support the theory of spontaneous generation.
>
> ...
>
> Spontaneous Generation
>
> The more rational elements of society [i.e those that didn't believe supernatural explanations], however, tended to take a more naturalistic view of the matter. One had only to accept the evidence of one's senses to know that life arises regularly from the nonliving: worms from mud, maggots from

decaying meat, mice from refuse of various kinds. This is the view that came to be called spontaneous generation. Few scientists doubted it. Aristotle, Newton, William Harvey, Descartes, van Helmont all accepted spontaneous generation without serious inquiry. Indeed, even the theologians – witness the English priest John Turberville Needham – could subscribe to this view, for Genesis tells us, not that God created plants and most animals directly, but that he bade the earth and waters to bring them forth; since this directive was never rescinded, there is nothing heretical in believing that the process has continued.

But step by step, in a great controversy that spread over two centuries, this belief was whittled away until nothing remained of it. First the Italian Francisco Redi showed in the 17th century that meat placed under a screen, so that flies cannot lay their eggs on it, never develops maggots. Then in the following century the Italian Abbe Lazzaro Spallanzani showed that a nutritive broth, sealed off from the air while boiling, never develops micro-organisms, and hence never rots. Spallanzani could defend his broth; when he broke the seal of his flasks, allowing new air to rush in, the broth promptly began to rot. He could find no way, however, to show that the air inside the flask had not been vitiated. This problem was finally solved by Louis Pasteur in 1860, with a simple modification of Spallanzani's experiment. Pasteur too used a flask containing boiling broth, but instead of sealing off the neck he drew it out in a long, S-shaped curve with its end open to the air. While molecules of air could pass back and forth freely, the heavier particles of dust, bacteria, and moulds in the atmosphere were trapped on the walls of the curved neck and only rarely reached the broth. In such a flask, the broth seldom was contaminated; usually it remained clear and sterile indefinitely.

...

This great controversy ended in the mid-19th century with the experiments of Louis Pasteur, which seemed to dispose finally of the possibility of spontaneous generation. For almost a century afterward biologists proudly taught their students this history and the firm conclusion that spontaneous generation had been scientifically refuted and could not possibly occur. Does this mean that they accepted the alternative view, a supernatural creation of life? Not at all. They had no theory of the origin of life, and if pressed were likely to explain that questions involving such unique events as origins and endings have no place in science." [46]

As you can see biology is indeed moving somewhere in this area, science can rightly say it is banishing the mists of the unknown and establishing the truth, which is that the spontaneous creation of any lifeform is impossible! (Actually scientists now have a Law of Abiogenesis, based on Pasteur's work, which is that life cannot arise except via other life.) We know this because the experiments of Pasteur et al are by no means the last word on our understanding of lifeforms. To cut a long story very short, the fact is that in the century and a half since Pasteur's, and Darwin's time, our knowledge of the cell and other aspects of lifeforms has increased exponentially but always by adding on more complexity to it, making it less and less likely that it could have come about by chance. Here is a simple quote on this by Dr David Berlinski (1942 -). He is of German Jewish heritage, a postdoctoral fellow in mathematics and molecular biology at Columbia University, an author of many books on mathematics and teacher at numerous universities including Stanford and the University of Paris, and was asked at one point:

"That if he [Darwin] thought of the cell as being a Buick [car], what is the cell now in terms of its complexity by comparison?"

and answered:

"A galaxy." [47]

That sums it up, but that in turn means that we know now it is far less likely that life could have ever arisen by any random means, than was known to be the case during the time when Darwin put forward his theories.

Hence the more you consider it the more you realise that the current trends of scientific discovery are pushing you further and further away from the possibility that evolution could work as a theory, because you cannot even start the process with the first lifeform. As time goes on it seems to this observer that there are more and more serious implications for the theory of Evolution thrown up by the advance of our knowledge of genetics and biology:

As our knowledge has increased over the last few years we have gone from appreciating a kind of plain and simple DNA to understanding more of the vast complexity involving it and the requirement for "interpretation by the highly dynamic cellular systems that control DNA packaging, imprinting, replication, transcription, translation, splicing, signal transduction, morphogenesis, and so forth." Don't forget that the latest developments in cloning and designing new living organisms – by slicing in and out DNA sequences from other organisms via virus vectors etc – are all done on the base of an original living organism. Scientists nowadays make absolutely no attempt to create from scratch a living organism, no matter how simple, because even with all the advances in computers and Nanotechnology the mystery of creating life continues to elude science.

Another important point is that we are now almost a century and a half in the midst of this often heated debate on evolution and surely it is high time to see to what extent the theory has been proven via the fossil record. In the late 70s it was reported that there are now as many as 250,000 fossil samples scattered across the great institutions of the world and yet we are still arguing about a mere handful of very controversial, and implausible, supposed 'missing links.' The simple reality is that no proof backing up Darwin's theory has been found in the fossil record, the 'missing links' are still missing! But they shouldn't be after this length of time and that amount of research, unless it is the case that the theory is just not right and does not explain the complexity of biological systems in life on earth.

You can see this in the following quotes from a molecular biologist and two paleontologists, respectively

> "Fossils have ... failed to yield the host of transitional forms demanded by evolutionary theory...the absence of transitional forms is dramatically obvious."

Actually this biologist, Dr Denton, feels so strongly about this that he has gone on to say that:

> "The Darwinian theory of evolution is no more nor less than the great cosmogenic myth of the twentieth century." [48]

Also, from paleontologist Dr David Raup:

> "250,000 species of plants and animals recorded and deposited in museums throughout the world did not support the gradual unfolding hoped for by Darwin." [49]

See also the comments by Dr Stephen J Gould, a well known academic in this field who formulated the theory of Punctuated Equilibrium:

> "The extreme rarity of transitional forms in the fossil record persists as the trade secret of paleontology. The evolutionary trees that adorn our textbooks have data only at the tips and nodes of their branches; the rest is inference, however reasonable, not the evidence of the fossils." [50]

So as time has gone on the evidence accumulated is not backing up Darwin at all. The interesting thing here is that in the last 15 years or so the pace of change and increase in knowledge of genes and gene expression in both modern and indeed ancient plant and animal specimens – via bones etc, many dating a long time hence – has increased exponentially. A geneticist can now, via a few mouse clicks on his computer, instantly check the molecular structure or DNA sequence that is of interest to him on huge international databases that hold vast biological data from both the current and historical eras. Only two decades ago this would have involved months of work, which can now be compressed into a few hours. With all that data then surely the pattern of evolution would now be very obvious to us all? The truth is that if the theory was true at this stage we would have very clear lines of animals and their DNA sequences going from simple to complex up the line of evolution, and it is just not there. No such examples have come forward. If you don't believe me you should watch this video and see how Dr Richard Dawkins was stumped when asked to give just such an example: http://www.youtube.com/watch?v=zaKryi3605g . In fact over the last few decades of the 20th century and into the 21st quite a bit of the trend has been the other way, refuting some of the old standbys of the evolutionist critique, as can be seen in this quote from the 1976 Presidential Address to the Geological Society by Dr Derek Victor Ager (1923-1993), Professor of Geology, University College of Swansea,:

> "It must be significant that nearly all the evolutionary stories I learned as a student, from Truman's Ostrea/Gryphaea to Carruthers' Zaphrentis delanouei, have now been 'debunked'. Similarly, my own experience of more than twenty years looking for evolutionary lineages among the Mesozoic Brachiopoda has proved them equally elusive." [51]

This can be seen in what happened to the famous peppered moths, previously the main stalwart used to show evolution in action, as outlined here by the Sunday Telegraph journalist Robert Matthews:

> "Evolution experts are quietly admitting that one of their most cherished examples of Darwin's theory, the rise and fall of the peppered moth, is based on a series of scientific blunders. Experiments using the moth in the Fifties and long believed to prove the truth of natural selection are now thought to be worthless, having been designed to come up with the 'right' answer." [52]

So the onward march of science, and specifically the onward

galloping it is doing in the genetic area, is moving us to believe less in the Darwinian interpretation and in consequence should lead us to believe more in the ancients and their feeling that it points towards the ordering and governorship of God.

But yet there are many who will just wait for science to solve these problems. They will admit that yes science has not solved the problem of the first lifeform etc but they are confident that this will happen in the future. In otherwords some people seem to have a blind faith in some kind of future scientific advance, which is certainly not proven by science now, while po-facedly telling the rest of us not to believe in God because it's existence is not proven by science! Is the logic not going around in circles here? And on that I will leave you with some thoughts by the famous British mathematician and astronomer Sir Fred Hoyle. Hoyle, who was described in the Guardian in 2001 as "one of the 20th century's leading scientists" [53] and is generally conceded was unfairly cheated out of a Nobel Prize in 1983,[54] here describes his view of how people are dealing with the absence of scientific proof – or even a credible theory – for the origin of life on this planet:

> "The concept of 'evolution,' to which I have already referred, serves very much like a primitive god. 'Chance' is another god of modern science. However improbable a situation may be, the argument is that, if it hadn't been so, we wouldn't be here to know about it. Since we are indeed here, 'therefore' it had to be so, even to the extent of explaining away a number with 40 000 digits. Astronomers are permitted to contemplate the state of affairs outside the Earth, but only on the condition that they see the universe as a purposeless meaningless affair.
>
> ...
>
> The likelihood of the formation of life from inanimate matter is one to a number with 40 thousand naughts after it. It is big enough to bury Darwin and the whole theory of evolution. There was no primeval soup, neither on this planet nor on

any other, and if the beginnings of life were not random they must therefore have been the product of purposeful intelligence." [55]

CHAPTER 3
Evidence of the Supernatural in general

But maybe there is another, simpler, way of looking at all this. Clearly the great problem that the rational mind has in believing in the existence of God is that most people do not accept the existence of anything supernatural. In otherwords all the stuff about ghosts and souls and demons and all that is taken as bunkum and that being the case its very difficult to accept any similar sounding 'hocus pocus' when somebody comes along and says that God exists. In otherwords, clearly if you were to believe in the existence of the supernatural at all then its only a short enough stretch to believe in God? Hence maybe we can just widen this debate somewhat and see is there proof of supernatural phenomenon at all because if so most people would be prepared to believe in God I think.

Certainly in history, maybe particularly Irish history, you cannot but be impressed by the overwhelming amount of detailed eyewitness accounts of supernatural incidents. The Confessions of St Patrick for example, a very respected very authentic document in the opinion of all Irish historians I would suggest, describes how he found his way at one point by taking directions from the guardian angel of Ireland, Victor, who came to him in a dream. Adamnán's Life of St Colmcille, another greatly respected work, sometimes considered the first great biography of these islands, describes how the great saint's death was supernaturally held up by the prayers of his friends.[56] If you don't just want Irish sources you could consider the autobiography of Guibert of Nogent, who died in 1124 in Northern France, another highly respected medieval source, which similarly abounds in supernatural incidents.[57]

Anyway anybody who has ever read extensively the original writings of our history will tell you that these things are very extensively documented. The question then is how does modern science treat these references? Well obviously some scientists take the view that they couldn't have happened, because there is no such thing as God or the supernatural, and therefore the writers are lying, exaggerating, hallucinating, or suffering from some other unfortunate psychological problem! But if you think about it that is not a very scientific way to examine evidence. It makes more sense to just take these eye witness accounts for what they are i.e. eye witness evidence that the supernatural exists, and consequently if they are in such abundance, and in otherwise authentic sources, maybe you should just come away with the impression that the supernatural does indeed exist?

Of course what we also hear from some scientists is that these references are not compiled in proper laboratory or even legal conditions and hence we cannot accept this as proper evidence. But, to take one example, the traditional process of beatifying Catholic saints involved compiling documented proof of at least two miracles performed by the candidate. And this was quite a serious and important piece of evidence gathering and proof weighing because, for example, it involved, since 1587, famously a 'devil's advocate' who argued against the credibility of the saint and the authenticity of the miracles. There are thousands of miracles carefully documented by the Bollandists (a group that over the course of four centuries meticulously compiled the various saints' lives) for example.[58] There are also facts related to the miracles, not just eyewitness accounts, that can be used to verify what happened. You can see videos and photographs of those saints who had stigmata like Padre Pio. Many of the people who received miraculous cures at Lourdes were examined by a neutral commission – including Protestant and Jewish doctors – of medical experts who examined X-rays etc and pronounced many cases as true supernatural miracles. The witnesses to what happened at Knock were formally examined and questioned, even on their death beds, as to what happened and authentic records of this have been kept. Meanwhile the miracle at Fatima was witnessed by some 70,000 people, including by a number of reporters who wrote about it in their newspapers.[59]

In order to give a proper flavour of the kind of historical accounts of miracles that abound in recorded Irish history, and in international sources like the Bollandists, I thought I would give you here a few quotes from some books written by Irish authors in the early to mid 17th century:

(a) The following quotation was written by Dr Henry Fitzsimon (c.1566 - c.1643) S.J. who prepared most of the text in this book while imprisoned in Dublin Castle as a Catholic in 1600-4. A son of the Lord Mayor of Dublin, he was very well educated in places like Oxford – where he was a committed Protestant, he was beaten in a controversy with a Jesuit and that is why he became a Catholic – and Paris and throughout many adventures in Ireland and across Europe – he served as a chaplain in Bohemia in the 30 years war for example – he was always fearless in standing up for his country and his religion:

"In Dona moore [Donaghmore presumably, possibly the townland 2 miles south of Ashbourne], seven miles from Dublin in Ireland, Mr Richard Bealing [doubtless Bellings, in all probability the grandfather of the secretary of the Supreme Council of the Confederation of Kilkenny, who lived near Mulhuddart] Justice of peace dwelled, when Catholics were persecuted under the Lord Gray, about the year of Christ 1580. He being an eminent person, was accused (by Sir R[obert] D[illon] the blind knight, and blood sucker) that he harboured one Patrick Nigram a priest; even then to be found in his house. Searchers being in all haste sent (for at that time James FitzMaurice, Doctor Sanders, and divers others, coming into the country, had made the state jealous toward matters of religion) as they environed the house, the Mother of God, our Blessed Lady appeared to Mistriss Bealing saying: 'sayeth [abbreviation 'sed' expanded here] instantly to Sir [sic] Patrick Nigram, that he descend into a cave, or cellar, and that removing a stone in such a corner, he further descend by stairs, where they shall conduct him'. Which she, although once, or twice admonished (supposing it to be a dream) neglected, till at length in visible manner, with admirable beauty and brightness, the immaculate Queen of heaven objected herself, and renewed the commandment so distinctly, that she promptly procured it to be fulfilled. Nigram was a Godly priest of unspotted life, and rare zeal, my quondam school fellow, whom of purpose, I visited upon his death bed, and from himself, beside all others, received the assurance of this declaration. When he removed the stone, he found indeed the degrees, or stairs, of five or six steps, guiding him to a small neat chamber, of some 20 foot long, and 12 foot broad, wherein a bed, and chair was duly placed. He being bestoyed in his cabinet, the searchers coming in, with all diligent inquiry, sought every place of the house, every cellar, and corner, but all in vain. After three days, frantic to be frustrated, and weary to inquire without hope of their purpose, they departed. Nigram by Mistress Bealing, being repealed out of his cell (wherein he had all that time, abounded with spiritual delight) they covering again the place, never after by any inquiry, were able to find so much as any show thereof remaining. Wherefor, at least some times, narrow, and unnatural places, may by God's divine providence, serve, to conceal miraculously what he would not have discovered. Whereof innumerable like instances might, if brevity permitted, be alledged." [60]

(b) This following incident has been mentioned by five separate accounts written or published in the mid to late 17th century.

(i) Firstly I will give you the quote from Fr John Lynch (1599-1673), who is a very well respected Irish historian – and Bishop of Killala – of the period, originally from Galway and writing here in a published book in 1667:

"Lavallin Nugent, refusing the opulent inheritance of Dysert [immediately north of Lilliput on the western shores of Lough Ennell in

Co. Westmeath] which came to him on his brother's death, associated himself with the Order of the Capuchins. He was so pious that he became the institutor of the Capuchin missions to Germany and Ireland. And at the consecration of the host, which he exhalted as was his custom while performing his office, Our Saviour having put on the form of a little child manifested himself visibly to a woman who was a heretic. [This] so influenced her mind that having adjured her heresy she joined herself to the Catholics." [61]

Remarkably it seems that Lynch had this from an independent source and not from the two main histories of the Irish Capuchins which were, and remain, only available in manuscript form. (I say that because the long account of this family in Lynch's Alithinologia doesn't seem to have had its source in O'Connell's work, who in turn would have drawn on Archbold.) These two historians mention this incident in some depth from which we find that it occurred in the St Servatius' Church in Cologne, in or around 1612, and the woman in question, who was a sister of the dean of the collegiate church of St George the Martyr in that city, witnessed it when Nugent was saying mass before the sermon which was to be given by Fr Bonaventura von Wuerzburg OFM (Cap.). Just to clarify then you have these two corroborating manuscript accounts:

(ii) Fr Nicholas Archbold OFM (Cap.) (1589-1650), *Historie of the Irish Capucins*, completed in 1643, now in the Municipal Library in Troyes, France, Ms 1103, p.20-2. Archbold was from a well known family in Dalkey and he was actually an eyewitness to the incident, being in the church at the time. He also tells us that the lady testified as to what happened to her in a legal document which was deposited in the city archives.

(iii) Fr Robert O'Connell OFM (Cap.), *Historia Missionis Hibernicae Capucinorum* authenticated 26th Sept 1654, also in the above library, Ms706, p.67. O'Connell was the joint author of the famous *Commentarius Rinuccinianus* and as such needs little mention here. He was from Kerry as it happens, near where the liberator was from, and his real first name was Daniel. Forty years after the incident happened he interviewed the lady as part of his research into his history of the Irish Capuchins and she, then an old woman, absolutely confirmed the story.

Then on top of that you have it mentioned in two other contemporary accounts:

(iv) *Origines et memorabiliora Prov. Rhenanae*, written about 1629 and published in Arsenius von Losheim Jacobs, *Die Rheinischen Kapuziner, 1611-1725* (Munster, 1933), i, W, p.126.

(v) Aegidius Gelenius, *De admiranda, sacra, et civili magnitudine Coloniæ Claudiæ Agrippensis Augustæ Ubiorum urbis* (Cologne, 1645), p.525.

Its curious too how each of these seem to be separate independent accounts of the incident, rather than just copies of each other, bearing in mind that the two Capuchin histories are not well known, and not widely copied, manuscripts which were never published. O'Connell did have access to Archbold's account though, but, as we have seen, adds separately sourced information to it.[62]

(c) This is by Fr Daniel Daly O.P. (1595-1662) writing in 1655 and referring to the time of the 1651 siege at Limerick:

> "The second is the apparition of the blessed mother of God at about three o clock in the afternoon on the summit of the great church dedicated to her. She was seen by some simple people who were at work in the fields accompanied by St Francis and St Dominick, and five other heavenly beings, who seemed to follow her to the convent of the Dominicans, and thence to the Franciscan church without the walls. From those who were spectators, Father James Dooley received information of the circumstances as I have narrated them, and he himself is yet living." [63]

Fr Daly was a larger than life Kerryman who, among many other things, was entrusted with intricate diplomatic negotiations involving the Spanish and British governments,[64] was also appointed ambassador from Portugal to the court of Louis XIV, and his epitaph reads: "Successful in the royal legations he undertook, he was conspicuous for prudence, learning and piety."

The aforementioned Fr James Dooley, who had a doctorate in theology, was a reasonably prominent figure at the time, with some letters of his existing at Rome, and also was, at the time that Daly was writing, the Vicar Apostolic of Limerick and later Bishop of same, and around this time, rector of the Neophytes College at Madonna dei Monti in Rome.

(d) The following account comes from Fr Anthony Bruodin (or MacBrody) OFM, a Franciscan writing at their house in Prague in 1669. He was a great author who did his best in gathering together details on the Irish Franciscan martyrs of the Cromwellian period but he was far away in Prague and unfortunately got some details wrong, hence its helpful that here, in contrast, he was an eyewitness to the incident. By the way the MacBrody's were the hereditary family of historians in Clare:

> "Beside these, and several other gifts of nature, Thomond is also blessed with supernatural gifts, such as several wells formerly made holy by saints. People who drink of the water from these wells with devotion are cured of various ills, as the daily experience of several centuries testifies. One of these wells is called Tobar Rian Douin, from which the town takes its name, not far from the house of my father Miler Brouder in Ballyogan. He died in 1668, the year I wrote these things; he was then in the 81st year of his age and the 58th of his marriage with my mother Margaret Moloney. There are also wells dedicated to Saints Senan, Donatus, Caimin and Cronan, and two to St Brigid. St Michael's well was first found 36 years ago, and since God worked many miracles through it (as everyone in Ireland knows, even the heretic English), I shall say a few words about how it was found, lest the memory of it perish.
>
> A lady of ancient lineage, Lady Marian O'Gorman, lost her husband Sir Thomas O'Gorman, Lord of Tullycrine in the barony of

Clondegad in Thomond. She was about fifty-two years old at the time; I knew her well as she was a close relative. She suffered so much from sciatica and a stone in the kidney that she could not sleep day or night with the pain. She tried several doctors, but in vain; the human skills of the doctors could do nothing to relieve the pain. The devout Lady Marian left aside vain hope in human medicine, and drawing on her Catholic faith, she sought divine help through the intercession of St Michael, the most glorious prince of archangels. Michael, commander of that angelic army, hastened to the aid of the suppliant lady. The pain lessened. The following night he appeared to Marian in a dream and spoke these words to her: 'Tomorrow, you will go to the shrine dedicated to my name'. (In Irish it is called Cill Mhichil, which means the shrine dedicated to St Michael, where there is a chapel dedicated to his name). 'When you have heard mass, you will go the cemetery and where you see a clump of reeds you will dig the ground. When you have done that, a copious flow of health-giving water will flow forth. As soon as you drink of this water, and wash your hands and feet in it, you will be completely cured.'

Good Catholic that she was, Marian paid no heed to the angel's advice the first time, for she knew that dreams were not to be trusted unless they were clearly from God. The prince of angels appeared to her a second time in her sleep, and warned her to give top priority to what he had previously ordered her to do. Still, on her confessor's advice, she wanted further proof of whether this inspiration was coming from God or not. So, in spite of increasing pain, she declined to carry out the order. But at the same time she continued to pray to St Michael for help. The Archangel appeared a third time; if she did not heed the divine warning this third time, he said, she would suffer irreparable damage.

Next morning, Marian called her confessor and her son Thomas O'Gorman, and told them of what she had seen and heard in her third dream. With the consent of both men, she had herself driven immediately to the designated place, about an Irish mile from her home. There, she first went to confession and received holy communion. Then, in the presence of many people, she ordered the earth to be dug up. The parish priest, Mr Dermot O'Queely, took up the spade in the name of God, and he had no sooner sunk it in the ground than a spring of the clearest water gushed forth. All the Catholics sank to their knees at the sight of this miracle, and gave thanks to God for this unexpected grace. Marian wept for joy and, calling on further help from her heavenly protector and the assistance of her servants, she approached the full well. She tasted the water, washed her hands and feet, and she was instantly restored to full health as if she had never been ill. That same week, so greatly did the devotion of the people to the glorious prince of angels and to the recently blessed water increase, two people who had been blind from birth had their sight restored. Three cripples also walked; one of whom could only crawl about on his hands and knees for the previous fifteen years.

The fame of the miracles worked at the new well increased daily, and a huge crowd began to gather there from all over Thomond and the whole of Munster. Eventually they came from all the provinces of Ireland, especially on the feast of St Michael and on the anniversary of the apparition; there were times when as many as 6,000 received holy communion there on one day.

As God continued to favour the place with

miracles, the faith and devotion of the people grew towards this sacred place. In the first year alone, the parish priest listed out 300 miracles to the late bishop of Killaloe, the most reverend John O'Molony, a cousin of mine. All of these were people who has tasted the water from St Michael's well with devotion and were restored to their former health by the power of God. The following years too, up to my departure from the country in 1643, an equal number of miracles were authenticated by a notary public appointed for this purpose.

The only miracle I witnessed with my own eyes happened on the feast of St Michael in 1642. A poor man called Donatulus (little Donat, or Donnachin) was so crippled from birth that his heels were attached to his buttocks. For many years he used to be carried about Clanricard and Thomond from house to house on a horse, or sometimes propelled himself in a little hand driven cart, in search of food. With the assistance of some devout people he was present at St Michael's shrine, along with thousands of others from all over Ireland, on the day and year I mentioned. About 11 o'clock in the morning, just after the sermon, Donat (I forget his surname) was brought to the well by some devout person, in spite of the milling crowd, and washed in its waters. No sooner had he done so that Donat suddenly stood up before all those people, rejoicing and praising God as if he had never been crippled. He did the customary rounds of the church and cemetery on his bare feet in the most lively fashion.

I was already a Franciscan at that time, and I was able to see for myself the marks of his heels and calves on his buttocks; I even touched them out of curiosity. Nor must some heretic say that several such ailments can be cured by the natural powers of water. No, it was not customary for the sick to bathe there as they do at the Caroline Spa and elsewhere here in Bohemia and at the various healthgiving waters around Europe where doctors send people. Here, people first armed themselves with firm faith in God, and hope in the invocation of the Blessed Archangel Michael, and then drank a little of the water and wet their faces with it rather than washed themselves properly. The power by which they were healed came from elsewhere, not from the natural properties of that water. But let's get back to the subject." [65]

If you are interested in fascinating international examples of supernatural activity I would point you in the direction of the approved visions of Mother Mariana de Jesus Torres in Ecuador and Anne Catherine Emmerich in Germany as examples that are not easily explained away. In the case of the former, a number of her visions – the dates of which are given in square brackets below – were well documented long before the events described seem to have come about:

"[16th Jan 1599:]

In the 19th century, a truly Christian president [Gabriel Garcia Moreno] will come; a man of character whom God Our Lord will give the palm of martyrdom on the square adjoining this Convent of mine. He will consecrate the Republic of Ecuador to the Sacred Heart of my Most Holy Son and this consecration will sustain the Catholic Religion in the years that will follow, which will be ill-fated ones for the Church.

These years, during which the accursed sect of Masonry will take control of the civil government, will see a cruel persecution of all religious communities, and will also strike out violently against this one of mine.

[21st Jan 1610:]

Thus, I make it known to you that from the end of the 19th century and from shortly after the middle of the 20th century, in what is today the Colony and will then be the Republic of Ecuador, the passions will erupt and there will be a total corruption of customs, for Satan will reign almost completely by means of the Masonic sects. They will focus principally on the children in order to sustain this general corruption. Woe to the children of these times!

It will be difficult to receive the Sacrament of Baptism and also the Sacrament of Confirmation. They will receive the Sacrament of Confession only if they remain in Catholic schools, for the Devil will make a great effort to destroy it through persons in position of authority.

...

As for the Sacrament of Matrimony, which symbolises the union of Christ with His Church, it will be attacked and deeply profaned. Freemasonry, which will then be in power, will enact iniquitous laws with the aim of doing away with this Sacrament, making it easy for everyone to live in sin and encouraging the procreation of illegitimate children born without the blessing of the Church. The Catholic spirit will rapidly decay; the precious light of Faith will gradually be extinguished until there will be an almost total and general corruption of customs. Added to this will be the effects of secular education, which will be one reason for the death of priestly and religious vocations.

The Sacrament of Holy Orders will be ridiculed, oppressed, and despised, for in this Sacrament, the Church of God and even God Himself is scorned and despised since He is represented in His priests. The Devil will try to persecute the ministers of the Lord in every possible way; he will labor with cruel and subtle astuteness to deviate them from the spirit of their vocation and will corrupt many of them. These depraved priests, who will scandalise the Christian people, will make the hatred of bad Catholics and the enemies of the Roman Catholic and Apostolic Church fall upon all priests.

This apparent triumph of Satan will bring enormous suffering to the good Pastors of the Church, the many good priests, and the Supreme Pastor and Vicar of Christ on earth, who, a prisoner in the Vatican, will shed secret and bitter tears in the presence of his God and Lord, beseeching light, sanctity and perfection for all the clergy of the world, of whom he is King and Father.

Further, in these unhappy times, there will be unbridled luxury which will ensnare the rest into sin and conquer innumerable frivolous souls who will be lost. Innocence will almost no longer be found in children, nor modesty in women.

[2nd Feb 1610:]
Know, beloved daughter, that when your name will become known in the 20th century, there will be many who will not believe, claiming that this devotion is not pleasing to God.
...
A simple, humble faith in the truth of my apparitions to you, my favoured child, will be reserved for humble and fervent souls who are docile to the inspirations of grace, for our Heavenly Father communicates His secrets to the simple of heart, and not to those whose hearts are inflated with pride, pretending to know what they do not or infatuated with empty science.

[December 1624:]

As you see, St. Gabriel also carries a ciborium filled with Hosts: this signifies the most august Sacrament of the Eucharist, which will be distributed by my Catholic priests to faithful belonging to the Holy Roman, Catholic and Apostolic Church, whose visible head is the Pope, the King of Christendom. His pontifical infallibility will be declared a Dogma of Faith by the same Pope [Pius IX] chosen to proclaim the Dogma of the Mystery of my Immaculate Conception. He will be persecuted and imprisoned in the Vatican by the unjust usurpation of the Pontifical States through the iniquity, envy and avarice of an earthly monarch." [66]

Remember these visions was completely recorded and documented long long before the modern era. She even names the country Ecuador long before it was actually called that.

The visions of Anne Catherine Emmerich are possibly even more remarkable. She was one of the many fully documented stigmatics – 360 of whom have been approved by the Church –, i.e. she bled in her hands, feet and side in the same way as Our Lord on the cross, and she was examined not only by Church but even by secular authorities to rule out any possible foul play. Although nearly illiterate, and not even remotely a biblical scholar, she has left us many books full of magnificently detailed accounts of the events of biblical times. These visions are so highly thought of that Mel Gibson used them in his film on the Passion and her account has even been used to find an archaeological site at Ephesus in modern day Turkey. [67]

Many other people have had these stigmata like, as mentioned, Padre Pio, Theresa Neumann [68] and St Gemma Galgani.[69] In case you are wondering, there are so many well documented stigmatics that most atheist commentators do not doubt there existence, they only try to come up with non-supernatural explanations for the phenomenon, but not with great success as you can read here: http://www.newadvent.org/cathen/14294b.htm . Also don't think for a minute that these cases haven't been investigated by science and found to be authentic, in the sense that there is no logical scientific explanation for what happens. These cases have long ago being examined in great depth by scientists, for example you have the agnostic Dr Pierre Janet (1859-1947) who published the results of his experiments on Madeleine le Bou (c.1857 -1918), a stigmatic from a traditional Catholic family in Western France, in: "Un Cas du phenomene des Apports," *Bulletin de l'Institut Psychologique International*, I (1900-1901), p.329-335, and by the same author: *De l'angoisse à l'extase* (Paris, 1928) vol 2, p.304. He did everything to try and come up with a simple scientific explanation for her stigmata, including going to the length of encasing one of her feet in a copper shoe with a window installed, whereby he could see the progress of the wound of the stigmata and at the same time prove that nobody could be tampering with it, i.e. creating the wound. He didn't find any scientific explanation and just ends up with a Freudian analysis as regards the power of imagination etc, which seems a very weak explanation for these phenomenon.

In more modern times you can read about the investigations of people like Dr. Ricardo Castanon Gomez [70] and Mike Willesee. Dr. Castanon was working on biochemistry in Germany for a book on the evolution (which he now doesn't believe in) of the brain when, as a committed atheist, he decided to look into some of these cases of stigmata etc in order to disprove them. In fact he has found many of these cases to be perfectly genuine, although he has also found some charlatans as well. Of the cases he has investigated, using the full battery of scientific tests, he has found about 7 complete frauds but over 50 completely authentic ones – and hence he has now become a Catholic – although it must be said that he only tries to test properly cases that seem authentic on the surface. In otherwords excluded from those figures are many other cases which he didn't bother to look at in depth because the people involved were clearly exaggerating, mentally unbalanced, or suspiciously fond of making money, and in some cases he felt the subjects were too fanatical, meaning that they may have been hoping too much for a sign from God.

Michael Willesee is a well known investigative journalist in Australia who had left the faith but believed again after doing some investigations into these cases. For his pains on doing these documentaries he actually went from being awarded journalist of the year by the Australian Skeptics Association, "for his critical approach to dubious claims", to then receiving their Bent Spoon Award! He is particularly well known for his 1998 work on the 'Signs of God' documentary for the Fox TV network in the US.[71] In any case there are countless modern examples of cases like these who are indeed subject to the best that science can offer and the only explanation seems to be a supernatural one, for example here is a list of specialists who examined Nancy Fowler, a stigmatic in Conyers, Georgia, USA, including the aforementioned Dr Castanon, who is a Professor of Neuropsychophysiology,:

> "Neurologist, Dr Ramon Sanchez of Atlanta, a specialist in Neurology and Epileptology;
> Neurologist, Dr Norma Augosto Maury of Puerto Rico;
> EEG Technicians, Scott Prandy and Ted Blume;
> Dr. George Hogben, Psychiatrist from New York;
> Dr. Philip Callahan, now retired, a former research scientist and professor with the University of Florida;
> Umberto Velasquez, a radiation scientist from the Florida State Department of Health;
> William Stellar, Cameraman and Documentary Producer, formally of Australian ABC Television;
> Australian Attorney Ron Tesoriero who arranged for the recording of the testing for a video and a book documentary." [72]

The point being that there is no point in coming up with simple puerile explanations for these incidents, the usual explanations have been scientifically tested to death by these experts and have been found wanting, and hence the only answer left seems to be the supernatural.

In any case the point obviously is that there are a lot of clear, well authenticated, and not so easily dismissed accounts of miracles in Irish and obviously international history. It seems then to this writer that you cannot keep trotting out 'mass psychosis' or some other piece of pop psychology to trash these eyewitness accounts. The proper, scientific, approach, it seems to me, is to consider them carefully, and if the authors are respected serious people, as they are, then maybe we should take on board these incidents as having actually happened?

Also it is not just in the case of the Catholic Church where you can see evidence of the existence of the supernatural. There are countless well documented cases of Near Death Experiences as another example.[73] If you'd like a scientific take on this phenomenon you might like to see this by Dr Lloyd Rudy, 'a legend in the field of cardiac surgery, credited with the discovery that heart attacks and strokes are caused by blood clots': http://www.youtube.com/watch?v=JL1oDuvQR08 .
Unfortunately from the Occult world you can get very specific eye witness accounts of demons being raised and possessions etc. See for instance the testimony of Doreen Irvine from London,[74] Bill Schnoebelen [75] and Jeff Harshbarger [76] from the US, and Roger Morneau from Canada.[77]

The Exorcist film was based on a true story and is one of a huge number of examples where you get the usual demonic practices, like bodies being elevated into the air and people speaking in languages they don't know etc, all carefully documented in demon possessed people. The real story of this case centres on Robbie Doe, or Mannheim, – which are pseudonyms, the Church protected his identity – who was born on the 1st of June 1935 into a German Lutheran family and grew up in Cottage City in Maryland. He got possessed when he was using a ouigi board on the 15th of January 1949 and was finally delivered from these demons in St Louis on the 18th of April 1949. He was such a celebrated case that the successful exorcism was reported in the newspapers at the time (e.g. on the 19th August 1949 in the Evening Star, Washington DC).

As pointed out, his case manifested the supernatural occurrences common to many exorcisms including speaking in strange languages, objects moving across rooms of their own accord and in this case writing which manifested itself on the skin of the boy. No less than 48 witnesses – who witnessed the events in two different locations, St Louis and the suburbs of Washington DC, and at different times – signed the final ecclesiastical report on the case, testifying to the supernatural nature of the occurrences. "Terry D. Cooper, Ph.D., a psychologist, as well as Cindy K. Epperson, a doctoral fellow at the University of Missouri, analysed the case and came to the conclusion that normal psychological explanations cannot account for the claimed events." In the book they wrote on the subject these authors went through all the possible psychological disorders that could account for what happened, and rejected all of them as impossible in this case. In fact exorcisms, and manifestations of demons in general, have occurred all throughout history, after all even King James I wrote a book on demonology.[78]

In Ireland it is not just all fairytales where Irish people said they saw ghosts etc, these are in many cases real stories that are handed down because they genuinely happened. Any middling sized parish or old family in Ireland abounds in such cases.

Furthermore this is not all old history where very credible people talk about their experiences with the supernatural. I just thought I would leave you with two recent cases from Irish policemen who wrote their memoirs in the last few years. The first is by Gerard MacManus, a nephew of the writer Terence MacManus, from Dundalk, and secondly by Gerry O'Carroll who frequently writes in the Evening Herald on security issues.

In any case at some point when you read all this stuff you have to accept that there actually is quite a lot of credible evidence out there that the supernatural exists, and its only a short step from that to believing in God and the religion of our ancestors.

Gerard MacManus:

> "The occupied cells [in Arbour Hill, where he was serving as an Irish Army MP] took up a small part of the prison interior, so I roamed around exploring. Certain locked rooms, when I walked past them, caused my body to shiver. This did not happen once, nor was it my imagination. Each time I passed by those rooms and cells, my body would shiver, night after night, and I wondered what it

was. Later when I was a homicide detective in Atlanta, then the murder capital of America, I discovered what it was: a death shiver. I would experience the same shiver when I was in a room with a murder victim, not once but many times.

There is nobody in this world who can convince me that when we die our souls just evaporate. Think about yourself as you sit reading this book. Without your soul you are just an empty vessel sitting in a chair. Our soul is a powerful force which controls our brain and our body. When the body dies, the soul has to find someplace to go, because it is not a physical thing; it is just out there. I trust that I have not 'weirded you out', as they say, but I believe that our souls are powerful forces.

When my shift was over in the morning, I would walk across the street to Collins barracks and sleep until about three in the afternoon and then lie in my cot thinking about things. I know that spooky places tend to feed the imagination and hidden fears, but in the case of Collins barracks and Arbour Hill Prison, I truly believe that something or someone was with me on those long quiet nights. If it was the souls of our nation's tortured past, then I pray they find peace, for when I was there I felt no peace in them, none at all, just an unhappy coldness. I wish I could bring them peace, I truly do. They say that few people experience these chills – something to do with their sensitivity. Frankly I would rather that I had not been bestowed with that 'blessing', which is why I never attend funerals – I make everybody nervous." [79]

Gerry O'Carroll:
[In the old Garda Station in Kildare Town:] "On entering the hall, I saw an elderly man through the

glass door, standing at the counter in the public office. He was no more than six feet away from me. He was a tall man, slightly stooped and appeared to be in his early 60s. His face was pale and careworn. He had a serious, sad and gentle appearance about him. He had a full head of greying black wavy hair.

He wore a beige trench coat buttoned up to his neck and stood facing the station orderly, who was seated behind a table at the other end of the room. There was a turf fire lighting in the grate. For some reason that I will never know, I went back out the front door and walked down the side of the station. Through the side windows, I saw that the man in the trench coat was still standing at the counter. The television was on under the counter and the station orderly was deeply engrossed in what he was watching. I could see quite clearly that it was The Riordans, a series based on a farming community in rural Ireland. I went down to the yard and lit myself a cigar. After a few minutes, I decided to go back to the station. I again walked up to the side entrance and saw the elderly man was still standing there and the station orderly was in his position by the fire.

I walked around the corner back into the station and pushed back the glass door into the public office. There was no sign of the man in the trench coat. I asked the station orderly where the man had gone. He replied that nobody had been in the station for the past 25 minutes. For reasons that I cannot explain, I realised in that instant that the visitor in the beige trench coat was not of this world.

As if I was being led by an unseen hand, I took down a Sacred Heart badge that was wedged behind a socket over the fireplace. On the reverse side of the badge, there was a photograph of the man I had seen standing at the counter for nearly ten minutes. The text under the photograph read: 'Father John Sullivan, died Sunday, February the 19th 1933.'

The photograph of the priest on the badge was identical in every respect to the man I had seen. I had no doubt then, or now, that Father John Sullivan had appeared to me that night in the flesh. I froze at the thought and experienced an emotional shock, but no fear. Although I was supposed to be a hard-bitten detective who had never been prone to a fevered imagination, something had happened to me that defied all logic and understanding.

As I was standing there clutching the photograph, a local detective who was working on the investigation walked into the public office and stood exactly on the spot where I had seen Father Sullivan. I told him what had happened. He looked at me in disbelief and told me that he had been present in his official capacity at the ceremony of exhumation of the mortal remains of Father John Sullivan on 27 September 1960 at Clongowes Wood College, County Kildare. It was the first stage in the process of canonisation for that holy man. His body lies in a lead casket in the Jesuit Church in Gardiner Street. It has become a shrine for thousands of Dubliners. I left the station shortly afterwards. I was in no mood to conduct any further interviews that night.

This strange occurrence was the final link in a chain of events that began one beautiful Saturday in June 1968. It was early morning and I had just said goodbye to my girlfriend, Kathleen, who was on her way to Scotland to see her parents. I was taking a leisurely stroll past the Green Cinema on St Stephen's Green when I felt a tug on my jacket. It was a very old man with a white beard, wearing a black overcoat. He was sitting on the granite steps outside the cinema.

I took a coin from my pocket and handed it to him. He pushed it aside and I realised he was no beggar. In a firm but gentle voice, he asked me to sit down. I sat down beside him on the steps, although feeling a little self-conscious. There was something about him that compelled me to listen to what he had to say. He told me that his name was Mr Ffrench and that he had a lifelong devotion to Father John Sullivan, the Jesuit priest. He showed me a miraculous medal and other religious items that he said Father John Sullivan had blessed and given to him.

He told me that the coat on his back was also given to him by Father Sullivan, and he asked me to touch it, which I did to humour him. He then said the country would become a sea of tears and a vale of suffering if we didn't pray for deliverance through the intercession of Father Sullivan to the Sacred Heart of Jesus. He gave me details of the saintly life that Father John Sullivan had led and his selfless devotion to the poor. He asked me to pray to him and to encourage others to do likewise, and to never forget what he had told me that morning. The sincerity and conviction in that old man's words and the air of sanctity he had about him moved me deeply.

When I walked away from him that morning, I felt some of the warmth had gone out of the day. I never again thought about that fateful meeting until my experiences in Kildare Garda Station all those years later.

In the course of the Clerkin investigation, another remarkable coincidence that ties this tale together took place. During the case, it was necessary to interview the director of the Salts Textile factory in Tullamore regarding the movements of an employee who was believed to have been involved in the periphery of a crime. We were shown into a plush office, where we introduced ourselves and explained the nature and importance of this inquiry to the overall investigation.

Mr Pocock, the director, was a large genial man with a round face and a bald head on which were deep indentations. We had finished our conversation and were about to leave his office when I noticed a framed picture of Father John Sullivan. It was identical to the one I had seen in the station. A votive lamp was lighting the photograph from underneath. I was stunned to see such a shrine and I turned to Pocock and asked him about his interest in Father Sullivan. His face became animated. He told me that Father Sullivan had been a living saint and he had devoted his life to the cause of his canonisation. He went on to tell me an incredible story.

Some years before, he had been diagnosed with inoperable tumours on his brain. The doctors had given up all hope of a recovery and, in effect, he was waiting to die. He said that he had received a visit from his wife and children, and as they left the room he knew that he would never see them again. He prepared himself for the inevitable and as he lay hovering between life and death, drifting in and out of consciousness, he heard a voice call his name. He looked and saw a man standing at the end of the bed. The man said, 'I'm Father John Sullivan, don't worry.'

When he woke up that morning, he thought at first that he had dreamt it all. He then realised with total clarity his mysterious visitor had brought him a miraculous gift. He suddenly felt physically well and experienced a peace he had never known. He rang the bell for breakfast and got out of bed. The nurse called the doctors. He was brought for X-rays, which showed no trace of the tumours. Within three days, he was back home with his family. Doctors agreed that what had taken place was a miracle.

I told him of my encounter in the Garda station. He left his desk with tears in his eyes and, grabbing me by the hands, said that I was a very privileged person. Later, he sent me a relic of Father Sullivan and a book, both of which I treasure to this day.

There was one more fascinating twist in this strangest of tales. Before leaving Kildare, I was told a story by a retired colleague, who had been stationed in Kildare Garda station in the early '70s. He told me that one bad winter's night he was station orderly and was about to lock up when he found an old man sheltering in the little hallway inside the front door. He described him as being very old and frail with a long, white beard and wearing a heavy, black overcoat. He took pity on him, made him a cup of tea and allowed him to stay in a cell for the night. He said that the next morning he'd had to turn him out of the station before the sergeant in charge arrived or he would have got into trouble for his act of kindness. As he was leaving, the old man told him that his name was Mr Ffrench and handed him a Sacred Heart badge with the photograph of Father John Sullivan, the same one that I had discovered on the mantelpiece in the station.

All my life, I have been a spiritual person but a rather lukewarm Catholic. In November 1976, I was the last man that anybody would have imagined to have a 'road to Damascus' type of experience. I cannot explain what happened. It defies all logic and reason; however, I know that what my eyes saw convinced me beyond any doubt of the existence of a divine being and the certainty of life after death. I retain a deep and lasting devotion to Father John Sullivan not just because I have become familiar with his extraordinary saintly existence but most of all, despite all the horrors and inhumanity I have witnessed in my life, this encounter renewed my faith in the basic goodness of mankind." [80]

CHAPTER 4
Importance of Christianity to a Nation

Finally there is one other important point that needs to be made here. The reality, although few seem to realise it, is that the question of the growth of atheism in society is a very political one, in otherwords it has political consequences. It is in fact the case that the enemies of a given state will often try to increase the level of atheism in that country because it can help to destroy the moral fabric and courage of the people in that targeted nation. And, frankly, speaking for myself, I would say that the media in Ireland is at least as controlled and manipulated as any in the advanced Western world and consequently their ongoing ludicrously exaggerated reporting of religious issues in Ireland must be part of a wider, corrupt, political agenda. It might be interesting to read here then the experiences of many great thinkers on this question in the past and the present.

This is the view of Edmund Burke, the great Irish philosopher of course, giving his assessment of the importance of the deliberate fostering of atheism and anti-clerical hatred in bringing about the massacres in France in the late 18th century:

> "It is thus, and for the same end, that they endeavour to destroy that tribunal of conscience which exists independently of edicts and decrees. Your despots govern by terror. They know, that he who fears God fears nothing else; and therefore they eradicate from the mind, through their Voltaire, their Helvetius, and the rest of that infamous gang, that only sort of fear that generates true courage. Their object is, that their fellow citizens may be under the dominion of no awe, but that of their committee of research, and of their lantern." [81]

Professor Max Planck, the father of Quantum Physics, outlines here his view of what was happening during the rise of Nazism in Germany in 1937:

> "Under these conditions it is no wonder, that the

> movement of atheists, which declares religion to be just a deliberate illusion, invented by power-seeking priests, and which has for the pious belief in a higher power nothing but words of mockery, eagerly makes use of progressive scientific knowledge and in a presumed unity with it, expands in an ever faster pace its disintegrating action on all nations of the earth and on all social levels. I do not need to explain in any more detail that after its victory not only all the most precious treasures of our culture would vanish, but – which is even worse – also any prospects at a better future." [82]

This is from a document prepared in the US under the auspices of the notorious Soviet secret police chief, Beria, who along with Stalin presided over the terrible genocide in Russia in the 30s, and shows that the Communists themselves were very clear in why they hated the Church:

> "As it seems in foreign nations that the church is the most ennobling influence, each and every branch and activity of each and every church, must, one way or another, be discredited. Religion must become unfashionable by demonstrating broadly, through psychopolitical indoctrination, that the soul is non-existent, and that Man is an animal. The lying mechanisms of Christianity lead men to foolishly brave deeds. By teaching them that there is a life here-after, the liability of courageous acts, while living, is thus lessened. The liability of any act must be markedly increased if a populace is to be obedient. Thus, there must be no standing belief in the church, and the power of the church must be denied at every hand." [83]

This is echoed by the great Alexander Solzhenitsyn, a Nobel prize winner obviously, who wrote an article called: *'Godlessness, The First Step to the Gulag'*, giving his thoughts on the real origin of the disaster that fell on the Russian people in the early 20th century:

"Over a half century ago, while I was still a child, I recall hearing a number of old people offer the following explanation for the great disasters that had befallen Russia: "Men have forgotten God; that's why all this has happened." Since then I have spent well-nigh 50 years working on the history of our revolution; in the process I have read hundreds of books, collected hundreds of personal testimonies, and have already contributed eight volumes of my own toward the effort of clearing away the rubble left by that upheaval. But if I were asked today to formulate as concisely as possible the main cause of the ruinous revolution that swallowed up some 60 million of our people, I could not put it more accurately than to repeat: "Men have forgotten God; that's why all this has happened."

...

By the time of the Revolution, faith had virtually disappeared in Russian educated circles; and amongst the uneducated, its health was threatened.

It was Dostoevsky, once again, who drew from the French Revolution and its seeming hatred of the Church the lesson that "revolution must necessarily begin with atheism." That is absolutely true." [84]

In modern times this recent quote from a member of the Chinese Academy of Social Sciences shows that they also see the importance of religion:

"One of the things we were asked to look into was what accounted for the success, in fact, the pre-eminence of the West all over the world.

We studied everything we could from the historical, political, economic, and cultural perspective. At first, we thought it was because you had more powerful guns than we had.

Then we thought it was because you had the

best political system. Next we focused on your economic system.

But in the past twenty years, we have realised that the heart of your culture is your religion: Christianity. That is why the West is so powerful.

The Christian moral foundation of social and cultural life was what made possible the emergence of capitalism and then the successful transition to democratic politics. We don't have any doubt about this." [85]

Doesn't it mean then that its absence will lead to a collapse of what makes a country work, and hence weaken its ability to stand up to its enemies like the ever more powerful EU and other supranational entities?

Footnotes

1. For which see: http://www.allaboutarchaeology.org/biblical-archaeology.htm and http://www.aboutthejourney.org/new-testament-archaeology.htm .

2. http://en.wikipedia.org/wiki/Mesha_Stele .

3. Gleason Archer, *A Survey of Old Testament Introduction* (Chicago, 1974), p. 25.

4. http://www.leaderu.com/orgs/probe/docs/bib-docu.html .

5. www.earlychristianwritings.com/yonge/book40.html .

6. http://www.allaboutthejourney.org/flavius-josephus.htm .

7. http://www.allaboutthejourney.org/suetonius.htm .

8. http://www.allaboutthejourney.org/cornelius-tacitus.htm .

9. http://en.wikipedia.org/wiki/Suetonius .

10. Like Augustus 87-88, http://www.gutenberg.org/files/6400/6400-h/6400-h.htm#2H_4_0003 .

11. *Annals* 5.4, http://www.sacred-texts.com/cla/tac/a05000.htm .

12. http://www.sacred-texts.com/cla/tac/a15070.htm .

13. http://www.livius.org/su-sz/suetonius/suetonius.html .

14. Justin the Martyr (103-165) an early Christian writer from Nablus in Palestine who later travelled to Rome, writing before 165 AD:
"And after Jesus was crucified they cast lots upon his vesture, and they that crucified him parted it among them. And that these things did happen, you can ascertain from the Acts of Pontius Pilate.
...
There are these words: 'At his coming the lame shall leap as an hart, and the tongue of the stammerer shall be clear speaking: the blind shall see, and the lepers shall be cleansed; and the dead shall rise, and walk about.' And that he did those things, you can learn from the Acts of Pontius Pilate."
(*First Apology* Chapters xxxv and xlviii, and another translation is available at http://www.ccel.org/ccel/schaff/anf01.viii.ii.xxxv.html
and http://www.ccel.org/ccel/schaff/anf01.viii.ii.xlviii.html . These 'Acts of Pontius Pilate' are not to be confused with the later 5th century forgery, as is noted in a footnote at the former website. Justin is certainly referring here to Roman records which he seems to have actively sought and consulted for his

books, for example at one point he says: "Now there is a village in the land of the Jews, thirty-five stadia from Jerusalem, in which Jesus Christ was born, as you can ascertain also from the registers of the taxing made under Cyrenius, your first procurator in Judæa." (*First Apology* Chapter xxxiv, available at http://www.ccel.org/ccel/schaff/anf01.viii.ii.xxxiv.html .))

Tertullian (c.160-c.220) a lively fascinating writer from Carthage who is famous as the first Christian father who wrote in Latin as opposed to Greek, in c.197 AD mentioned an old Roman law requiring that any God to be worshipped within the Empire needed first the approval of the Senate, and it seems that Tiberius approved worship of the Christian God, having received a report from Pontius Pilate:

"Tiberius, in whose time the Christian name first made its appearance in the world, laid before the Senate tidings from Syria Palestina which had revealed to him the truth of the divinity there manifested, and supported the motion by his own vote to begin with. The Senate rejected it because it had not itself given its approval. Caesar held to his own opinion and threatened danger to the accusers of the Christians.

...

All these things Pilate did to Christ; and now in fact a Christian in his own convictions, he sent word of Him to the reigning Caesar, who was at the time Tiberius."
(*The Apology* chapter 5 and chapter 21, available at:
http://www.ccel.org/ccel/schaff/anf03.txt .)

Eusebius of Caesarea (c.263-369 AD), a Roman historian and early Church father also known as Eusebius Pamphilius, agreed with the idea of such a report from Pilate:
"And when the wonderful resurrection and ascension of our Saviour were already noised abroad, in accordance with an ancient custom which prevailed among the rulers of the provinces, of reporting to the emperor the novel occurrences which took place in them, in order that nothing might escape him, Pontius Pilate informed Tiberius of the reports which were noised abroad through all Palestine concerning the resurrection of our Saviour Jesus from the dead."
(*Church History*, book 2, chapter 2, 1, available at:
http://christianbookshelf.org/pamphilius/church_history/chapter_ii_how_tiberius_was_affected.htm .)

15. http://www.allaboutthejourney.org/pliny-the-younger.htm .

16. http://www.allaboutthejourney.org/jewish-tradition.htm .

17. By the way if you wish to understand Aquinas' proofs in more depth you should read the first few chapters of his book 'Contra Gentiles,' available here: http://dhspriory.org/thomas/ContraGentiles1.htm . This is a better starting point

than his 'Summa Theologica', because the latter is a very concise laconic work, intended to be fleshed out by teachers previously schooled in the doctrines of Aristotle et al. Also a long detailed exposition of these five proofs is available in Franz Clemens Brentano, trans. by Susan F Kranz, *On the Existence of God* (Dordrecht, 1987).

18. Aristotle, Physics, book 8, pt 6, available at:
http://classics.mit.edu/Aristotle/physics.8.viii.html .

19. http://classics.mit.edu/Aristotle/metaphysics.2.ii.html .

20. This is a quote from him on the subject:
"...it is necessary that there should be an eternal unmovable substance. For substances are the first of existing things, and if they are all destructible, all things are destructible. But it is impossible that movement should either have come into being or cease to be (for it must always have existed), or that time should. For there could not be a before and an after if time did not exist." (Metaphysics, book XII, pt 6, available at:
 http://www.intratext.com/IXT/ENG2242/__P35.HTM .)

21. 3.25 at http://www.abu.nb.ca/courses/grphil/philrel/ScotusLecture.htm .

22. http://engforum.pravda.ru/index.php?/topic/156507-plotinus-and-the-trinity-of-god/ .

23. In his book *Mere Christianity*, available at: http://www.full-proof.org/wp-content/uploads/2010/04/Mere-Christianity-Lewis-chapters.pdf .

24. In the section entitled 'Natural Religion,' available at:
http://www.newmanreader.org/works/grammar/chapter10-1.html#section1 .

25. Xenaphon, *Memorabilia of Socrates*, Book I Chapter IV available at:
http://thriceholy.net/Texts/Memorabilia.html .

26. Epistles, *On Real Ethics as Superior to Syllogistic Subtleties*, vol III, 117, available at: http://www.stoics.com/seneca_epistles_book_3.html .

27. Rene Descartes, Third Meditation, in *Meditations on First Philosophy*, first published as *Meditationes de prima philosophia* (Paris, 1641), available at: http://www.earlymoderntexts.com/pdfbits/dm2.pdf , p.14.

28. Francis Bacon, *On Atheism*, No.16 in, *The Essays of Lord Bacon* (Philadelphia, c.1900), p.88-94.

29. http://www.proofthatgodexists.org/favourite-quotes.php .

30. Abraham de Moivre, *The Doctrine of Chances* (London, 1756), p.v.

31. John Leslie, Professor Emeritus at the University of Guelph, Canada, and Fellow of the Royal Society of Canada, elaborates here about some of the mechanisms that illustrate the Fine Tuned Universe Argument:
"1) The principle of special relativity ensures that forces such as electromagnetism have an invariable effect regardless of whether they act at right angles to a system's direction of travel. This enables genetic codes to work and planets to hold together when rotating.

2) Quantum laws prevent electrons from spiraling into atomic nuclei.

3) Electromagnetism has one-force strength, which enables multiple key processes to take place: it allows stars to burn steadily for billions of years; it enables carbon synthesis in stars; it ensures that leptons do not replace quarks, which would have made atoms impossible; it is responsible for protons not decaying too fast or repelling each other too strongly, which would have made chemistry impossible.

How is it possible for the same one-force strength to satisfy so many different requirements, when it seems that different strengths would be required for each one of these processes?"
(http://answers.yahoo.com/question/index?qid=20091216050659AA2yQ9P)

32. A few of the laws of physics that are relevant to this question are described here: http://www.allaboutphilosophy.org/teleological-argument.htm .

33. Stanley Gudder, *A Mathematical Journey* (London, 1994), p.xv. Incidentally this quote was also attributed at one time to Kepler.

34. http://www.allaboutthejourney.org/miracle-of-life.htm .

35. Harold J. Morowitz, *Energy Flow in Biology* (New York, 1968, republished 1979), p.99.

36. Dr Francis Crick, *Life Itself: its origin and nature* (London, 1981), p.51-52. Also a very elaborate discussion of the probabilities for the formation of human life is provided in Dr James F Coppedge, *Evolution: Possible or Impossible?* (Zondervan, 1973), available online at
http://creationsafaris.com/epoi_toc.htm .
Here is an online video that covers the same subject:
http://www.metacafe.com/watch/6332250/stephen_meyer_proteins_by_design_doing_the_math/ .

37. Emile Borel, *Probability and Life* (New York, 1962), p.28, translated from the French of Emil Borel, *Les Probabilite et la Vie* (Paris, 1943).

38. *Physics Today*, Vol. 25 (1972), p.23-28.

39. *De Natura Deorum*, ii. 34-35, available at: http://ia600302.us.archive.org/27/items/denaturadeorumac00ciceuoft/denaturadeorumac00ciceuoft.pdf .

40. Antony Flew, *There is a God* (New York, 2008), p.75.

41. Metaphysics, book 12, pt 7, available at: http://classics.mit.edu/Aristotle/metaphysics.12.xii.html .

42. Ibid.

43. Duncan Aikman in an article entitled "Lemaitre Follows Two Paths to Truth," in the *New York Times Magazine* Feb. 19, 1933, pp. 3, 18, quoted in *The Literary Digest*, vol 115, Jan-June 1933, p.23, and you can see a picture from that magazine here: http://cgi.ebay.com.sg/ws/eBayISAPI.dll?VISuperSize&item=370159382590 .

44. Antony Few, *There is a God* (New York, 2008), p.135-6.

45. In a chapter entitled Dr Arno Penzias, Vice President, Research, AT&T Bell Laboratories, *Creation is supported by all the data so far*, in Henry Margenau and Roy Abraham Varghese, ed., *Cosmos, Bios, and Theos* (La Salle, 1992), p. 5 and 83.

46. George Wald, The Origin of Life, *Scientific American* August 1954, p.44-53, quoted at http://www.talkorigins.org/faqs/quotes/mine/part1–4.html .

47. http://www.youtube.com/watch?v=Yx5BwnwUDjo&NR=1 .

48. Dr Michael Denton, M.D., Ph.D., a molecular biologist at the University of Otago, New Zealand, writing in *Evolution: A Theory in Crisis* (Bethesda, 1985), p.157-198; and p.358.

49. Dr. David Raup, curator of geology at the Field Museum of Natural History in Chicago, "Conflicts Between Darwinism and Paleontology," *Chicago Field Museum of Natural History Bulletin* 50, January 1979.

50. From "Evolution's Erratic Pace", *Natural History*, vol. 86 (May 1977), p.14.

51. Ager, D V, *The Nature of the Fossil Record,* in *Proceedings of the Geological Association* (1976) 87 (2) 131-159.

52. http://en.wikipedia.org/wiki/Peppered_moth_evolution .

53. http://www.guardian.co.uk/education/2001/aug/23/highereducation.peopleinscience .

54. http://www.guardian.co.uk/science/2010/oct/03/fred-hoyle-nobel-prize .

55. First part from Sir Fred Hoyle, *Facts and Dogma in cosmology and elsewhere* (Cambridge, 1982), p.14, which prints the Rede Lecture delivered at Cambridge on the 7th of May 1982; and the second part quoted at: http://www.guardian.co.uk/education/2001/aug/23/highereducation.peopleinscience .
You can find out more about these criticisms of evolution by looking at an interesting film called, *Expelled: No Intelligence Allowed*, narrated by Ben Stein, available at: http://www.youtube.com/watch?v=cEvq4xIHmH4 ; and another good documentary, narrated by Lee Strobel and entitled, *The Case For a Creator*, is available at: http://www.youtube.com/watch?v=lJNgTUhTJvg .
Also this lecture by Dr George Sim Johnston gives a good background to the general state of play as regards Evolution:
http://www.thomasaquinas.edu/news/newsletter/1999/fall/johnston.htm .

56. http://www.fordham.edu/halsall/basis/columba-e.html .

57. http://www.fordham.edu/halsall/basis/guibert-vita.html .

58. You can read about a few at this site: http://www.miraclesofthesaints.com/ .

59. http://en.wikipedia.org/wiki/Our_Lady_of_F%C3%A1tima and a list of the famous apparitions is available here:
http://www.unitypublishing.com/Apparitions/TrueApparitions.html .

60. Dr Henry Fitzsimon S.J., *A Reply to M Rider's Rescript and a Discovery of Puritan Partiality in his Behalf* (Rouen [although actually it says 'Roan'], 1608), p.93-4.

61. Fr John Lynch, *Supplementum Alithinologiae* (St Omer, 1667), p.188-9, translated from the Latin at PRONI D/3835/A/1/82.

62. This list of references is from F X Martin, *Friar Nugent* (London, 1962), p.127.

63. Fr Daniel Daly O.P., translated by Fr Charles Meehan OFM, *The Geraldines* (Dublin, 1847, while the original Latin book was titled '*Initium, incrementa, et exitus familiae Geraldinorum*' and published at 'Ulyssippone' in 1655), p.209; and see also *Commentarius Rinuccinianus*, Vol IV, 651-652.

64. See: http://www.dominicans.ie/friars/communities/tralee/history.html?start=3 .

65. Fr Antonius Bruodinus OFM, *Propugnaculum Catholicae Veritatis* (Prague 1669), p.958-71, quoted in the very good pages of Clare Library at: http://www.clarelibrary.ie/eolas/coclare/history/strangers_gaze/strangers_macbrody.htm .

66. http://www.ourladyofgoodsuccess.com/frames-3-4-2005/chiesa-viva/chiesa-viva-413-english.pdf .

67. You can read one of her books, *The Dolorous Passion of Our Lord Jesus Christ*, here: http://www.gutenberg.org/cache/epub/10866/pg10866.html , and for an account of the Ephesus site see:
http://www.catholictradition.org/Assumption/ephesus1.htm and
http://www.ephesustravelguide.com/houseofmary.htm and
http://www.unitypublishing.com/Apparitions/EmmerichGreatMystic.htm .

68. http://en.wikipedia.org/wiki/Therese_Neumann .

69. You can read here the testimony of many witnesses to her stigmata: http://www.stgemmagalgani.com/2009/01/stigmata-scourgings-crown-of-thorns.html .

70. http://video.google.com/videoplay?docid=9179467206976930820 .

71. http://www.youtube.com/watch?v=g_X3zHKRB6w .

72. http://www.ultimatedressage.com/forums/viewtopic.php?f=9&t=49186&start=50 .

73. See e.g. http://www.neardeathexperiencers.org/page20a.html . You can see some video testimonies of these experiences at:
http://www.youtube.com/watch?v=NPabMyVvC9s ,
http://www.youtube.com/watch?v=DOVawdK06HY ,
http://www.youtube.com/watch?v=jvIbqf7MuE0 ,
http://www.youtube.com/watch?v=8vj0qKthCgg ,
http://www.youtube.com/watch?v=nTqVHibyZXM and
http://www.youtube.com/watch?v=qWPuRpNHFuk .

74. http://www.youtube.com/watch?v=6C3vXif1LoQ .

75. http://video.google.com/videoplay?docid=7672003660947890622 .

76. http://www.youtube.com/watch?v=9lvZlHyY8sg .

77. http://www.youtube.com/rogermorneau#p/u/9/0CLAye_rEik .

78. Terry D. Cooper, Cindy K. Epperson, *Evil: Satan, Sin, and Psychology* (2008, Mahwah, New Jersey), p.26 and 31. As regards more modern cases of exorcism, you can see this documentary by ABC's 20/20 team from 1991: http://www.youtube.com/watch?v=kn9GaVqeAEs , and by the same program in 2007: http://www.youtube.com/watch?v=KC5O2jS3P64&NR=1 .

79. Gerard Mac Manus, *Dark Corners* (Cork, 2008), p.84-85.

80. Gerry O'Carroll, *The Sheriff: A Detective's Story* (London, 2006), p.137-141.

81. Edmund Burke, ed. by W King and F Laurence, *The Works of* (London, 1792), p.353.

82. http://www.angelfire.com/folk/infidel/MaxPlanck.html , quoting his lecture entitled: *Religion and Science* (Leipzig, 1958, but first delivered in 1937), p.7.

83. Document prepared for the US Communist party in the 30s and endorsed by Beria: http://www.indymedia.ie/article/84203 .

84. http://www.zimbio.com/member/jimpfaff/articles/6080506/Alexandr+Solzhenitsyn+Godlessness+First+Step .

85. http://www.ionainstitute.ie/index.p

APPENDIX A
Frequently Asked Questions

Just hoping to address a few questions that frequently turn up in relation to this issue.

Look, if there was a God could he not just come out and say so, reveal himself and stop this circus of people trying to prove his existence?

To answer that maybe it might help to begin at the beginning here and outline, what seems to the current writer anyway, the basic model of humans and earth and the Christian concept of free will.

First of all we have God creating the universe and mankind etc etc. Then God sets a test for mankind and uses their time on earth as the proving ground for this test. Obviously he provides a kind of set of instructions, scripture etc, which you are to follow and if you do so, at the end of the test you get to heaven, and if not you fall to hell. The road that ultimately gets you to heaven is reckoned to be the rocky road, the narrow path, and in your way you have the devil firing live ammunition at you to make it very difficult to get there. That is what its all about and you have free will here on earth which makes it a proper test, .i.e. you can, if you want to, choose the good or the bad road, God allows you that choice, because by doing so he makes it a proper test. The concept of 'free will' is crucial to understanding the traditional Catholic outlook on God.

Now the point is that if the man above came down and sat beside you right now then you would have no trouble believing in his existence and in his Revelation. You would certainly then get full marks on the first question on the paper, the first of the ten commandments, you would naturally believe in and honour God, and hence it wouldn't be much of a test, everybody would pass then! So that's the way to understand how Our Lord and Our Lady intervene in the world now. They coax and clarify points for people who want to seek out the truth (e.g. in the voluminous approved writings of Anne Catherine Emmerich, including *The Dolorous Passion of Our Lord Jesus Christ*, *The nativity of our Lord Jesus Christ*, and *The Lowly Life and Bitter Passion*) and provide supernatural aids to help people to get to heaven, by providing the Rosary and, in the case of Our Lord, by providing the Eucharist and Confession to help people, but nonetheless they are usually just a little off the radar, you have to seek them out and 'believe,' they are not in your face obvious.

Why? Again, because if they were obvious it would invalidate God's plan of providing a test for our souls on earth. The way to understand it is to imagine Our Lady and Our Lord as very sympathetic and enthusiastic teachers who are walking up and down as pupils take an exam. Yes they might throw in a hint now and again, where they see a pupil who has nearly got the answer, and they might be particularly sympathetic to some person whose heart is in the right place and who is clearly trying his best, but no, whatever they do they will never go to the point of actually answering the questions for you. They couldn't do that because if they did it would make a mockery of the exam process, the whole idea of humans going through life on earth is that they make their own mistakes and will get punished for them at the end, you cannot make the process too easy for them.

So your proof is based on the universe needing a cause, because everything needs a cause, so what caused God then?

If you find yourself asking that then you have misunderstood the deductions of Aristotle and Plato et al and their logic with respect to the origin of the universe. And incidentally there is no point in disparaging these great philosopher's sense of logic, these guys didn't just use logical methodology in their work, they invented it!

Again, what Aristotle and nearly all the great philosophers concluded was that you cannot have an infinite series of causes and effects, you need to ground the sequence on an 'uncaused cause' or an 'unmoved mover', to coin a famous summary of Aristotle's logic. They are not saying that everything needs a cause, they are saying that everything other than the very first cause needs a cause, that there was an original being, which Aristotle concluded was God, which was itself uncaused. You have to imagine a sequence of dominos falling, with one knocking over the next but with some non-domino being starting the sequence going in the first place, a kind of circular or infinite series of dominos is not possible.

Hence the 'first cause', and the 'first mover' – which he is saying is God – is outside the cause and effect sequence. The great philosophers also concluded that this being was eternal, which means it doesn't have a beginning, which in turn means it doesn't need any outside agency to bring it into existence.

Ok say we admit that there is some being like that which is eternal and infinite and omnipotent etc, how do we know that it isn't the devil then? Maybe the grand architect of the world is the personification of evil? And how do you explain the existence of evil in the world anyway?

Well actually many great philosophers have considered that question too. Descartes, for example, entertains the notion that he was possibly being fooled by God and Plotinus wrote a whole document exploring the idea that the supreme being was a kind of devil.[1] Ultimately both rejected this idea, as have all the great philosophers we have examined. It seems that this supreme being, that the philosophers have worked out exists, must also be a kind of perfect being and an evil entity doesn't seem to fit that description.

On the overall question of why there should be evil in the world I will just refer you to the first question above, on the idea of free will etc, and then leave you with this long quote from Plotinus, an Egyptian philosopher from the later Roman Empire who is sometimes called a Neo-Platonist. I hope I will be forgiven for quoting him at such length, I do so because since Plotinus was not a Christian what you are getting here is a very exact interpretation of the accumulated wisdom of the ancient Greek and Roman philosophers, in otherwords their deductions of the world as derived by pure logic and reason, not influenced at all by the Christian religion or Church hierarchy:

> "But there is still the question as to the process by which the individual things of this sphere have come into being, how they were made.
>
> Some of them seem so undesirable as to cast doubts upon a Universal Providence; and we find, on the one hand, the denial of any controlling power, on the other the belief that the Kosmos is the work of an evil creator.
>
> This matter must be examined through and through from the very first principles.
>
> ...
>
> The conflict and destruction that reign among living beings are inevitable, since things here are derived, brought into existence because the Divine Reason which contains all of them in the upper Heavens – how could they come here unless they were There? – must outflow over the whole extent of Matter.
>
> Similarly, the very wronging of man by man may be derived from an effort towards the Good; foiled, in their weakness, of their true desire, they turn against each other: still, when they do wrong, they pay the penalty – that of having hurt their Souls by their evil conduct and of degradation to a lower place – for nothing can ever escape what stands decreed in the law of the Universe.
>
> This is not to accept the idea, sometimes urged, that order is an outcome of disorder and law of lawlessness, as if evil were a necessary preliminary to their existence or their manifestation: on the contrary order is the original and enters this sphere as imposed from without: it is because order, law and reason exist that there can be disorder; breach of law and unreason exist because Reason exists – not that these better things are directly the causes of the bad but simply that what ought to absorb the

Best is prevented by its own nature, or by some accident, or by foreign interference. An entity which must look outside itself for a law, may be foiled of its purpose by either an internal or an external cause; there will be some flaw in its own nature, or it will be hurt by some alien influence, for often harm follows, unintended, upon the action of others in the pursuit of quite unrelated aims. Such living beings, on the other hand, as have freedom of motion under their own will sometimes take the right turn, sometimes the wrong.

Why the wrong course is followed is scarcely worth enquiring: a slight deviation at the beginning develops with every advance into a continuously wider and graver error – especially since there is the attached body with its inevitable concomitant of desire – and the first step, the hasty movement not previously considered and not immediately corrected, ends by establishing a set habit where there was at first only a fall.

Punishment naturally follows: there is no injustice in a man suffering what belongs to the condition in which he is; nor can we ask to be happy when our actions have not earned us happiness; the good, only, are happy; divine beings are happy only because they are good.

Now, once Happiness is possible at all to Souls in this Universe, if some fail of it, the blame must fall not upon the place but upon the feebleness insufficient to the staunch combat in the one arena where the rewards of excellence are offered. Men are not born divine; what wonder that they do not enjoy a divine life. And poverty and sickness mean nothing to the good – only to the evil are they disastrous – and where there is body there must be ill health.

Besides, these accidents are not without their

service in the co-ordination and completion of the Universal system.

One thing perishes, and the Kosmic Reason – whose control nothing anywhere eludes – employs that ending to the beginning of something new; and, so, when the body suffers and the Soul, under the affliction, loses power, all that has been bound under illness and evil is brought into a new set of relations, into another class or order. Some of these troubles are helpful to the very sufferers – poverty and sickness, for example – and as for vice, even this brings something to the general service: it acts as a lesson in right doing, and, in many ways even, produces good; thus, by setting men face to face with the ways and consequences of iniquity, it calls them from lethargy, stirs the deeper mind and sets the understanding to work; by the contrast of the evil under which wrong-doers labour it displays the worth of the right. Not that evil exists for this purpose; but, as we have indicated, once the wrong has come to be, the Reason of the Kosmos employs it to good ends; and, precisely, the proof of the mightiest power is to be able to use the ignoble nobly and, given formlessness, to make it the material of unknown forms.

The principle is that evil by definition is a falling short in good, and good cannot be at full strength in this Sphere where it is lodged in the alien: the good here is in something else, in something distinct from the Good, and this something else constitutes the falling short for it is not good. And this is why evil is ineradicable: there is, first, the fact that in relation to this principle of Good, thing will always stand less than thing, and, besides, all things come into being through it and are what they are by standing away from it.

...

Bad men rule by the feebleness of the ruled: and this is just; the triumph of weaklings would not be just.

It would not be just, because Providence cannot be a something reducing us to nothingness: to think of Providence as everything, with no other thing in existence, is to annihilate the Universe; such a providence could have no field of action; nothing would exist except the Divine. As things are, the Divine, of course, exists, but has reached forth to something other – not to reduce that to nothingness but to preside over it; thus in the case of Man, for instance, the Divine presides as the Providence, preserving the character of human nature, that is the character of a being under the providential law, which, again, implies subjection to what that law may enjoin.

And that law enjoins that those who have made themselves good shall know the best of life, here and later, the bad the reverse. But the law does not warrant the wicked in expecting that their prayers should bring others to sacrifice themselves for their sakes; or that the gods should lay aside the divine life in order to direct their daily concerns; or that good men, who have chosen a path nobler than all earthly rule, should become their rulers. The perverse have never made a single effort to bring the good into authority, nor do they take any steps to improve themselves; they are all spite against anyone that becomes good of his own motion, though if good men were placed in authority the total of goodness would be increased.

In sum: Man has come into existence, a living being but not a member of the noblest order; he occupies by choice an intermediate rank; still, in that place in which he exists, Providence does not allow him to be reduced to nothing; on the contrary he is ever being led upwards by all those varied devices which the Divine employs in its labour to increase the dominance of moral value. The human race, therefore, is not deprived by Providence of its rational being; it retains its share, though necessarily limited, in wisdom, intelligence, executive power and right doing, the right doing, at least, of individuals to each other – and even in wronging others people think they are doing right and only paying what is due.

Man is, therefore, a noble creation, as perfect as the scheme allows; a part, no doubt, in the fabric of the All, he yet holds a lot higher than that of all the other living things of earth.

Now, no one of any intelligence complains of these others, man's inferiors, which serve to the adornment of the world; it would be feeble indeed to complain of animals biting man, as if we were to pass our days asleep. No: the animal, too, exists of necessity, and is serviceable in many ways, some obvious and many progressively discovered – so that not one lives without profit to itself and even to humanity. It is ridiculous, also, to complain that many of them are dangerous – there are dangerous men abroad as well – and if they distrust us, and in their distrust attack, is that anything to wonder at?

...

Are we, then, to conclude that particular things are determined by Necessities rooted in Nature and by the sequence of causes, and that everything is as good as anything can be?

No: the Reason-Principle is the sovereign, making all: it wills things as they are and, in its reasonable act, it produces even what we know as evil: it cannot desire all to be good: an artist would not make an animal all eyes; and in the same way, the Reason-Principle would not make all divine; it makes Gods but also celestial spirits, the intermediate order, then men, then the animals; all is graded succession, and this in no spirit of grudging but in the expression of a Reason teeming with intellectual variety.

We are like people ignorant of painting who complain that the colours are not beautiful everywhere in the picture: but the Artist has laid on the appropriate tint to every spot. Or we are censuring a drama because the persons are not all heroes but include a servant and a rustic and some scurrilous clown; yet take away the low characters and the power of the drama is gone; these are part and parcel of it." [2]

But look, faith is what religion is all about, and faith is the opposite to reason and logic and science and on those sentiments I would prefer to ground my life and my view of the universe etc.

This gets to the heart of many peoples objection to religion and I thought maybe it might help to go into this in a little detail. First of all lets think about what 'faith' is exactly. It seems it has two meaning in this context:

a) Firstly it means trusting people, I guess in this context 'experts' if you like, as opposed to seeing or doing a thing for yourself. So sometimes you work out a mathematical calculation by hand yourself, or do a chemical experiment and see the results yourself, in which case you don't need faith. On the otherhand sometimes you cannot do these calculations yourself and so rely on others, they tell you what they have done, or you have read about people who have done these things, and if you go by that and believe them then you are putting your 'faith' in those people. At one level, that's all that faith is, if you think about it, and you do this pretty much every minute of every day. You cannot obviously do everything or see everything yourself, I don't care how brilliant a scientist you are you have to rely, a lot I would suggest, on the work and observation of others.

For example, consider if you are an historian, or a student of history, and you are trying to understand the events in the life of Socrates. Since you are not actually there in ancient Greece, you have to rely on, at least:

i) the testimony of linguists who have translated ancient Greek texts;

ii) historians who have transcribed texts that appear in documents that are dated typically long long after the death of Socrates;

iii) scribes who typically will have copied out – adding some mistakes maybe – the above texts many times before the modern historian gets to see them;

iv) on second or third hand sources who describe what Socrates told them or others – there are no first hand accounts of Socrates, because he never wrote anything down himself, or at least no such writings have survived.

You rely heavily on 'faith' then if you are finding out about Socrates and clearly that type of situation is quite similar to a biblical scholar or theologian working out the provenance or influences on some Christian text or passage in the Bible.

So theology does not really look much different to any other science or discipline in its use of 'faith', in this sense.

b) But obviously there is another sense by which people understand the word 'faith.' Clearly sometimes it carries almost a mystical meaning, the same meaning as the Irish words 'An Creideamh', 'the belief', maybe. Its sometimes taken as a statement that a person believes in the mysteries of the Christian religion, that they have 'the' faith.

So maybe to simplify things we will define that type of 'faith' as a 'belief in the mysteries of the Christian religion.' This obviously begs the next question:

What do you mean by mysteries exactly? Surely if a person believes in something as nebulous and as devoid of human reason as a 'mystery' then this kind of illogical and

unreasonable 'faith' is exactly what I have been referring to?

Ok, well there is another concept that comes in here. To recap, what the Greeks, and I would say all the great philosophers, have agreed on is that there is some supernatural, eternal, infinite, perfect etc being out there responsible for the creation of the universe, and the order within it, etc etc. Now, in a way, a lot of theological work centres around trying to feel our way into identifying the nature and practices of this being, but this is clearly very difficult. Because it is supernatural and omnipotent etc, and we are on the otherhand only natural and have only limited intelligence, we can only feel our way in the dark trying to understand this being, we cannot expect to know all the details and motives of such a being.

The analogy here might be if you had two intelligent mice debating the nature of these humans that they are observing from their mouse hole in the kitchen. Some things they can understand about these humans, even though they have only a mouse like perspective. The humans seem to eat and drink much like we (!) mice do. They walk around in much the same way that we do, except they use two legs. They bleed like we do, go fast in response to danger, sometimes anyway, much like we do. But then sometimes they seem to spend their time tapping their fingers on these kind of panels they call keyboards while looking at a screen. Among the mice nobody can figure out what all that means, they have reached the limit of their natural intelligence in accessing the nature of humans – even the somewhat expanded intelligence we are giving them here!

So how should the mice rationalise all that? What they presumably should logically conclude is that some things about humans they can understand, given their limited intelligence, and some things they just cannot and these they could call mysteries. The other option is that they could arrogantly dismiss as non-existent those qualities about humans that they do not understand. In otherwords some mice could say that they are doing nothing significant at those keyboards, they are just passing the time drumming their fingers the same as we do swishing our tail, contrary to reports some mice have made that it seems important to these humans. They could say all this because after all what could they be at that is all that important? In otherwords they could just dismiss completely as nonsense that which they do not understand, or, in the first scenario, they could just recognise the limits of their intelligence and simply call this process of tapping on keys a 'mystery.'

Now this is clearly very analogous to how humans should treat this being the Greeks described as omnipotent, supernatural and infinite etc. Obviously we are not omniscient in understanding this being so we are very like those mice trying to understand humans, it is logical to assume that there are some things we can understand about such a being and some we cannot, and to call the latter a mystery seems as good a way as any of terming it. If you think about it, that is much more preferable in logic and reason than to somehow assume we know everything, and with that dismiss things as non-existent just because we don't understand them.

Another analogy here might be of helpful: Imagine we could time travel and brought forward from the 17th century some great scientists like Boyle or Newton and plonked them on Hawaii in 1945. So they find out about this smallish bomb that the US used, which was simply a mechanism to split almost the smallest thing known to man at the time, the atom, and when they split that smallest thing they created a gigantic explosion which destroyed a whole city. What are these brilliant scientists going to make of that, you split the smallest thing and by that create the largest bomb ever made, with huge gigantic releases of energy etc? Isn't that going to go contrary to their knowledge of science? Maybe they might dismiss the thing as ridiculous and unscientific rubbish etc? When they hear from the pilots about what happened they might call them loonies and when later all these victims of radiation poisoning pass by them they might dismiss them as suffering from some sort of psychological delusion? The whole idea of this bomb going off like this is contrary to scientific reason, and therefore it cannot happen?

But of course a wise and intelligent scientist in that position would hear the stories coming back and start pulling on his chin and sagely recognise that maybe science has progressed in the meantime and maybe then there is something he doesn't understand about all this. So he will stop dismissing the stories coming back and will recognise the limits of his scientific knowledge. To do that is to use your reason and logic, not to put it aside. Scientific knowledge is a great thing, usually anyway, but a little humbleness about these things, i.e. the limits of current scientific knowledge, can also be, and in fact usually is, the mark of really great intelligence and logic.

So, I would postulate, that that is what is happening when some people dismiss the concept of 'mysteries.' Scientists are seeing this parade of people walking in front of them, miraculous cures at Lourdes with full test results by medical experts – half of whom are non-Catholic – testifying to their miraculous character, videos and pictures from hundreds of people afflicted with stigmata, testimonies, given sometimes in semi legal settings, of people who say they saw approved apparitions etc etc and many of these scientists are quick to dismiss it all as some kind of psychological mass hysteria or some other patently threadbare explanation. The clever, the logical, the intelligent scientist, will pull on his chin and will at some point accept that there maybe things happening which are outside the bounds of at least his natural reason, i.e. a 'super'natural being or event, and that recognition is very far from being an illogical one, if you think about it.

Such then is the explanation for these issues in traditional theology. If you read somebody like St Thomas Aquinas he is normally quite clear about what can be proven about God by natural reason alone and what cannot and hence needs to rely on supernatural aids or Revelation. i.e. Some parts of theology, like the existence of God and some of his attributes like infiniteness, can be proven using logic alone while others, such as the Trinity, will require you to believe supernatural sources such as the Bible. Its also felt that supernatural aids, like prayer by you or by others on your behalf, will aid you in understanding these more in depth theological matters.

But theology is really all about pushing this story drawn up

in scripture etc that has nothing to do with human reason and logic. Science, and indeed philosophy, are logical disciplines that work completely differently to theology, which is a kind of dictatorially imposed literary criticism!

But here you are also misunderstanding the different branches of theology. Simplistically put, theologians often will condemn a given practice as contrary to either: 'Divine law', meaning a practice condemned in a passage by Our Lord in the Bible maybe, and sometimes known as 'Revelation'; 'Ecclesiastical law', possibly in breach of the numbered Canon laws of the Church, or the decrees of the various Councils like Trent or Nicea etc; or 'Natural law', meaning contrary to a kind of obvious 'natural order' or smooth working society.

Its the latter type of law that maybe you don't understand. What the church is getting at here is that if you think profoundly about the society you live in you should be able to see, even if you are a pagan say, a kind of natural smooth working structure that if unbalanced will lead to negative consequences for everybody. For example it might be claimed that if anybody could indulge in murder, or lying, or warfare for little reason or excuse, then society could clearly not function very well to the detriment of everybody. Hence the Church might claim that it is obvious that these things are contrary to a 'Natural law' and therefore that the divine and ecclesiastical prohibitions on these practices are demonstrably good or logical to everybody, even to a non believer or pagan. It might be felt as well that this kind of logic extends to the idea of a society where children are brought up in monogamous marriages rather than a sexual free for all to the detriment of the stability of marriages, and hence to the ability to bring up children and support the young and the old in a family structure. Remember that Natural Law deliberately provides a kind of sandbox where theologians can work out questions and discuss issues without making any reference at all to Scripture or what theologians would call supernatural aids. In otherwords they discuss the different issues as if God didn't exist, its a branch of theology that was used and drawn up to allow theologians that kind of freedom to put the tenets of their religion to one side, as it were, in order to give free scope to one's human logic and reason, which after all are God given.

Anyway these are the kind of arguments that you see discussed in traditional theological literature. As a simple example of this here is a short quote from *'A Handbook of Moral Theology'* by Fr Dominic M. Prummer O.P. on the church prohibition on interest:

> "Principle. Usury in its strict sense is contrary to Divine positive law, to Ecclesiastical law, and to Natural law.
>
> a) Divine law commands: "Lend to them (your enemies) without any hope of return" (Lk.vi, 35; cf. Ex. Xxii, 25; Lev. Xxv, 35-37; Ez. Xviii, 8, 13).
>
> b) Ecclesiastical law has severely forbidden usury in five Ecumenical Councils (Lateran III, IV, V; Lyons II; Vienna) and in several condemned propositions (cf. c. [Canon law number:] 1543.)
>
> c) Natural law forbids selling the same thing twice. But in fungible goods which are also consumed at their first use, the goods themselves and their use are morally the same – that is to say, they do not possess separate prices. Therefore a person who demands a price both for the thing he loans and for its use is selling the same thing twice and thus offends against Natural law. Accordingly S. Leo the Great well says: 'Foenus pecuniae funus est animae.'"

Meaning 'The Interest of money is the funeral of the soul.' And that last reference from Natural law was indeed first articulated by the pagan Aristotle, a very popular philosopher with Catholic theologians, especially Aquinas who draws on him very extensively. Contrary therefore to its many modern critics, Catholic theology does indeed ask that people use their reason and intellect to see this 'natural order' of the world, and hence God's plan for humans, not just to understand issues on 'faith' alone.

This then is where St Thomas Aquinas, and so many other theologians who unfold for us this 'Natural law', are coming from. They are not just saying 'do this' or 'believe this' because it is written in Scripture etc, they are trying to trace out a logical and scientific approach to understanding the world and the best way to organise human society etc, quite consciously building on the earlier works of the Greek philosophers.

Ok have you read then these....[fill in here the usual passages in the Bible that atheists like to quote] ...lines from scripture? Is that what you believe? Unscientific rubbish like this?

Which brings us to the question of literal readings of the Bible. Obviously this is one of the classic differences between most Protestant faiths and the traditional Catholic one. The latter faith tends to emphasise that the Bible should be read through the prism of tradition and the magisterium of the Church, rather than just believing in a literal translation of the Bible.

Hence if you want to find out whether a Catholic believes in doctrine expressed in a given passage in the Bible, you have to take that passage you are focusing on and see if it was mentioned approvingly by the early Church Fathers – like St Augustine – or the very important later ones, like St Thomas Aquinas, or maybe see if it was referred to in one of the important councils of the Church, like Nicea and Trent, and if so then we can say that that passage passes the test in the sense of being approved by the magisterium. (By 'magisterium' it is meant a sense of the teaching authority of the Church, basically the accumulated wisdom of the Church Fathers and the important Councils.) Then we would look at how that passage fares in tradition: maybe it is incorporated in an early prayer, or maybe it is read out at mass on an important feast day etc etc.

Only when a given passage of the Bible passes these tests can we say for sure that we are talking about Catholic doctrine, the literal passage alone, not backed up by tradition or the magisterium, is not of itself Catholic doctrine. So you cannot just quote a given passage from the Bible and accuse a Catholic of believing that, without going through the aforementioned exercise first.

Oh I see, so you want to censor the Bible then, in a way, only certain passages meet your approval, can the word of God not stand on its own two feet? Can you not just read and then believe what you say is the word of God, without needing this control mechanism you mention?

Well this is a very complicated issue but basically there are a number of good reasons why taking the literal word in the Bible is maybe not the best way to proceed. A few points would include:

a) Considering the New Testament for example, it makes sense that tradition would contain a better and more rounded account of Our Lord's teaching than the Gospels alone. The Gospels are obviously only four shortish texts which are trying to cram into a few pages the life and teachings of Our Lord over approximately three years. These books, and the rest of the Bible, clearly cannot capture all of the details of that teaching in this short space and in fact it might be said that some quotes here and there are in some cases superficially contradictory.

So it makes sense that we could be helped out in interpreting this text by tapping into tradition as preserved by the Disciples of Our Lord and passed on by them to the early Church Fathers and adherents. Those Disciples, and Apostles obviously, in many cases must have listened at length to Our Lord's teaching, attending lecture type sessions over many hours doubtless, and so they must have been able to pass on to the early Christians what exactly that teaching was. Hence we are right in being guided by them in this way by reading the early Church Fathers and noting tradition that wasn't written down at this period, rather than seeking to make sense of those, sometimes contradictory, few quotes which is at times all we get in the Gospels.

b) Obviously a lot of what is written in the Bible takes the form of parables, allegories and analogies, as opposed to straight forward factual accounts and it can be difficult to determine sometimes which is which. There is nothing wrong with there being allegories in the Bible, because after all many of the great philosophers and scientists use analogies like these all the time, but in the form it comes down to us it can clearly be difficult to separate out what we should take as literal facts and what we should presume to be fictional stories that only illustrate certain truths. Hence its helpful again to have the accumulated wisdom of the Church, the magisterium, to guide us here.

c) Even putting aside all questions of translation difficulties, there are always going to be problems with interpreting the literal words of texts that can date back as far as two and a half millennia or so.

Take a simple word like 'slave' for example. If you now, in 2011, were to give a speech on slaves then people will naturally interpret you as referring to slaves imported from Africa into the US in the 18th century say, and that will be their mental image when the word is spoken. Fair enough but if I give the same speech in 300 BC my reference to slaves could create a different impression on my listeners, in practice the word might have a different meaning even if it is correctly translated between the different languages. If, for example, it happened to be the case that virtually all people who did the on the ground manual labour on farms and in houses were slaves in that society then using the word slaves would just mean the same as 'labourers' or 'workers' in our language, in otherwords people who did the more menial chores for pay. In 300 BC the words 'slave' and 'labourer' could be interchangeable, because in practice all the labourers might be slaves, hence the mental picture that is in the heads of the listeners to that speech in 300 BC could be a lot different to the listeners of that speech in 2011 AD. Therefore if you are reading that speech now you might end up misinterpreting the sense that the speaker was trying to convey .i.e. he could be making a point applicable to all labourers, not just slaves as we would interpret the word. In practice its going to be very difficult for an ordinary person to accurately follow a speech made in 300 BC if he doesn't have also a good background knowledge of the history of the period, which many of the experts who inputted their knowledge into that magisterium did have.

Here again then we can see the pitfalls of rushing into our literal reading of the Bible, as opposed to drawing on the authoritative interpretations of people like St Augustine.

d) Finally I would point out that some atheist commentators can be very impractical in their literal interpretations of the Bible, and this pitfall is also avoided by drawing on the wisdom of the magisterium and tradition.

Most of the Bible is obviously an historical account of the Jewish race and then of the early Christians. Its an historical narrative where you get good and bad Jews and Christians and some important speeches made by prophets and by Our Lord, trying to put the populace back on the correct path. But an historical account is just that, its not a scientific thesis.

Think about this for a minute, say I read the collected speeches of some Irish politician writing in the 20th century and we say that in one of those speeches he sweeps his arm over the horizon and says "just as the sun rises in the morning and moves over to set in the evening, I will...." Are we going to conclude from that that (a) the politician is a liar because he says that the sun moves when it does not, or (b) that he is scientifically illiterate etc etc? No, what we would conclude is that he is drawing a figure of speech in his oratory, it would be a bit much to expect him to draw a diagram and give the latest thinking on astronomy when he is just illustrating a point in what he is saying. Its perfectly fair for speakers to do that because not every speech has to be a science lecture, and consequently it is perfectly fair to read such speeches in the Bible without over-interpreting the scientific data contained therein.

You also have to factor in the state of knowledge of the listeners. If Moses, or somebody inspired by God in the Bible, is giving a speech to the Jews where he is trying to get them to mend their ways he cannot be expected to launch into a detailed scientific digression on some point, because after all it might make no sense to his listeners and then they might not heed the rest of it.

Incidentally this idea that you have to take regard of the degree of learning of the listeners also extends to us in our reading of the Bible now. For example at the beginning of the Bible we are told that the order in which our earth came about was: first came the heavens and the earth, then water and dry land, then animals fish and birds etc, and then humans. In otherwords an order of creation that only makes sense now after the discovery of the Big Bang theory and which must have puzzled readers of the Bible before its discovery. So, in short, when some commentators wax lyrical about how God is omniscient, and therefore couldn't have got anything wrong in the Bible, remember to factor in that you are not omniscient and could be interpreting the facts wrong or not with complete understanding.

But there are lots of gods worshiped down through history, its just a superstition that seems to be inherent in humans, and why should the one real God, if you say there is one, not emerge clearly instead of this colourful array of imposters?

Some argument on those lines seems to have been popularised by Dawkins, and atheists in general always seem to want to boast of rejecting 'God or gods.'

Firstly I will refer you back to the first answer on free will, its entirely compatible with this important Christian concept of free will that you get a choice of religions and 'gods.'

And in fact the notion that there has always been a belief in God or gods among all races through history, which indeed is true enough, has usually being held to be one of the proofs of God's existence. To quote the aforementioned C.S. Lewis, the Belfast author of 'The Chronicles of Narnia,' where he is referring to the hunger man feels towards the divine:

> "Creatures are not born with desires unless satisfaction for these desires exists. A baby feels hunger; well, there is such a thing as food. A dolphin wants to swim; well, there is such a thing as water. Men feel sexual desire; well, there is such a thing as sex. If I find in myself a desire which no

experience in this world can satisfy, the most probable explanation is that I was made for another world." ³

Another way of looking at it is that presumably all humans have this 'want' if you like, a looking upwards towards the divine which needs to be satisfied. So its a bit like any practical human problem faced through history, like needing bridges wherever humans encounter rivers. That requirement has always been there in history and every race has tried to address it. The Romans built bridges in a certain way, the ancient Celts built them another way – sometimes by making fords shallower by throwing in detrimus into the river – etc etc. Then in our modern times we hope to be a bit more advanced but nonetheless we do indeed draw on a few Roman and Greek influences in building our own bridges now. Then if I was to stand back and see how humans have addressed the problems of bridge building over the centuries you will see quite a few similarities, between the way the different races addressed the problem and the way we do now, and indeed some dissimilarities. They would be similar, at least partly, because each race is trying to solve the exact same problem and maybe there is only one sensible solution to it, like building the bridge end on solid ground where the river is narrow, and it will be different because each race had and has their own skill set and tools and special way of doing things. Obviously this divine 'need' in humans works itself out much the same way, you will see similarities in the way different races addressed the issue over the centuries as opposed to the way it is done now, and some differences. Hence you will find temples and sacrifices, similar to our churches and the sacrifice of the mass, maybe because it always made sense to build a nice building to worship the divine, and then there are differences between the different races and between the past and now.

Fascinating stuff but what does all that amount to? A Christian is saying that God has been around all the time and that man has been made in his image, albeit also that man is a fallen race after Adam, and hence it is natural to suppose that earlier pre Christian races would also have recognised this divine spark somehow, and indeed that current primitive races will feel the need to acknowledge the same thing. I don't follow why any of that gives comfort to the atheist position? As pointed out, this is usually held up as a proof of theism and it does seem to be so and not the opposite?

Ok, maybe we could concede that Our Lord in the Bible seems to be a person worth following but what about the Old Testament God? Does he not come across as a strict heartless type of fellow? And as a Christian you are tied to the Old Testament as much as to the New, you cannot disown that God?

I would answer this two ways:

a) First of all I think it is fair and reasonable for a Christian to hold up the example of Our Lord in the New testament as the basic model to follow, rather than the Old Testament. After all there are clearly some differences between what Our Lord says and what was important to the Jews in the Old Testament. Surely that is reflected in the fact that the Jewish priests, and Pharisees and the Sanhedrin, were the bitter enemies of Our Lord in the Gospel. He outlined a somewhat different and better way of practising religion than was the case in the Old Testament and a Christian is following his example rather than the old one. In short that's what the word Christian implies, if you wanted to go by the Old Testament alone you would be a Jew, not a Christian. So in fact a Christian is entitled to put the emphasis on the New Testament rather than the Old, if you think about it.

b) I would make another point though. It seems to this observer that the post Vatican II Catholic Church has erred somewhat in presenting God as a warm cuddly fellow that you just have to ask favours from that will automatically be answered. This image is different from traditional Catholicism which emphasised maybe that God was a kind of just king, a strict and exact being that jealously guarded his prerogatives, rather than just a warm friendly person. It seems to me anyway that this kingly God, which some people would say then is a kind of Old Testament God, is simply nearer to the truth. You don't want to mess with an all powerful and omniscient king, you would naturally be afraid of him, and have reason to be if you follow the pre Vatican II emphasis on hell and purgatory etc.

So maybe when people make this distinction between an Old Testament and New Testament God actually they should acknowledge that at least a whiff of the punishing and scolding power of the Old Testament God is simply closer to the truth than what has been preached post Vat II?

Incidentally the Old and New Testaments are also linked in another curious way. A lot of people find it very interesting that the Old Testament contains specific and detailed prophecies foretelling the life of Our Lord e.g does this foretell the crucifixion, which occurred many hundreds of years after this was written in the Psalms:

> "O God my God, look upon me: why hast thou forsaken me? Far from my salvation are the words of my sins. O my God, I shall cry by day, and thou wilt not hear: and by night, and it shall not be reputed as folly in me. But thou dwellest in the holy place, the praise of Israel. In thee have our fathers hoped: they have hoped, and thou hast delivered them. They cried to thee, and they were saved: they trusted in thee, and were not confounded. But I am a worm, and no man: the reproach of men, and the outcast of the people. All they that saw me have laughed me to scorn: they have spoken with the lips, and wagged the head. He hoped in the Lord, let him deliver him: let him save him, seeing he delighteth in him. For thou art he that hast drawn me out of the womb: my hope from the breasts of my mother. I was cast upon thee from the womb. From my mother's womb thou art my God, Depart not from me. For tribulation is very near: for there is none to help

me. Many calves have surrounded me: fat bulls have besieged me. They have opened their mouths against me, as a lion ravening and roaring. I am poured out like water; and all my bones are scattered. My heart is become like wax melting in the midst of my bowels. My strength is dried up like a potsherd, and my tongue hath cleaved to my jaws: and thou hast brought me down into the dust of death. For many dogs have encompassed me: the council of the malignant hath besieged me. They have dug my hands and feet. They have numbered all my bones. And they have looked and stared upon me. They parted my garments amongst them; and upon my vesture they cast lots." (Psalms 21:2-19)

Isaias, or Isaiah, flourished about 750-700 BC, and is he here foretelling the demise of our Lord, who was despised by the people after he was scourged and looked ragged, and who said nothing in his own defence when questioned by Pilate?

"Therefore the Lord himself shall give you a sign. Behold a virgin shall conceive, and bear a son and his name shall be called Emmanuel.

...

Despised, and the most abject of men, a man of sorrows, and acquainted with infirmity: and his look was as it were hidden and despised, whereupon we esteemed him not. Surely he hath borne our infirmities and carried our sorrows: and we have thought him as it were a leper, and as one struck by God and afflicted. But he was wounded for our iniquities, he was bruised for our sins: the chastisement of our peace was upon him, and by his bruises we are healed. All we like sheep have gone astray, every one hath turned aside into his own way: and the Lord hath laid on him the iniquity of us all. He was offered because it was his own will, and he opened not his mouth: he shall be led as a sheep to the slaughter, and shall be dumb as a lamb before his shearer, and he shall not open his mouth. He was taken away from distress, and from judgment: who shall declare his generation? because he is cut off out of the land of the living: for the wickedness of my people have I struck him. And he shall give the ungodly for his burial, and the rich for his death: because he hath done no iniquity, neither was there deceit in his mouth. And the Lord was pleased to bruise him in infirmity: if he shall lay down his life for sin, he shall see a longlived seed, and the will of the Lord shall be prosperous in his hand. Because his soul hath laboured, he shall see and be filled: by his knowledge shall this my just servant justify many, and he shall bear their iniquities. Therefore will I distribute to him very many, and he shall divide the spoils of the strong, because he hath delivered his soul unto death, and was reputed with the wicked: and he hath borne the sins of many, and hath prayed for the transgressors."

(Isaias 17:14 and 53:3-12)

Remember that fragments of most of the books of the Old Testament, including a full copy of the Book of Isaiah, have turned up among the Dead Sea Scrolls and the physical paper, actually parchment and papyrus, that they are written on has been dated to c.350-100 BC. In otherwords they are dated, at minimum, 100 years before the events of the New Testament, hence nobody is saying that our copies of the Old Testament books were in any way doctored after the fact to agree with the events of the New Testament. Since the basic facts of the events of the historical Jesus are agreed by, I would say, all serious scholars as having taken place, bearing in mind that they are verified by so many different writers in the New Testament and, in the case of the resurrection for example, by outside writers like Josephus, then if you try to explain away the above prophecies in the Old Testament you are left with maybe only one other explanation: you have to say that Our Lord was deliberately or fraudulently copying the prophecies of the Old Testament throughout his life. Actually it does seem that he was at times conscious of these prophecies and, for some reason, anxious to fulfil them but he hardly brought about his own virgin birth or the fact of the soldiers casting lots for his clothes?

Yes but if you do believe in the supernatural at all then you have to believe in all of that stuff, the tooth fairy, the leprecán at the end of the road etc etc.

I don't think that follows at all. Say I never believed that America existed and I rejected as nonsense anybody that came along saying they were from there. Then, for some reason, I changed my mind and believed that the US existed, it doesn't follow from that that everybody that I come across with a 10 gallon hat has to come from America. Presumably I will believe some stories, that seem plausible, and reject some that don't. So in this case, if you do believe the supernatural is possible, then the next step would be to weigh up the evidence of God's existence, and there happens to be a lot of such evidence, through Revelation over the course of history and presumably you might also feel that Our Lord exists based on believing the Gospel account to be authentic, etc etc. While on the otherhand you might reject the existence of the tooth fairy, based on the lack of evidence. The issue of leprecáns obviously depends on where you are, if you happen to live in the Burren, for example, then the chances of a leprecán being around is not all that remote!

You list the laws of physics as an example of intelligent design, but they are just mathematical constructs which scientists use to explain the universe, just like the number seven or the pocket calculator! Scientists just use these as tools to help them to do their job, it is no reflection of whether or not the universe itself is ordered, it only helps physicists to do their calculations quicker.

I think maybe another analogy might help here. Imagine if you were a scientist who was asked by the police to examine some kind of runaway train, whose origin they hoped to trace. This is a bit like the theoretical physicist trying to trace, from clues in the modern world, whence the universe had come from. So our scientist gets the train taken apart and he tries to read some clues from it. Now we will say that this train works on the Swiftline Network, headquartered at Ballymagash. One of the great characteristics of that famous network is that they always send their trains on the straightest line on their network, without stops, on any given journey, and they always start the journey with full tanks of diesel. So our scientist, knowing this, will hence find out how much diesel was left in the tank of the train, and how many miles per gallon the train does, and then by looking at a map of the network system he can say with certainty where the train originated.

This, I think, is quite analogous to our Hawkins type figure trying to understand the origins of the universe from the clues around us now. And if you consider it for a minute, you can see that the scientist couldn't tell us where the train had come from unless the Swiftline Network had very definite rules as to how the trains ran. He can have as many statistical graphs and as many fancy equations as he likes but if those trains do not always start with full tanks, and run completely straight, then he just won't be able to tell where the train comes from. The rules and laws of the train system, which he is relying on, are inherent to the train system itself, they are not just his own statistical or mathematical aids. This is clearly what it is like with the universe, the laws of physics are built into the universe structure, and we are just discovering them, but clearly some clever and coherent builder had constructed them. Hence you cannot get away from the concept of an intelligent designer in the universe and in nature.

But why would this being, that you say is so omnipotent – i.e. all powerful obviously – and omniscient, then respond to prayers for example? Why would he stoop to listen to just me, if he is so powerful? And anyway if he knows everything and can mould the future then why isn't everything preordained

on earth? Why would he would he want to set up this 'test', that you describe in the first answer, since he knows, being omniscient, the outcome? This whole model of the earth is counter intuitive if you believe that he is an omnipotent being, why would he bother setting up this earth, humans and souls business, at all?

Just to clarify again what we mean by omnipotent: according to the proofs of God's existence we are concluding that he can do anything he wants, that he has complete power over us and can look into our souls and see what we are really thinking etc etc. But remember that's all we have concluded on this score, what you are actually talking about in that question are ways that God's power should seem limited. You are saying that he couldn't be expected to respond to prayers, he couldn't want to set up the earth and he wouldn't wish to give humans free will and the test described. So you are saying he cannot, or at least surely he would not, wish to do x, y and z. But remember the doctrine of omnipotence is only telling us that he can do everything, so obviously, by that doctrine, he can if he wants to set up the earth and agree to answer prayers, – which the lives of the saints [4] show are always considered by God – etc. So if you consider it for a minute you will have to agree that these concepts are at least *not strictly incompatible with the theory of omnipotence*, if you are saying he can do everything then he can do these things if he wants to?

But I totally concede that it sounds *unintuitive to the doctrine of omnipotence* that he would want to set up earth and listen to prayers etc. But when we are in the business of talking about an intuitive understanding of God's actions we are now trying to second guess this hugely intelligent being. We are now like those mice looking at humans, as in the above analogy, and we just cannot hope to be able to figure out, using our limited intelligence, all that they are up to.

If you think about your intuitive guess work here it really sounds a bit like some guy working in a diner in the mid-West in the US who is told that the President just dropped in unannounced for a hamburger and fries. To you he must seem omnipotent and you are probably incredulous that this happened, thinking why would he want to do that, it doesn't make sense? He could arrange any type of meal he wants with his vast kitchen and cooks, he could even fly in from Paris the latest cooking if he wanted to, why would he possibly want to call in here? But how do you know the real life goings on of the President in the White House, maybe he gets bored sometimes of a Friday evening and just wants to go out, who knows. Sure he can do almost whatever he likes but we cannot go from that concept and then reject the idea that he calls into a small diner from time to time, we just accept that we cannot hope to second guess his thinking and actions in that way.

That is, I think, the way to understand this question, we don't twist the doctrine of omnipotence around and start saying that God cannot – or surely wouldn't want to – do x or y, or z. How can we, with our limited intelligence, hope to know all his thinking on these matters?

Modern cosmology does not support Aristotle or Aquinas. Unlike them, it considers time a facet of the universe, hence the idea of space-time. It considers it illogical to speak of time before the universe in much the same way that we don't speak of letters of the alphabet before A.

You may be wrong in assuming that Aristotle, and Aquinas who follows him, did not take into account the problems with time when they drew up their theories on the origin of the universe. This is a summary of Aristotle's opinions on the subject, which is not quite the way that Einstein would have put it but its not all that far off it either:

> "Time is a constant attribute of movements and, Aristotle thinks, does not exist on its own but is relative to the motions of things. Time is defined as "the number of movement in respect of before and after," so it cannot exist without succession; but he also seems to say that to exist time requires the presence of a soul capable of "numbering" the

movement." [5]

The fact is that this time issue does not invalidate their arguments. They base their arguments on causality which still works even if time is not working as we understand it. Its a bit like if we lived in an era when time didn't exist somehow and we saw a black car. Having seen a black car, and knowing something of how cars are made, we can say that at some point somebody painted that car black i.e. we see the 'effect', the black paint on the car, which must have been 'caused' by some person painting it. We can bring along the logic of this 'cause' and 'effect' even when time is not present as such, in otherwords if time is all at sea we don't know whether the car was painted black simultaneously, or before, or after the time we saw the car but nonetheless, even allowing for all that confusion, we can say that at some point the car was painted black. And we can go along from there, and say that since a car exists then at some point in time somebody made the car and then made the components that the car was made of etc etc, we can go along doing this 'cause' and 'effect' thing even where we are lost as regards our normal concept of time.

If we believe your outside sources listed above which corroborate the Bible, and then accept from that that the Bible may be authentic as regards most basic facts it nonetheless does not follow that all, or any, of the miraculous and Godlike events in the Bible really happened. It could be written like a work of modern fiction on something like the 1916 rising, say, where an author might have wrote into the story Patrick Pearse, and the basic historical facts, but then wrote about a fictional family and events on top of that.

But this idea presents not a few difficulties. Looking firstly at the:

Old Testament
You have to ask yourself how this race of the Jews has spent so much time and effort perpetuating fiction, and fiction that they at all times claimed as fact. Remember at that time you don't

actually have fiction writers in the way you have now, I don't think they felt they were very useful, whereas of course you do have chroniclers who preserve the ancient history of the race, which all races value and promote.

Then you have to think about how the documents were preserved. What happens is that somebody writes it at the time and then it is read out in temples etc over the years and copies are made etc etc. Well obviously at the time the events happened many of the audience know they are untrue, in this scenario, and remember they are certainly claiming them to be true, and this includes many of the miraculous events which were observed by numerous people. So our chronicler, who has secretly turned fiction writer, presents this document which is read out at the temple and it is completely untrue and everybody is reading it out loud – as happens at Jewish religious meetings – and there is no problem at all?

Anyway if you really think about these things you find that this isn't actually very likely, the idea that what is written is simply true is certainly the most likely explanation, now that we can rule out any idea that it was a modernish forgery, or a text heavily corrupted by bad translations or bad copies, which we can certainly now do via the Moabite Stone and the Dead Sea Scrolls etc.

New Testament

Then as regards the New Testament you can find yourself twisting through very tight knots in trying to get this theory off the ground. Effectively then the four Evangelists are lying, in this scenario. The four Gospels are pretty clear documents which are explicitly written as authentic accounts of events in Israel c.30 AD, you certainly cannot say that the authors intended to write fiction which people should read now as fiction. Clearly, under this theory, they would have to be writing fiction that they are consciously passing off as fact. The problem with this is that there was a large community of early Christians, at the time the Gospels were written, who knew perfectly well the basic facts of the life of Our Lord and hence could expose the fiction for what it was. So presumably they are in on the act, what you are saying is that they are involved in this huge wide conspiracy? And as late as the early 2nd century, at the same period when even physical fragments of the Bible have turned up (e.g. fragment P52, part of the Gospel of St John, dated to roughly 125 AD), you had a number of men still living who had lived in close quarters with the Disciples who personally knew Our Lord. Just to emphasise that point I might as well describe these three men in particular:

St Polycarp (69-155 AD), a martyred disciple of John the Apostle, and he knew others that knew Our Lord, wrote a Letter to the Philippians of c.110-140 AD, from which:

> "Now He that raised Him from the dead will raise us also." [6]

St Ignatius of Antioch (born c.35 or 50 and martyred at Rome c.108 AD), who succeeded St Evodius as Bishop of Antioch c.67 AD, personally knew the Apostles Paul and John and was appointed to that bishopric by Peter, wrote:

> "Take note of those who hold heterodox opinions on the grace of Jesus Christ which has come to us, and see how contrary their opinions are to the mind of God. ... They abstain from the Eucharist and from prayer because they do not confess that the Eucharist is the flesh of our Savior Jesus Christ, flesh which suffered for our sins and which that Father, in his goodness, raised up again. They who deny the gift of God are perishing in their disputes." [7]

St Clement of Rome (fl 96 AD and died c.110 AD, martyred by Trajan), personally knew the Apostles Peter and Paul and we are also told, by St Irenaeus, that he "saw the blessed Apostles and conversed with them, and had yet ringing in his ears the preaching of the Apostles and had their tradition before his eyes, and not he only for many were then surviving who had been taught by the Apostles." He wrote a famous letter from which this quote comes:

> "Let us understand, dearly beloved, how the Master continually showeth unto us the resurrection that shall be hereafter; whereof He made the Lord Jesus Christ the first fruit, when He raised Him from the dead." [8]

So now your conspiracy stretches into the best part of a hundred years or so with a huge wide circle of people being hoodwinked by our crafty Evangelists and Apostles and Disciples? The whole thing gets very convoluted if you try to claim that the authors of the New Testament were making it up. That's why there is so much interest in the archaeological evidence, and the writings of the Roman and Jewish historians which corroborate the New Testament, because in practice most serious scholars, looking at the atheist thesis, would have only entertained the idea that the Bible may be a bad copy, or translation, or later forgery, and which the above evidence now refutes. The idea that it was all along deliberate fiction is too hard to sustain. And after all look at the numbers of these 'conspirators' who were martyred for their faith, they are dying for their belief in a work they know to be fiction?

There is no point also is going down the road of these 'conspirators' making loads of money on the back of their new Church etc etc because actually they were heavily persecuted during those years of course. Their rich churches were only caves underground and they at all times stood a good chance of being executed for their beliefs, rather than gain from them.

Also, before leaving this point, note that the quotes above constitute three independent second hand accounts corroborating Our Lord's resurrection, and these statements come to us outside of the Bible accounts. There is no point in people being so po-faced in their dismissal of second hand sources of information, that is quite an authoritative source in any discipline. If you read a newspaper or watch a journalist on the news the best you can hope for is that it would be second hand information, i.e. the journalist telling you what somebody told them about a given incident, but most of the time it would be at least third hand information, e.g. where a policeman would have observed a given incident and then related that to the press officer who in turn related it to the journalist, its virtually never better than second hand. Remember that in the cases outlined above the writer is telling you directly what they were told by eyewitnesses to the events that they lived with for many years, its a perfectly good standard of information for your average historian or journalist.

It is up to religious people to prove that God exists, not up to atheists to prove the opposite, and remember that extraordinary claims require extraordinary evidence.

I don't think that "extraordinary claims require extraordinary evidence" has any counterpart as a way of weighing proof in law or anywhere else. On the contrary, many people have found from their experience that strange things happen, and "the truth is stranger than fiction."

In any case this balance of proof thing is a hoary old debating point and which I think should be viewed in common sense terms. The way I see it what is happening in modern Ireland could be phrased like this:

> "Nowadays, with the onward march of science, we are able to brush apart the old superstitions and show how a belief in God is contrary to human reason."

That I think is in practice what many modern atheists are saying. The natural common sense reply to that is: "Ok, well why do you say that? Can you show us what you mean?" Then it is behoven upon atheists to show that, to indicate where in science it proves or indicates anything like that. That's where the burden of proof comes from in this question, it comes from people using science to say that God does not exist.

If, on the otherhand, you are to say that science cannot prove that then I believe it should be logically looked upon as neutral on this question. In otherwords then science can be expected to go off and do its own thing and not step into an area that clearly is not natural to it. In otherwords unless it found the 'God molecule' or whatever, and show how God doesn't exist, then you would expect it to leave this question to the philosophers and theologians etc, which it currently isn't doing.

But those historical scientific writers that you quote in

Appendix B obviously had to say nice things about theism because otherwise they would have been executed for heresy!

Its amazing how many people are deluded with such crazily exaggerated notions like that about the Inquisition and Church history. For example, as far as I know, in the entire long recorded history of the Catholic Church in Ireland – some 1600 years – only four people were ever executed for heresy in any proceedings that could be described as a type of inquisition. (I.e. Petronella de Meath, executed in 1324 in connection with the case of Alice Kyteler in Kilkenny, Adam Duff executed on foot of an order by a civil court in Dublin in 1327,[9] and there is a reference to two men of the 'Clankellans' sentenced to be burnt in Bunratty in 1353, having been tried by Roger Craddock, the Franciscan Bishop of Waterford, who was accompanying the Justiciar, Thomas de Rokeby, in a campaign into Thomand. This incident did not meet with the approval of his superior, Ralph Kelly the Carmelite Archbishop of Cashel, however, who as a result came down with a troop of armed men to Craddock in Waterford, asaulted him and seized his goods.[10])

On the otherhand the number of people executed in this country because they tried to stay Catholic, in the teeth of state oppression, is very large, while the number of people executed around the world by atheists because they retained their faith, especially in the 20th century in places like Russia, China and even Spain, is obviously a huge figure.

The critics of evolution do admit that a type of evolution and natural selection does take place within species – which indeed they do – but then why not accept that that similar type of evolution takes place across species? After all the species barrier is not such a magical thing set in stone (although it must be admitted that the fact that species cannot mate across the species barrier is significant) so why not just accept that the same mechanism can occur across species, if you are prepared to accept that it does occur within species?

Now this is where you have to understand where the critics of evolution are coming from. You see these critics stand square on the old and irrefutable logic that you cannot get order, design and great complexity, arising spontaneously and randomly out of chaos and chance. So hence you cannot get new genes and gene structures – which are massively complex things, as complex as a skyscraper – arising out of nowhere by chance and giving you progressively complex beings up the line of the tree of life of evolution.

It might help here then just to rehash the basic model of evolution + natural selection. What evolutionists are saying is that randomly, just to take one hypothetical example, a lion could be born with an extra claw on his foot. Then, under natural selection, this new breed of lions with an extra claw should win out, over 1,000s of years, over the lions without that asset, because obviously they should be better able to kill predators etc, and hence we get up the evolutionary tree of life creating more complex beings through initially random changes i.e. the first lion being born with the extra claw, which are then 'held' by natural selection, reaching a shelf or plateau on the upward push of the evolutionary tree of life. The critics of evolution are saying that that initial step, the lion born with an extra claw, could not happen by chance because we know now that even a simple thing like a new claw requires a massive series of interlocking and complex genes to arrive, magically, from nowhere, and random mutations could never create that.

But, and this is what's happening here, they do allow that it can happen in reverse i.e. you can get 'progress' in a sense backwards, by creating slightly new types of life forms through a process of random mutations hitting and then degrading the previously complex forms.

Maybe a simple analogy might explain this better. This analogy by the way I appreciate is just all conjecture and implausible fiction, apart from the first bit of course! We will say that Paris Hilton falls madly in love with me, gets married, and from that I own 100 skyscraper hotels across the world earning so much money a year. 99.99% of the time having all hundred hotels up and running obviously leads to more money for me of course.

Now imagine we hit our hotel structure with a random mutation, meaning a random act changing some part of the structure, say in Hotel A somebody pulls out a girder. Now remember that's what random mutations look like in the eyes of the knowledgeable scientists who don't go with evolution, they say the random mutation is just hitting and degrading, making worse, some part of the structure of the DNA, whereas the evolutionists are talking about a random change which will magically create a shining new hotel overnight, with all its interdependent complexities arising like this out of chance. Now of course after this girder has been pulled out of one my hotels I am at least 99.99% of the time going to be worse off, because I have lost the use of the hotel. But, conceivably, in very rare occasions it could be to my advantage. Maybe that hotel was in some country which was going to pass some new horrendous laws which could affect the whole corporation, so I might have been lucky having it closed down at that time like that. So in those rare occasions I am better off, i.e. advancing a step forward in the law of Natural Selection, by losing some part of my hotel structure, the opposite of what would normally the case.

Now if you can follow that, this is what's happening sometimes in the case of DNA being hit by a random mutation. Even though it only can degrade and worsen the DNA structure, for some reason nonetheless it might in fact help the species and hence they will move forward in this new evolved state. So, to take a simple example, say we have a bird species that obviously relies on a huge complex structure of DNA to grow and move its wings. Now we will hit it with a random mutation on that DNA structure and this effect was so catastrophic that now it cannot fly anymore. Most of the time then that new bird or birds will just die off, because they need the wings to survive. But, conceivably, there could be a 1 in a 1000 – or much longer odds – chance where losing their wings was useful to them. Maybe they are on an island somewhere where there is a huge quantity of deadly hawks who kill basically anything that makes it into the air, so if they evolved to walking on the ground only they are more likely to survive, so natural selection can then kick in and we can get at least a new type of bird within a species.

Hence that's what the critics of evolution are saying can happen as regards natural selection and a limited form of evolution. You see its a very limited and slight form of evolution because it couldn't lead to radical changes in the type of lifeform you are looking at. If you follow the logic of what happens above you cannot get from a fish to a bird or something, it doesn't allow for those kind of radical changes, only a change that would be a gradual diminution of the original complexity of the organism.

So hence again you can observe this kind of limited 'evolution' in some species and no it does not follow that this will give you any comfort in trying to justify the overall large macro evolution picture.

And otherwise you say then that evolution doesn't happen? But what about the development of bacteria which are resistant to antibiotics? Isn't that a clear example of evolution in action?

The above scenario is the answer then to this question, these bacteria are losing the use of some complex genes that they had but in this instant are more useful for them to have in a broken – post a genetic mutation – rather than working state. This is because the antibiotic will work its killing properties on the structures created by those genes, and so, like the bird with broken wings, its more useful to the bacteria to have lost those genes.

If you still say that antibiotic resistant strains of bacteria are a sign of evolution rather than the above process, then maybe we could formulate here two hypotheses which, if proved true, could show that the above mechanism was occurring as opposed to evolution:

a) We might expect under our hypothesis that bacteria would have shown antibiotic properties in the past, considering how easy it is for the bacteria to display that state, in our scenario, as opposed to evolution which would require the bacteria to stretch up along the tree of life, creating new complexity in adapting to the antibiotics.

Well it turns out that bacteria from 150 years ago, frozen in ice, show the same antibiotic resistance properties of modern bacteria, clinching our hypothesis.[11]

b) We would expect that the antibiotic resistant bacteria would be handicapped in some way, under our thesis. In otherwords, just like the bird with non-working wings, we are talking about a broken gene sequence, which was otherwise useful for the bacteria, in the antibiotic resistant strain so surely some part of the bacteria will now not work as well as before.

In fact an example of that can be seen in bacteria which are resistant to Quinolone type antibiotics, which work against bacteria by binding to a bacterial protein called gyrase, which the bacteria needs to reproduce.[12] Hence the quinolone resistant bacteria has a mutation in the gene responsible for making gyrase, so now the quinolone cannot bind to it properly and then kill the bacteria, but, and this is the hypothesis we are making, the bacteria then reproduces more slowly, because the altered gyrase is not as good as the previous type from the point of view of bacterial reproduction. So again it is as you would expect under our scenario, whereas if you are talking about a better stronger bacteria, caused by evolutionary forces creating more complex mechanisms, then you would not expect that, you would expect it to evolve into a better state with antibiotic resistant properties but also able to reproduce as well as before.

Q.E.D.!

Are there any other 'Proofs of God's Existence' or have you covered them all?

No, there are plenty of others out there. For example here is another one that has not been much mentioned recently, and I will finish this appendix by describing this little known proof and answering some obvious questions on it:

The Sex Ratio: Proof of God's Existence from the Balance of the Sexes at Birth

The question is how come we have pretty much an even balance of male and female births in the population? Since there are known to be specific factors influencing the likelihood of a male or female birth occurring, not just random chance in the selection of a male or female birth, then how or why does it end up so even across the population?

So just to take a pretty random quote from a parenting site which lists some natural factors that are known to influence this selection:

> "there are few things you could try naturally, that can help you improve the odds of having either a boy or a girl.
>
> The methods depend on the fundamental differences in X and Y chromosomes of the sperm.
>
> ...
>
> Diet: To conceive a boy, a diet rich in sodium and potassium helps. This includes foods like red meat, bananas, peaches and sausage.
>
> For a girl, diet rich in calcium and magnesium provides the necessary pH level. Recommended foods include broccoli, apples, fish and dairy products." [13]

It is accepted by science that some factors like these will change and effect significantly the gender of a soon to be conceived child. But then why would it all end up roughly half in half in the whole population, why a set ratio at all? Presumably its quite random the amount of fertile couples that are eating red meat as opposed to fish or whatever – and there is no reason for a half in half split here – according to the above list, so why then do we end up with such a uniform figure down through history for the balance of male and female births?

There is no point in waving at us some kind of natural selection explanation here because no less a figure than Darwin himself tried to marry this with his theory of evolution and failed. He wrote extensively on it in his first edition of *The Descent of Man* but by the second edition he ended up writing:

> "I formerly thought that when a tendency to produce the two sexes in equal numbers was advantageous to the species, it would follow from natural selection, I now see that the whole problem is so intricate that it is safer to leave its solution for the future." [14]

What makes this proof so interesting, and plausible, is that the ratio at birth of males and females is *not* an exact 50:50 split, as you would expect if it was random, but rather it is always slightly more boys than girls, enough to correct for the greater likelihood of boys dying young so that in the marrying population you get an even enough male/female balance. Its as if somehow the man above knows this and is compensating for it? And furthermore, and even more intriguingly, it has been well known since at least the mid 18th century that at times of war, both during and after it, the ratio of boys born will increase, to compensate for the men lost in the war? [15]

In a recent book on this sex ratio it is conceded that:

> "Nowadays, following Ronald A Fisher (1890-1962), the view is taken that the trend of the sex ratio is, in principle, to adjust towards a balance of the two sexes." [16]

The intricacies of Fisher's work are by no means accepted nowadays but the principle, that nature will adjust the sex ratio of births to bring us back in the direction of a "Fisherian" 1:1 male female balance in the population, is, as you can see in the above quote, the accepted scientific principle here. Is this not nature then using some kind of mysterious 'intelligence' in correcting the birth ratio to give us this balance?

In any case this proof of God's existence has been known from at least the very early 18th century, as you can see in a quote from this 1710 publication by Dr John Arbuthnot (1667-1735), a physician, polymath and good friend of Swift and Pope:

> "*II. An Argument for Divine Providence, taken from the Constant Regularity observed in the Births of both Sexes. By* Dr. John Arbuthnot, *Physician in Ordinary to her Majesty, and Fellow of the College of Physicians and the Royal Society.*

AMONG innumerable Footsteps of Divine Providence to be found in the Works of Nature, there is a very remarkable one in the exact Balance that is maintained between the Numbers of Men and Women; for by this means it is provided, that the Species may never fail, nor perish, since every Male may have its Female, and of a proportional Age. This Equality of Males and Females is not the Effect of chance but Divine Providence, working for a good End, which I thus demonstrate:

Let there be a Die of Two sides, M and F...[goes on to describe the laws of probability here]...

It will be easy by the help of Logarithms, to extend this Calculation to a very great Number, but that is not my present Design. It is visible from what has been said, that with a very great Number of Dice, ... and consequently (supposing M to denote Male and F Female) that in the vast Number of Mortals, where would be but a small part of all the possible Chances, for its happening at any assignable time, that an equal Number of Males and Females should be born.

...we must observe that the external Accidents to which Males are subject (who must seek their Food with danger) make a great havock of them, and that this loss exceeds far that of the other Sex occasioned by Diseases incident to it, as Experience convinces us. To repair that Loss, provident Nature, by the Disposal of its wise Creator, brings forth more Males than Females; and that in almost a constant proportion. This appears from the annexed Tables, which contain Observations for 82 years of the births in London. Now, to reduce the Whole to a Calculation, I propose this

Problem. A lays against B. that every Year there

shall be born more Males than Females: To find A's Lot, or the Value of his Expectation.

It is evident from what has been said, that A's lot for each year is less than 1/2 (but, that the Argument might be stronger) let his Lot be equal to 1/2 for one year. If he undertakes to do the same thing 82 times running, his Lot will be 1/2 divided by 82, which will be easily found by the Table of Logarithms to be 1 / 4 8360 0000 00000 00000 00000 0000 . But if A wager with B, not only that the Number of Males shall exceed that of Females, every Year, but that this Excess shall happen in a constant Proportion, and the Difference lie within fix'd limits; and this not only for 82 Years, but for Ages of Ages, and not only at London, but all over the World; which it is highly probable is the Fact, and designed that every Male may have a Female of the same Country and suitable Age; then A's Chance will be near an infinitely small Quantity, at least less than any assignable fraction. From whence it flows, that it is Art, not Chance, that governs." [17]

And incidentally much the same argument was used by Johann Peter Süssmilch (1707-1767), a member of the Prussian Academy of Sciences, writing in 1741:

"that four to five per cent more boys than girls are born, thus compensating for the higher male losses due to the recklessness of boys, to exhaustion and to dangerous tasks, to war, to sailing, to emigration, and Who thus maintains the balance between the two sexes so that everyone can find a spouse at the appropriate time for marriage." [18]

When I toss a coin a thousand times, the heads and tails will approximate 50-50, and God was nowhere to be seen and not involved, thanks.

Obviously its not anyway a true 50/50 split, as already described, but anyhow I also think you missed the significance of the first few paragraphs in the original outline of this proof above. There I was talking about how this breakdown, i.e. the odds of a child being conceived as male or female, isn't a random thing at all in the face of modern science, we know about numerous factors that impinge on this ratio. Since it isn't random, we are not bringing in therefore the rules of probability, which would only apply if there was a genuinely random process involved in the conception of males or females, which there isn't.

Maybe I could make that a bit clearer. Leaving aside the diet one already discussed, lets look at the factors that influence this natural – i.e. ignoring abortion, which particularly skews figures in China – ratio of male/female births. Here is a major study published in 2007 which examined births over a period of 1940 and 1949, over a large population of 523,671, and then matched the data to the occupatation of the fathers in the 1960 Census: http://www.ncbi.nlm.nih.gov/pubmed/17957828 . It found that "Agricultural owners/managers and office managers were both statistically significantly more likely to have male offspring with adjusted odds ratios (and 95% confidence intervals) of 1.045 (1.024-1.066, $p < 0.001$) and 1.021 (1.003-1.039, $p = 0.022$), respectively." In short they found that "Father's occupation level, even 10-20 years after childbirth...is associated with the sex ratio of offspring."

Countless studies have shown the same thing, that the occupation of the father has a major impact on whether or not they will have male or female offspring, for example here is another one, this time from 2011 in relation to basketball players in Spain, wherein it is said that: "In conclusion, a significant increase in the sex ratio value in favour of female offspring was observed in the group of CAU professional basketball players." [19] In fact the figures there are amazing, no way is that some statistical quirk, the occupation here makes a pretty huge difference in the sex ratio of the children.

There are plenty of other factors that have been shown to influence this, including for example the menarcheal age – age at which menstruation begins – of the mother.[20] But in turn the menarcheal age worldwide is changing quite dramatically and is also influenced by things like "social class, parents' ethnic origin, educational institution, and home living area".[21] Even smoking in mothers, allied to genetic issues of course, is a factor that will change the sex ratio of the offspring.[22]

It has also been shown, in a number of studies, that more girls are born to single mothers than is the case with two parent families, for example in this 2004 study published by the Royal Society:

> "In a sample of 86,436 human births pooled from five population-based surveys, I found 51.5% male births reported by respondents who were living with a spouse or partner before the child's conception or birth, and 49.9% male births reported by respondents who were not." [23]

As you can see in that paper, these studies that show a lower percentage of boys born to single mothers actually go back all the way to the late 19th century.

Now consider that the Sex Ratio at birth in the UK in 2001 was estimated at c.1,050 (i.e. the number of male births divided by the number of female births and multiplied by 1,000, as described here: http://www.cdc.gov/nchs/data/nvsr/nvsr53/nvsr53_20.pdf , which is also where that statistic comes from, p.5). Meanwhile the oldest figures we have for England, as far as I know, are those from Romsey for the period 1569-1658, which work out as a ratio of 1,056.[24] So we end up with only a difference between these two figures of about half of one percent, but how could that happen? 0.5% of a difference in some 400 years, in a figure everybody says is influenced by all these factors like the rise of single mothers, smoking, differences in the father's occupation etc etc? Do you not think these factors will have changed dramatically during the course of those 400 years? So why do we end up with such regularity over the centuries, virtually the same figure, despite all these various factors influencing that percentage? Bear in mind too that in some of these studies, like the Spanish basketball players, we are referring to quite huge variations in the ratio of the sex of the offspring, but how then could Tudor and Stuart England end up with the same figure when they certainly didn't have basketball players or the equivalent?

And that's without even going into the whole wartime rise issue. Interestingly, while the increase in the male birth rate during and after wartime is a very established fact, its also acknowledged that there is, amazingly enough, an increase in the female birthrate during times of natural disaster other than war (for example in the case of the smog in London in 1952, during the Brisbane flood in 1965, and after the Kobe earthquake in Japan in 1995).[25]

So we are left with the inevitable conclusion that there is some kind of 'intelligence' here, and, as you can see in the quote on Fisher above, modern science does recognise that there is some mysterious 'balancing' of this figure going on. In otherwords science does acknowledge that nature will strive to keep the figure in balance, and indeed to change the figure to recognise, in the case of war especially, an imbalance in the wider male/female population. Well how can that be, are they not acknowledging some kind of 'intelligence' in mother nature?

There is a huge variety of environmental factors and external conditions (such as the availability of food, the relative proportions of men and women, and varying hormonal conditions within the mother's body) that impinge on the Sex Ration. The environmental or external factors are therefore what determines the Sex Ratio, there is no need to bring God into it!

"external conditions"...."food"..."varying hormonal conditions within the mother's body" ...sure absolutely, bring them on, there is nothing in that that invalidates this argument. The point is that there is not a good, or any, answer there as to why that varying mass of factors – like the ones you mention – translates into such an exact and unusual figure, stable (but allowing for the war changes) over some 400 years?

While I am not dismissing these other factors I think it might be worthwhile going over again the occupations of the fathers. I say that because while other factors are indeed known to be issues here, as far as I know, based on the literature, by far the greatest changes in the statistics are seen in the case of the different trades and professions of the fathers. If you read these studies you notice a few percent of a change here or there usually but in this case the Sex Ratio can change very dramatically.

One of the first then to notice this was Marianne E Bernstein (1954), who, using the parents listed in Who's Who, found large differences in the Sex Ratio grouping around the occupations of the father. Following this W R Lyster, writing in the Lancet in 1982, found an "altered sex ratio in children of divers." The divers had 85 daughters and 45 sons. A few years before, the Director of the German Airforce Institute of Aviation medicine published a work on pilots and the Sex Ratio in *Aviation Space and Environmental Medicine* in August 1975. They showed that pilots with more than 2,000 hours flying time had significantly more daughters, while in regard to the ones with only 1,000 hours the phenomenon was less marked. By these means they showed that the stressfulness of the occupation was not a factor, because the first 1,000 hours are by far the most stressful.[26] Then there is the study by Bertis B Little, "Pilot and Astronaut offspring", published in *Aviation Space and Environmental Medicine* again, in 1987.[27] In astronauts and tactical pilots the figure was 66:100 as the proportion of sons to daughters, which again is a huge variation from the norm which should be about 105:100. We are told also that:

> "Pilots were not the only fathers to be investigated: there is evidence that anaesthetists and policemen also have more daughters, and these occupational effects are strong enough to reach statistical significance even in small samples" [28]

Meanwhile in the recent study among the basketball players they found it was a sex ratio of 0.42, with the national average being 1.06 (a figure over one means more males than females were born, and it is usually, as we have seen, something of the order of 105 males to 100 females).[29]

Anyway the more you read up the literature on this the more

you appreciate that this following piece of anecdotal evidence does seem to be what is actually occurring:

> "I recently retired after working for 45 years, the first 11 (peacetime) years in firstly the Navy and then the Air Force, the remaining 34 years as an accountant.
>
> During my time in the armed forces I noticed, beyond any reasonable doubt, that my colleagues collectively produced significantly more male offspring than female. During my time as an accountant the reverse was clearly obvious amongst my accountant colleagues, although not so amongst sales and engineering colleagues." [30]

So then you ask yourself the same question, how does it happen that with these kind of dramatic differences in the offspring of different occupations that we end up with a pure almost constant statistic over time, accurate to some 0.5% over c.400 years? Obviously the balance of these professions in society must have changed enormously over those 400 years?

Why do you say that natural selection and evolution do not work in regard to the Sex Ratio?

What happened was that Darwin ran with a theory on it for the first edition of his book *The Descent of Man* and then scrapped it for the second edition, as I said. But this theory was then resurrected by the aforementioned Ronald A Fisher, a big enthusiast of Darwin's and Eugenics and one of Richard Dawkin's favourite people, surprisingly enough! The way that Fisher put it became quite popular and, as I said, his overall idea, that nature will act with a kind of intelligence to give us a birth Sex Ratio that will lead to a balanced 1:1 for people of marrying age, continued and continues on today even though the evolutionary underpinnings of this have been scrapped. His theory was simply this (including a few later modifications to take out some financial issues that are not thought now to be so important):

We will say that whatever factor governs the Sex Ratio is inherited. Then we will say that, for the sake of argument, that in a population of 200 people, 100 males and 100 females, the 100 males had an inherited disposition to breed male offspring as opposed to females, while the females in that generation had no particular bias one way or the other. Ok, that being the case, the next generation, which we will say consists of 400 people, now has a balance of 300 males and 100 females say. This is because when the first generation mated the resulting offspring had a bias in favour of males, because in the parents here we had this bias to breed males. Fair enough, but now in this generation we can still only get 100 males and 100 females mating, presuming that we are talking about stable 2 parent families. This means that in this generation the females end up giving their genes disproportionally to the next generation, i.e. 100 females pass their genes on, but they are only one quarter of the total population here, as against 100 males passing on their genes, even though they are three quarters of the population. Remember as well that the females have no bias in favour of male offspring, so in this generation you are disproportionally favouring those that have no pro male offspring bias, correcting, somewhat, the imbalance that existed the last time. So what's happening is that its evening itself out as the generations cascade down. The bias in favour of males doesn't go on to lead to more males generation by generation because the fact that you always need one male matching with one female parent, and hence will discard the excess males or females, will bring you back towards a 1:1 balance.

That's the basic argument anyway, with a lot of other complications, and not a few other assumptions, but the whole argument is now discredited because whatever is the main factor impinging on the Sex Ratio in humans simply isn't inheritable. It doesn't pass from one generation to another anyway and hence all these evolution and genetic arguments completely break down. This became clear when a pupil of Fisher's, Anthony William Fairbank Edwards (1935-), examined a large data set in Sweden to try to prove Fisher's theories, and ended up concluding in his 1962 paper that:

"little progress has been made in establishing the heritability of the sex ratio" and "it must be concluded that, if genetic variability exists, it is of a very low order of magnitude." [31]

This was a large data set that he was using, on the offspring of Swedish Ministers of religion over many centuries, 5,477 Ministers from 1585-1920, but we are told that:

"The Swedish data (as well as two or three other large data sets) were carefully analysed for anything and everything that might provide a hint of hereditability, but not a single result was significant." [32]

And that's basically where we are now at on the subject of Natural Selection here, it is accepted that there is that 'very low order of magnitude' factor which seems to be inheritable, as seen in ethnic studies in multicultural societies for example, but it is known to be too small to be significant. Hence we have this abstract from a study by probably the leading expert on this area:

"It is suggested that the human sex ratio at birth is stabilized only to a minor extent by the direct processes of natural selection. Instead the major factors stabilizing sex ratio seem to be behavioural (coital rates) and psychological (parental perceptions of adult sex ratios). It is suggested that parental hormone levels are (a) a consequence of perceived adult sex ratios, and (b) a cause of sex ratio in the next generation, thus providing the basis for a negative feedback process stabilizing the sex ratio." [33]

As you can see this scientist, W H James, and another scientist and author, Dr Valerie J Grant, *do* have a theory, but a very faint one I would say, to explain the overall concept as to why the Sex Ratio should balance out over time, but remember they have *no* theory, as far as I have read in any case, to explain why it should break down in this exact way with a male birth bias of 105:100 century after century. The theory as to why it might tend to 1:1 is put forward in the latter's book, Valerie J Grant, *Maternal personality, evolution, and the sex ratio* (London, 1998), and it is admittedly at least quite interesting. It has to do with a concept of female selection of mates and subsequent theories on frequency of coitus, and also by postulating that the perceived Sex Ratio existing in society could psychologically affect parents and lead to an altered Sex Ratio in their offspring as a result of this psychological influence. So they speculate that maybe you would have more daughters among the occupations listed above because maybe those jobs are more 'manly' – and then attractive in a particular fashion to particular types of women –, with those fathers physically 'active' shall we say (!) more often or earlier in a marriage and hence leading to different gendered children according to the various hormonal cycles etc of the mother. Then they go on to talk about a possible balancing effect of the inheritance of these traits in the subsequent mothers etc. Anyway, as pointed out, none of this gets you anywhere in explaining the evenness and regularity over the centuries of the 105:100 discrepancy. You can see that from a quote from this website which is devoted to the Sex Ratio, which has a review of Grant's book as well as a list of the latest scientific papers on the subject:

"For every 100 baby girls, there are 105 baby boys. This is a fact.

Why more boys? Nobody knows! And it's a real puzzle because...

– Other animal species have half male and half female offspring.

– Men produce equal numbers of x-chromosome sperms (which make girls) and y-chromosome sperms (which make boys)." [34]

Of course the answer to this, like everything else, we will be told by those Star Trek type seers into the great wilderness of future scientific advances, is that scientists are on the job and any day now they will crack the thing, watch out, don't you worry. So again, to guard against this 'promissory materialism' stuff, I should point out that this subject is a well known scientific controversy, with countless theories coming and going among scientists ever since Aristotle reviewed the previous literature on the subject in the mid 300s BC. (He went with temperature as a factor by the way, which is not that bad a guess. Actually there is a bias in the statistics whereby people living at the Poles have proportionally more males and at the Equator more females.)

Arbuthnot's paper is very highly regarded actually, and is often held up as the first modern style scientific study of probability and statistics. It also generated a lot of interest, and some controversy, among scientists from the very beginning. So, for example, Nicolas Bernoulli in his two letters of 1712 and 1713, from London and Paris respectively, published in the Appendix to the *Analyse des Jeux de hazard*, 2nd Edition, had a go at him saying that if you had a dice with 35 faces, 18 representing males and 17 females, then chance would toss up the dice faces in the same order that Arbuthnot found in his statistics. Of course this is an outrageous misunderstanding of probability and a restrained Abraham de Moivre, in his great work on probability, the ground breaking *The Doctrine of Chances* (London, 1756), p.252, weighed in by pointing out the mistakes of Bernoulli and he confirmed that in his opinion it did indeed show the mark of our Maker. (Admittedly de Moivre might have misunderstood Bernoulli – a member of a famous family of mathematicians – here. If you were to speculate on a structured and stable biological trait that would favour male births – e.g. by saying that the Y chromosome sperm will swim consistently that little bit faster and hence a permanent but small bias in favour of male births – and then couple that with chance, and hence probability, for the remaining aspects of the male:female breakdown, then Bernoulli might have had something there. But all that is mute now because we know that the breakdown isn't by chance, it is decided by things like the father's occupation and hence should change in accordance with the occupational changes in the population. Incidentally de Moivre's comments are quoted in Appendix B infra.)

The point is that since you then end up with about 24 centuries of serious discussion of this topic among scientists, including intense modern style scientific research and analysis for 300 years since that paper of 1710, consequently it makes little sense to take again this familiar gamble that somehow the solution will arrive anytime soon via modern science. I think they will just end up with the same conclusion as Arbuthnot, that there is just no way that this mishmash of frequency of coitus or psychological factors etc could give you such a pure, and unlikely, statistic, statically even across populations over some four centuries.

There are obvious lines of enquiry for studying natural causes for changes in the proportion of male to female babies. Until you can exclude natural causes why should you leap to a supernatural cause?

Quite simply because you cannot get out of that boiling mass of factors this kind of ongoing stable figure, the odds against it, which Arbuthnot troubled to calculate for us, are too great. Its simply an impossibility, it doesn't matter now what other issue comes up, we just know, now that we can see the various factors that are impinging on the Sex Ratio – and hence its not random, or even random with a biological bias which could account for the 105 male birth thing – and that it isn't related to natural selection, long since discredited as an answer, that the various issues couldn't come together in such exact order as to translate into that exact statistic. When you hit these gigantic odds you are in the realm of design, intelligence, order, or whatever you want to call it.

Yes I know that's a familiar battleground from evolution but is true nonetheless. These high probabilities are just the polite scientific way of telling you that such and such an event is *impossible* to have come about by random means. That's what these high probabilities mean, if you understand probability, they are not to be taken as some excuse for somebody to run off and claim that over time such and such a thing is possible. You have to think about this question of randomness v design. If you are to say that complexity or design can come out of chaos that's the equivalent of saying that if you walked along a beach, that was beside a carrot patch, and you saw an elaborately designed sandcastle man with a carrot for its nose you would conclude that it may have come about from the action of the tides and the winds. That's just ludicrous, anything on those lines is a complete fallacy, if you have very large probability odds like this then you have design.

In otherwords our understanding of the natural world is at this point exhausted, since we know we cannot get order from chaos like that we are, so to speak, on the bank of a river we cannot cross. To add to our other proofs then, what we find is that we are beside three rivers that we cannot cross:

a) We have the beginning of the universe – remember it has a beginning, if you accept Big Bang – but we cannot get past the ex-nihilo thing (i.e. Ex nihilo nihil fit, nothing comes out of nothing.);

b) We cannot see how the first lifeform could have come about, because that would depend on a spontaneous creation of massive complexity and order arising from chance and randomness, which again is an impossibility, a logical fallacy;

c) and finally we have this mysterious regulated figure for the Sex Ratio, the probabilities of which arising by chance are far too great and hence cannot have arisen that way, and therefore also just cannot be explained by our natural reason, which dictates that you cannot get this kind of order from chaos.

So we really have three rivers here that we just cannot cross, we cannot see, using our knowledge of the way the world works and our use of logic and reason, how we can possibly cross these rivers. But of course we have crossed them, in the sense that they are there, we have a universe, we have lifeforms and DNA etc, and we have this consistent Sex Ratio figure. So what do we conclude from that? We conclude that there is something we haven't figured out yet, there is something beyond our ken of the natural world, beyond our reason. Of course a thing above and beyond the natural is what you call the 'super' natural, that's all the word means, and hence since these river crossings have happened, and must have used 'super'natural means as opposed to our natural knowledge, then we know that the supernatural exists.

This is just a little humbling for us and for scientists, we don't give up on our natural reason by any means but we recognise that there is something out there we don't get, that we don't understand. Now that we recognise that, we are in turn not so dismissive of reports of miracles or apparitions or indeed of miracles in the Bible. The new humble us is prepared to keep an open mind, now that we can see that there is something out there that we just don't grasp through the lens of our current state of natural reason. And obviously the traditional proofs, described above, go on to speculate as to why a particular being or entity would want to create the universe etc and then we get some of the various attributes of the Christian God from this kind of, complicated, but well studied analysis.

Footnotes
1. Plotinus' text, *Against the Gnostics: Against Those That Affirm the Creator of the Cosmos and the Cosmos Itself to Be Evil*, is available at: http://thriceholy.net/Texts/Plotinus5.html .

2. Plotinus, *Third Enneads* (Rome, c.253 AD), Second Tractate, On Providence (1), 1, 4, 5, 8, 9 and 11, available at:
http://classics.mit.edu/Plotinus/enneads.3.third.html .

3. C S Lewis, *Mere Christianity*, Bk. III, chap. 10, "Hope" quoted at http://www.peterkreeft.com/topics-more/20_arguments-gods-existence.htm .

4. For example in the *Life of St Columba*:
http://www.ucc.ie/celt/published/T201040.html .

5. http://en.wikipedia.org/wiki/Physics_(Aristotle) .

6. http://www.earlychristianwritings.com/text/polycarp-lightfoot.html .

7. Letter to the Smyrnaeans 6:2-7:1.

8. http://www.earlychristianwritings.com/text/1clement-lightfoot.html .

9. James Grace, *Annales Hiberniae* (Dublin, 1842), p.107.

10. Augustin Theiner, *Vetera monumenta hibernorum et scotorum* (Rome, 1864), p.269, JRSAI vol 6 1867 p.88,
http://www.carmelites.ie/PDF/PrereformationIreland.pdf p.7, which refers to Patrick Romaeus McCaffrey, *The White Friars* (Dublin, 1926), p.355 and Patrick Power, *Waterford And Lismore* (Cork, 1937), p.10-11, and finally see James Ware – who got it from Cotton Ms Vesp B. XI. f. 127v – *Antiquities and History of Ireland* (Dublin, 1705), p.24 under Waterford 1350.

11. As you can see in the New Scientist Magazine 11th of Feb 1989: http://books.google.ie/books?id=fA9tecLhj9wC&q=Franklin#v=snippet&q=Franklin&f=false .

12. Jonathan Heddle and Anthony Maxwell, Quinolone-binding pocket of DNA gyrase: role of GyrB, in *Antimicrobial Agents and Chemotherapy* 46(6):1805-1815, 2002; and Faye Barnard and Anthony Maxwell, Interaction between DNA gyrase and quinolones: effects of alanine mutations at GyrA subunit residues Ser83 and Asp87, in *Antimicrobial Agents and Chemotherapy* 45(7):1994-2000, 2001.

13. http://www.gettingpregnantquick.com/factors-affecting-the-gender-of-your-baby/ .

14. http://www.gutenberg.org/cache/epub/2300/pg2300.html .

15. http://www.time.com/time/magazine/article/0,9171,773794,00.html .

16. Éric Brian and Marie Jaisson, *The Descent of Human Sex Ratio at Birth: A Dialogue between Mathematics, Biology and Sociology* (Dordrecht, Springer, 2007), p.xv. This book by the way deliberately avoids discussing why this ratio should trend like this.

17. John Arbuthnot, "An argument for Divine Providence, taken from the constant regularity observed in the births of both sexes", published in the *Philosophical Transactions of the Royal Society of London* (1710) vol 27, p.186-190, available at: http://books.google.ie/books?id=1bijIzB8QokC .

18. Quoted in Valerie J Grant, *Maternal personality, evolution, and the sex ratio* (London, 1998), p.148.

19. http://www.ncbi.nlm.nih.gov/pubmed/21806664 .

20. http://www.ncbi.nlm.nih.gov/pubmed/21806664 .

21. http://www.ncbi.nlm.nih.gov/pubmed/2572476 .

22. http://www.ncbi.nlm.nih.gov/pubmed/2572476 .

23. http://www.jstor.org/pss/4142816 .

24. http://findarticles.com/p/articles/mi_qa3659/is_200108/ai_n8990886/ .

25. http://humrep.oxfordjournals.org/content/13/8/2321.full.pdf .

26. Mentioned in Valerie J Grant, *Maternal personality, evolution, and the sex*

ratio (London, 1998), p.161.

27. Ibid p.164.

28. Ibid p.165.

29. http://www.ncbi.nlm.nih.gov/pubmed/21806664 .

30. http://www.popsci.com/scitech/article/2008-12/why-does-war-breed-more-boys .

31. Grant op.cit. p.151.

32. Grant op. cit. p.150.

33. W H James, What stabilizes the sex ratio?, *Annals of Human Genetics*, 1995 Apr; 59 (Pt 2): 243-9, http://www.ncbi.nlm.nih.gov/pubmed/7625769 .

34. http://www.sexratio.com/facts.htm .

APPENDIX B
The Proofs by Philosophers and Scientists through history

This is just a list of famous philosophers and scientists who have looked at the Universe and its laws and concluded that there must have been an overall being who intelligently designed it all. I apologise for its length but while I have tried to concentrate only on the really famous scientists, like Nobel Prize winners and those who have given their names to units or laws in physics, it seems a large proportion of those were very interested in these wider questions. I have also added in some quotes from other scientists on the question of evolution and how it has been perceived by some over the ages.

Anaxagoras (c.500-c.428 BC)

Just a simple quote here, by Robert Boyle, summarising this ancient Greek philosopher's views, which shows the great antiquity of the teleological argument:

> *"The delineation and manner of all things he thought to be designed and made by the power and reason of infinite intelligence."*

Here this early Greek philosopher describes some of the attributes of God, who he called 'nous', by combining a very early cosmological and teleological argument:

"All other things partake in a portion of everything, while Nous is infinite and self-ruled, and is mixed with nothing, but is alone, itself by itself. For if it were not by itself, but were mixed with anything else, it would partake in all things if it were mixed with any; for in everything there is a portion of everything, as has been said by me in what goes before, and the things mixed with it would hinder it, so that it would have power over nothing in the same way that it has now being alone by itself. For it is the thinnest of all things and the purest, and it has all knowledge about everything and the greatest strength; and Nous has power over all things, both greater and smaller, that have soul. And Nous had power over the whole revolution, so that it began to revolve in the beginning. And it began to revolve first from a small beginning; but the revolution now extends over a larger space, and will extend over a larger still. And all the things that are mingled together and separated off and distinguished are all known by Nous. And Nous set in order all things that were to be, and all things that were and are not now and that are, and this revolution in which now revolve the stars and the sun and the moon, and the air and the aether that are separated off. And this revolution caused the separating off, and the rare is separated off from the dense, the warm from the cold, the light from the dark, and the dry from the moist. And there are many portions in many things. But no thing is altogether separated off nor distinguished from anything else except Nous. And all Nous is alike, both the greater and the smaller; while nothing else is like anything else, but each single thing is and was most manifestly those things of which it has most in it."

(The first quote is from Robert Boyle, *An Essay containing a requisite digression, concerning those that would exclude the Deity from intermeddling with matter* (1663), quoted in M. A. Stewart edit., *Selected Philosophical Papers of* Robert Boyle (Manchester, 1979), p.166, and the quote from Anaxagoras is from *Nous*, fragment 59 B 12, available at: http://www.ellopos.net/elpenor/greek-texts/ancient-greece/anaxagoras-nous.asp .)

Socrates (c.470-399 BC),

of course was the first of the really great Greek philosophers who went on to found so much of our Western system. Here he is talking to Aristodemus (c.450s-c.400 BC) (of Cydathenaeum, called 'the small') as related by Xenophon (c.430 -c.350 BC) who overheard the conversation which must have taken place in Athens at some time between c.410 and 401 BC. (Socrates never wrote anything down, all we know of him comes from a number of conversations of his that are handed down to us via his students, including Plato and Xenaphon.)

"I will first mention what I myself once heard him advance in a dialogue with Aristodemus, surnamed The Little, concerning the gods; for having heard that Aristodemus neither sacrificed to the gods, when engaged on any enterprise, nor attended to auguries, but ridiculed those who regarded such matters, he said to him, "Tell me, Aristodemus, do you admire any men for their genius?"

"I do," replied he.

"Tell us their names, then," said Socrates.

"In epic poetry I most admire Homer, in dithyrambic Melanippides, in tragedy Sophocles, in statuary Polycletus, in painting Zeuxis."

"And whether do those who form images without sense and motion, or those who form animals endowed with sense and vital energy, appear to you the more worthy of admiration?"

"Those who form animals, by Jupiter, for they are not produced by chance, but by understanding."

"And regarding things of which it is uncertain for what purpose they exist, and those evidently existing for some useful purpose, which of the two would you say were the productions of chance, and which of intelligence?"

"Doubtless those which exist for some useful purpose must be the productions of intelligence."

"Does not he, then," proceeded Socrates, "who made men at first, appear to you to have given them, for some useful purpose, those parts by which they perceive different objects, the eyes to see what is to be seen, the ears to hear what is to be heard? What would be the use of smells, if no nostrils had been assigned us? What perception would there have been of sweet and sour, and of all that is pleasant to the mouth, if a tongue had not been formed in it to have a sense of them?

In addition to these things, does it not seem to you like the work of forethought, to guard the eye, since it is tender, with eyelids, like doors, which, when it is necessary to use the sight, are set open, but in sleep are closed? To make the eyelashes grow as a screen, that winds may not injure it? To make a coping on the parts above the eyes with the eyebrows, that the perspiration from the head may not annoy them? To provide that the ears may receive all kinds of sounds, yet never be obstructed? and that the front teeth in all animals may be adapted to cut, and the back teeth to receive food from them and grind it? To place the mouth, through which animals take in what they desire, near the eyes and the nose? and since what passes off from the stomach is offensive, to turn the channels of it away, and remove them as far as possible from the senses?—can you doubt whether such a disposition of things, made thus apparently with attention, is the result of chance or of intelligence?"

"No, indeed," replied Aristodemus, "but to one who looks at those matters in this light, they appear like the work of some wise maker who studied the welfare of animals."

"And to have engendered in them a love of having offspring, and in mothers a desire to rear their progeny, and to have implanted in the young that are reared a desire of life, and the greatest dread of death?"

"Assuredly these appear to be the contrivances of some one who designed that animals should continue to exist."

"And do you think that you yourself have any portion of intelligence?"

"Question me, at least, and I will answer."

"And can you suppose that nothing intelligent exists anywhere else? When you know that you have in your body but a small portion of the earth, which is vast, and a small portion of the water, which is vast, and that your frame is constituted for you to receive only a small portion of each of other things, that are vast, do you think that you have seized for yourself, by some extraordinary good fortune, intelligence alone which exists nowhere else, and that this assemblage of vast bodies, countless in number, is maintained in order by something void of reason?"

"Yes; for I do not see the directors of these things, as I see the makers of things which are done here."

"Nor do you see your own soul, which is the director of your body; so that, by like reasoning, you may say that you yourself do nothing with understanding, but everything by chance."

"However, Socrates," said Aristodemus, "I do not despise the gods, but consider them as too exalted to need my attention."

"But," said Socrates, "the more exalted they are, while they deign to attend to you, the more ought you to honour them."

"Be assured," replied Aristodemus, "that if I believed the gods took any thought for men, I would not neglect them."

"Do you not, then, believe that the gods take thought for men? the gods who, in the first place, have made man alone, of all animals, upright (which uprightness enables him to look forward to a greater distance, and to contemplate better what is above, and to be less liable to injury, and have placed the eyes, and ears, and mouth); and, in the next place, have given to other animals only feet, which merely give them the capacity of walking, while to men they have added hands, which execute most of those things through which we are better off than they.

And though all animals have tongues, they have made that of man alone of such a nature, as, by touching sometimes one part of the mouth, and sometimes another, to express articulate sounds, and to signify everything that we wish to communicate one to another.

...

Nor did it satisfy the gods to take care of the body merely, but, what is most important of all, they implanted in him the soul, his most excellent part. For what other animal has a soul to understand, first of all, that the gods, who have arranged such a vast and noble order of things, exist? What other species of animal, besides man, offers worship to the gods? What other animal has a mind better fitted than that of man, to guard against hunger or thirst, or cold or heat, or to relieve disease, or to acquire strength by exercise, or to labour to attain knowledge; or more capable of remembering whatever it has heard, or seen, or learned?

...

Do you suppose, too, that the gods would have engendered a persuasion in men that they are able to benefit or injure them, unless they were really able to do so, and that men, if they had been thus perpetually deluded, would not have become sensible of the delusion? Do you not see that the oldest and wisest of human communities, the oldest and wisest cities and nations, are the most respectful to the gods, and that the wisest age of man is the most observant of their worship?

Learn also, my good youth," continued Socrates, "that your mind, existing within your body, directs your body as it pleases; and it becomes you therefore to believe that the intelligence pervading all things directs all things as may be agreeable to it, and not to think that while your eye can extend its sight over many furlongs, that of the divinity is unable to see all things at once, or that while your mind can think of things here, or things in Egypt or Sicily, the mind of the deity is incapable of regarding everything at the same time.

Socrates also felt that you didn't need to see the divine in order to believe in its existence, but rather you can know it exists from observing the effects of its actions.

And that I speak the truth, you yourself also well know, if you do not expect to see the bodily forms of the gods, but will be content, as you behold their works, to worship and honour them. Reflect, too, that the gods themselves give us this intimation; for the other deities that give us blessings, do not bestow any of them by coming manifestly before our sight; and he that orders and holds together the whole universe, in which are all things beautiful and good, and who preserves it, for us who enjoy it, always unimpaired, undisordered, and undecaying, obeying his will swifter than thought and without irregularity, is himself manifested (only) in the performance of his mighty works, but is invisible to us while he regulates them.

Consider also that the sun, which appears manifest to all, does not allow men to contemplate him too curiously, but, if any one tries to gaze on him steadfastly, deprives him of his sight. The instruments of the deities you will likewise find imperceptible; for the thunderbolt, for instance, though it is plain that it is sent from above, and works its will with everything with which it comes in contact, is yet never seen either approaching, or striking, or retreating; the winds, too, are themselves invisible, though their effects are evident to us, and we perceive their course. The soul of man, moreover, which partakes of the divine nature if anything else in man does, rules, it is evident, within us, but is itself unseen. Meditating on these facts, therefore, it behoves you not to despise the unseen gods, but, estimating their power from what is done by them, to reverence what is divine."

(Xenophon, *Memorabilia of Socrates*, Book I Chapter IV available at: http://thriceholy.net/Texts/Memorabilia.html . The last two paragraphs are from ibid Book IV Chapter III, available at: http://thriceholy.net/Texts/Memorabilia2.html .)</blockquote>

Hippocrates (c.460 BC - c.370 BC),

founder of the great medical school on the island of Kos in Greece is well known as the Father of Medicine and the source of the Hippocratic Oath.

"Near the place where the veins grow out of the heart are bodies bestriding the cavities – soft, spongy things called auricles, although they do not have channels in them as real ears do. In fact, these auricles do not take in sound, but rather are the organs by which nature captures the air. And I think this is the creation of a good hand-worker, for when he recognised that the viscus was going to be of a solid frame on account of the thickness of its substance, and then highly attractive, he added bellows to it, just as bronze smiths do to their melting-pots, in order that through these it would be able to handle the respiration. Proof of this theory: the heart, as you can see, moves as a whole, but the auricles inflate and collapse individually."

(Hippocrates, edit. by Paul Potter, *Hippocrates volume 9* (Harvard, 2010), p.65, Heart chapter 8.)

Plato (424/3 BC - 348/7 BC),

the great philosopher and mathematician from Athens who may be regarded as the first articulator of the idea of a Republic, here writes a fictional dialogue between an Athenian – in practice Plato himself – and Cleinias, an old Athenian politician.

"[Those who] have supposed one of three things—either that they [gods] did not exist—which is the first possibility, or secondly, that, if they did, they took no care of man, or thirdly, that they were easily appeased and turned aside from their purpose by sacrifices and prayers.

CLEINIAS: What shall we say or do to these persons?

ATHENIAN: My good friend, let us first hear the jests which I suspect that they in their superiority will utter against us.

CLEINIAS: What jests?

ATHENIAN: They will make some irreverent speech of this sort: 'O inhabitants of Athens, and Sparta, and Cnosus,' they will reply, 'in that you speak truly; for some of us deny the very existence of the Gods, while others, as you say, are of opinion that they do not care about us; and others that they are turned from their course by gifts. Now we have a right to claim, as you yourself allowed, in the matter of laws, that before you are hard upon us and threaten us, you should argue with us and convince us—you should first attempt to teach and persuade us that there are Gods by reasonable evidences, and also that they are too good to be unrighteous, or to be propitiated, or turned from their course by gifts. For when we hear such things said of them by those who are esteemed to be the best of poets, and orators, and prophets, and priests, and by innumerable others, the thoughts of most of us are not set upon abstaining from unrighteous acts, but upon doing them and atoning for them. When lawgivers profess that they are gentle and not stern, we think that they should first of all use persuasion to us, and show us the existence of Gods, if not in a better manner than other men, at any rate in a truer; and who knows but that we shall hearken to you? If then our request is a fair one, please to accept our challenge.

CLEINIAS: But is there any difficulty in proving the existence of the Gods?

ATHENIAN: How would you prove it?

CLEINIAS: How? In the first place, the earth and the sun, and the stars and the universe, and the fair order of the seasons, and the division of them into years and months, furnish proofs of their existence, and also there is the fact that all Hellenes [Greeks] and barbarians believe in them.

ATHENIAN: I fear, my sweet friend, though I will not say that I much regard, the contempt with which the profane will be likely to assail us. For you do not understand the nature of their complaint, and you fancy that they rush into impiety only from a love of sensual pleasure.

CLEINIAS: Why, Stranger, what other reason is there?

ATHENIAN: One which you who live in a different atmosphere would never guess.

CLEINIAS: What is it?

ATHENIAN: A very grievous sort of ignorance which is imagined to be the greatest wisdom.

CLEINIAS: What do you mean?

ATHENIAN: ...as to our younger generation and their wisdom, I cannot let them off when they do mischief. For do but mark the effect of their words: when you and I argue for the existence of the Gods, and produce the sun, moon, stars, and earth, claiming for them a divine being, if we would listen to the aforesaid philosophers we should say that they are earth and stones only, which can have no care at all of human affairs, and that all religion is a cooking up of words and a make-believe.

...

Yet the attempt must be made [to prove the existence of gods]; for it would be unseemly that one half of mankind should go mad in their lust of pleasure, and the other half in their indignation at such persons. Our address to these lost and perverted natures should not be spoken in passion; let us suppose ourselves to select some one of them, and gently reason with him, smothering our anger: O my son, we will say to him, you are young, and the advance of time will make you reverse many of the opinions which you now hold. Wait awhile, and do not attempt to judge at present of the highest things; and that is the highest of which you now think nothing—to know the Gods rightly and to live accordingly. And in the first place let me indicate to you one point which is of great importance, and about which I cannot be deceived: You and your friends are not the first who have held this opinion about the Gods. There have always been persons more or less numerous who have had the same disorder. I have known many of them, and can tell you, that no one who had taken up in youth this opinion, that the Gods do not exist, ever continued in the same until he was old; the two other notions certainly do continue in some cases, but not in many; the notion, I mean, that the Gods exist, but take no heed of human things, and the other notion that they do take heed of them, but are easily propitiated with sacrifices and prayers. As to the opinion about the Gods which may some day become clear to you, I advise you to wait and consider if it be true or not; ask of others, and above all of the legislator. In the meantime take care that you do not offend against the Gods. For the duty of the legislator is and always will be to teach you the truth of these matters.

CLEINIAS: Our address, Stranger, thus far, is excellent.

ATHENIAN: Quite true, Megillus and Cleinias, but I am afraid that we have unconsciously lighted on a strange doctrine.

CLEINIAS: What doctrine do you mean?

ATHENIAN: The wisest of all doctrines, in the opinion of many.

CLEINIAS: I wish that you would speak plainer.

ATHENIAN: The doctrine that all things do become, have become, and will become, some by nature, some by art, and some by chance.

CLEINIAS: Is not that true?

ATHENIAN: Well, philosophers are probably right; at any rate we may as well follow in their track, and examine what is the meaning of them and their disciples.

CLEINIAS: By all means.

ATHENIAN: They say that the greatest and fairest things are the work of nature and of chance, the lesser of art, which, receiving from nature the greater and primeval creations, moulds and fashions all those lesser works which are generally termed artificial.

CLEINIAS: How is that?

ATHENIAN: I will explain my meaning still more clearly. They say that fire and water, and earth and air, all exist by nature and chance, and none of them by art [by 'art' is meant something 'built' or 'designed' or 'created'], and that as to the bodies which come next in order—earth, and sun, and moon, and stars—they have been created by means of these absolutely inanimate existences. The elements are severally moved by chance and some inherent force according to certain affinities among them—of hot with cold, or of dry with moist, or of soft with hard, and according to all the other accidental admixtures of opposites which have been formed by necessity. After this fashion and in this manner the whole heaven has been created, and all that is in the heaven, as well as animals and all plants, and all the seasons come from these elements, not by the action of mind, as they say, or of any God, or from art, but as I was saying, by nature and chance only.

...

ATHENIAN: These, my friends, are the sayings of wise men, poets and prose writers, which find a way into the minds of youth. They are told by them that the highest right is might, and in this way the young fall into impieties, under the idea that the Gods are not such as the law bids them imagine; and hence arise factions, these philosophers inviting them to lead a true life according to nature, that is, to live in real dominion over others, and not in legal subjection to them.

CLEINIAS: What a dreadful picture, Stranger, have you given, and how great is the injury which is thus inflicted on young men to the ruin both of states and families!

...

ATHENIAN: Yes,...for if impious discourses were not scattered, as I may say, throughout the world, there would have been no need for any vindication of the existence of the Gods—but seeing that they are spread far and wide, such arguments are needed.

...

ATHENIAN: Well, then, tell me, Cleinias—for I must ask you to be my partner—does not he who talks in this way conceive fire and water and earth and air to be the first elements of all things? these he calls nature, and out of these he supposes the soul to be formed afterwards; and this is not a mere conjecture of ours about his meaning, but is what he really means.

CLEINIAS: Very true.

ATHENIAN: Then, by Heaven, we have discovered the source of this vain opinion of all those physical investigators; and I would have you examine their arguments with the utmost care, for their impiety is a very serious matter; they not only make a bad and mistaken use of argument, but they lead away the minds of others: that is my opinion of them.

CLEINIAS: You are right; but I should like to know how this happens.

ATHENIAN: I fear that the argument may seem singular.

...

ATHENIAN: If...we say that the whole path and movement of heaven, and all that is therein, is by nature akin to the movement and...calculation of mind, and proceeds by kindred laws, then...we must say that the best soul takes care of the world and guides it along the good path... And this soul of the sun ['and of the stars', moon, years, and months, and seasons]...ought by every man to be deemed a god.

...

ATHENIAN: Then all things which have a soul change, and possess in themselves a principle of change, and in changing move according to law and to the order of destiny: natures which have undergone a lesser change move less and on the earth's surface, but those which have suffered more change and have become more criminal sink into the abyss, that is to say, into Hades and other places in the world below, of which the very names terrify men, and which they picture to themselves as in a dream, both while alive and when released from the body. And whenever the soul receives more of good or evil from her own energy and the strong influence of others—when she has communion with divine virtue and becomes divine, she is carried into another and better place, which is perfect in holiness; but when she has communion with evil, then she also changes the place of her life.

'This is the justice of the Gods who inhabit Olympus.'

O youth or young man, who fancy that you are neglected by the Gods, know that if you become worse you shall go to the worse souls, or if better to the better, and in every succession of life and death you will do and suffer what like may fitly suffer at the hands of like. This is the justice of heaven, which neither you nor any other unfortunate will ever glory in escaping, and which the ordaining powers have specially ordained; take good heed thereof, for it will be sure to take heed of you. If you say: I am small and will creep into the depths of the earth, or I am high and will fly up to heaven, you are not so small or so high but that you shall pay the fitting penalty, either here or in the world below or in some still more savage place whither you shall be conveyed. This is also the explanation of the fate of those whom you saw, who had done unholy and evil deeds, and from small beginnings had grown great, and you fancied that from being miserable they had become happy; and in their actions, as in a mirror, you seemed to see the universal neglect of the Gods, not knowing how they make all things work together and contribute to the great whole. And thinkest thou, bold man, that thou needest not to know this? he who knows it not can never form any true idea of the happiness or unhappiness of life or hold any rational discourse respecting either.

...

For as we acknowledge the world to be full of many goods and also of evils, and of more evils than goods, there is, as we affirm, an immortal conflict going on among us, which requires marvellous watchfulness; and in that conflict the Gods and demigods are our allies, and we are their property. Injustice and insolence and folly are the destruction of us, and justice and temperance and wisdom are our salvation; and the place of these latter is in the life of the Gods, although some vestige of them may occasionally be discerned among mankind. But upon this earth we know that there dwell souls possessing an unjust spirit, who may be compared to brute animals, which fawn upon their keepers, whether dogs or shepherds, or the best and most perfect masters; for they in like manner, as the voices of the wicked declare, prevail by flattery and prayers and incantations, and are allowed to make their gains with impunity. And this sin, which is termed dishonesty, is an evil of the same kind as what is termed disease in living bodies or pestilence in years or seasons of the year, and in cities and governments has another name, which is injustice.

...

This ordered world is of mixed birth; it is the offspring of a union of Necessity and Intellect. Intellect prevailed over Necessity by persuading it to direct most of the things that come to be toward what is best, and the result of this subjugation of Necessity to wise persuasion was the initial formation of this universe."

(Plato, *Laws*, book X. The paragraph beginning with "If...we say that the whole path and movement of heaven" is quoted in William Lane Craig, *The Cosmological Argument from Plato to Leibniz* (London, 1980), p.3, the last quote is from his *Timaeus*, 48a, translated by Zeyl, quoted in: http://web.missouri.edu/~ariewa/Teleology.pdf , and otherwise these quotes are from: http://www.gutenberg.org/files/1750/1750-h/1750-h.htm#2H_4_0013 .)

Aristotle (384-322 BC),

"the father of the field of logic, he was the first to develop a formalized system for reasoning," here considers if nature is created by chance or for the sake of something, and deducts that "as in intelligent action, so in nature." Between these three men, Socrates, Plato and Aristotle, who preceded one another as the head of a philosophical school in Athens, you have the foundation of Western philosophy and the origins of the scientific method.

"We must explain then (1) that Nature belongs to the class of causes which act for the sake of something; (2) about the necessary and its place in physical problems, for all writers ascribe things to this cause, arguing that since the hot and the cold, &c., are of such and such a kind, therefore certain things necessarily are and come to be – and if they mention any other cause (one his 'friendship and strife', another his 'mind'), it is only to touch on it, and then good-bye to it.

A difficulty presents itself: why should not nature work, not for the sake of something, nor because it is better so, but just as the sky rains, not in order to make the corn grow, but of necessity? What is drawn up must cool, and what has been cooled must become water and descend, the result of this being that the corn grows. Similarly if a man's crop is spoiled on the threshing-floor, the rain did not fall for the sake of this – in order that the crop might be spoiled – but that result just followed. Why then should it not be the same with the parts in nature, e.g. that our teeth should come up of necessity – the front teeth sharp, fitted for tearing, the molars broad and useful for grinding down the food – since they did not arise for this end, but it was merely a coincident result; and so with all other parts in which we suppose that there is purpose? Wherever then all the parts came about just what they would have been if they had come be for an end, such things survived, being organized spontaneously in a fitting way; whereas those which grew otherwise perished and continue to perish, as Empedocles says his 'man-faced ox-progeny' did.

Such are the arguments (and others of the kind) which may cause difficulty on this point. Yet it is impossible that this should be the true view. For teeth and all other natural things either invariably or normally come about in a given way; but of not one of the results of chance or spontaneity is this true. We do not ascribe to chance or mere coincidence the frequency of rain in winter, but frequent rain in summer we do; nor heat in the dog-days, but only if we have it in winter. If then, it is agreed that things are either the result of coincidence or for an end, and these cannot be the result of coincidence or spontaneity, it follows that they must be for an end; and that such things are all due to nature even the champions of the theory which is before us would agree. Therefore action for an end is present in things which come to be and are by nature.

Further, where a series has a completion, all the preceding steps are for the sake of that. Now surely as in intelligent action, so in nature; and as in nature, so it is in each action, if nothing interferes. Now intelligent action is for the sake of an end; therefore the nature of things also is so. Thus if a house, e.g. had been a thing made by nature, it would have been made in the same way as it is now by art; and if things made by nature were made also by art, they would come to be in the same way as by nature. Each step then in the series is for the sake of the next; and generally art partly completes what nature cannot bring to a finish, and partly imitates her. If, therefore, artificial products are for the sake of an end, so clearly also are natural products. The relation of the later to the earlier terms of the series is the same in both. This is most obvious in the animals other than man: they make things neither by art nor after inquiry or deliberation. Wherefore people discuss whether it is by intelligence or by some other faculty that these creatures work, spiders, ants, and the like. By gradual advance in this direction we come to see clearly that in plants too that is produced which is conducive to the end-leaves, e.g. grow to provide shade for the fruit. If then it is both by nature and for an end that the swallow makes its nest and the spider its web, and plants grow leaves for the sake of the fruit and send their roots down (not up) for the sake of nourishment, it is plain that this kind of cause is operative in things which come to be and are by nature. And since 'nature' means two things, the matter and the form, of which the latter is the end, and since all the rest is for the sake of the end, the form must be the cause in the sense of 'that for the sake of which'.

Now mistakes come to pass even in the operations of art: the grammarian makes a mistake in writing and the doctor pours out the wrong dose. Hence clearly mistakes are possible in the operations of nature also. If then in art there are cases in which what is rightly produced serves a purpose, and if where mistakes occur there was a purpose in what was attempted, only it was not attained, so must it be also in natural products, and monstrosities will be failures in the purposive effort. Thus in the original combinations the 'ox-progeny' if they failed to reach a determinate end must have arisen through the corruption of some principle corresponding to what is now the seed.

Further, seed must have come into being first, and not straightway the animals: the words 'whole-natured first...' must have meant seed.

Again, in plants too we find the relation of means to end, though the degree of organization is less. Were there then in plants also 'olive-headed vine-progeny', like the 'man-headed ox-progeny', or not? An absurd suggestion; yet there must have been, if there were such things among animals.

Moreover, among the seeds anything must have come to be at random. But the person who asserts this entirely does away with 'nature' and what exists 'by nature'. For those things are natural which, by a continuous movement originated from an internal principle, arrive at some completion: the same completion is not reached from every principle; nor any chance completion, but always the tendency in each is towards the same end, if there is no impediment.

The end and the means towards it may come about by chance. We say, for instance, that a stranger has come by chance, paid the ransom, and gone away, when he does so as if he had come for that purpose, though it was not for that that he came. This is incidental, for chance is an incidental cause, as I remarked before. But when an event takes place always or for the most part, it is not incidental or by chance. In natural products the sequence is invariable, if there is no impediment.

It is absurd to suppose that purpose is not present because we do not observe the agent deliberating. Art does not deliberate. If the ship-building art were in the wood, it would produce the same results by nature. If, therefore, purpose is present in art, it is present also in nature. The best illustration is a doctor doctoring himself: nature is like that.

It is plain then that nature is a cause, a cause that operates for a purpose."

Aristotle articulated his theories of the divine across a number of books, including here in 'Nicomachean Ethics'.

"For this reason also the question is asked, whether happiness is to be acquired by learning or by habituation or some other sort of training, or comes in virtue of some divine providence or again by chance. Now if there is any gift of the gods to men, it is reasonable that happiness should be god-given, and most surely god-given of all human things inasmuch as it is the best. But this question would perhaps be more appropriate to another inquiry; happiness seems, however, even if it is not god-sent but comes as a result of virtue and some process of learning or training, to be among the most godlike things; for that which is the prize and end of virtue seems to be the best thing in the world, and something godlike and blessed....This is clear also from the praises of the gods; for it seems absurd that the gods should be referred to our standard, but this is done because praise involves a reference, to something else. But if praise is for things such as we have described, clearly what applies to the best things is not praise, but something greater and better, as is indeed obvious; for what we do to the gods and the most godlike of men is to call them blessed and happy. And so too with good things; no one praises happiness as he does justice, but rather calls it blessed, as being something more divine and better...But that perfect happiness is a contemplative activity will appear from the following consideration as well. We assume the gods to be above all other beings blessed and happy; but what sort of actions must we assign to them? Acts of justice? Will not the gods seem absurd if they make contracts and return deposits, and so on? Acts of a brave man, then, confronting dangers and running risks because it is noble to do so? Or liberal acts? To whom will they give? It will be strange if they are really to have money or anything of the kind. And what would their temperate acts be? Is not such praise tasteless, since they have no bad appetites? If we were to run through them all, the circumstances of action would be found trivial and unworthy of gods. Still, every one supposes that they live and therefore that they are active; we cannot suppose them to sleep like Endymion. Now if you take away from a living being action, and still more production, what is left but contemplation? Therefore the activity of God, which surpasses all others in blessedness, must be contemplative; and of human activities, therefore, that which is most akin to this must be most of the nature of happiness.

This is indicated, too, by the fact that the other animals have no share in happiness, being completely deprived of such activity. For while the whole life of the gods is blessed, and that of men too in so far as some likeness of such activity belongs to them, none of the other animals is happy, since they in no way share in contemplation. Happiness extends, then, just so far as contemplation does, and those to whom contemplation more fully belongs are more truly happy, not as a mere concomitant but in virtue of the contemplation; for this is in itself precious. Happiness, therefore, must be some form of contemplation.... Now he who exercises his reason and cultivates it seems to be both in the best state of mind and most dear to the gods. For if the gods have any care for human affairs, as they are thought to have, it would be reasonable both that they should delight in that which was best and most akin to them (i.e. reason) and that they should reward those who love and honour this most, as caring for the things that are dear to them and acting both rightly and nobly. And that all these attributes belong most of all to the philosopher is manifest. He, therefore, is the dearest to the gods. And he who is that will presumably be also the happiest; so that in this way too the philosopher will more than any other be happy."

An interesting quote from his book 'On the Heavens':

"The reasons why the primary body is eternal and not subject to increase or diminution, but unaging and unalterable and unmodified, will be clear from what has been said to any one who believes in our assumptions. Our theory seems to confirm experience and to be confirmed by it. For all men have some conception of the nature of the gods, and all who believe in the existence of gods at all, whether barbarian or Greek, agree in allotting the highest place to the deity, surely because they suppose that immortal is linked with immortal and regard any other supposition as inconceivable. If then there is, as there certainly is, anything divine, what we have just said about the primary bodily substance was well said. The mere evidence of the senses is enough to convince us of this, at least with human certainty. For in the whole range of time past, so far as our inherited records reach, no change appears to have taken place either in the whole scheme of the outermost heaven or in any of its proper parts. The common name, too, which has been handed down from our distant ancestors even to our own day, seems to show that they conceived of it in the fashion which we have been expressing. The same ideas, one must believe, recur in men's minds not once or twice but again and again. And so, implying that the primary body is something else beyond earth, fire, air, and water, they gave the highest place a name of its own, aither, derived from the fact that it 'runs always' for an eternity of time. Anaxagoras, however, scandalously misuses this name, taking aither as equivalent to fire."

From his book 'On the Parts of Animals':

"Continuous with the head and neck is the trunk with the anterior limbs. In man the forelegs and forefeet are replaced by arms and by what we call hands. For of all animals man alone stands erect, in accordance with his godlike nature and essence. For it is the function of the god-like to think and to be wise; and no easy task were this under the burden of a heavy body, pressing down from above and obstructing by its weight the motions of the intellect and of the general sense."

This following is from his book on Metaphysics, which he composed after he wrote his truly ground breaking and influential work on Physics, quoted from above. He obviously felt that discussing these subjects, like the origin of the Universe and the nature of God, was more important than mere physics.

"Since we are seeking this knowledge, we must inquire of what kind are the causes and the principles, the knowledge of which is Wisdom. If one were to take the notions we have about the wise man, this might perhaps make the answer more evident. We suppose first, then, that the wise man knows all things, as far as possible, although he has not knowledge of each of them in detail; secondly, that he who can learn things that are difficult, and not easy for man to know, is wise (sense-perception is common to all, and therefore easy and no mark of Wisdom); again, that he who is more exact and more capable of teaching the causes is wiser, in every branch of knowledge; and that of the sciences, also, that which is desirable on its own account and for the sake of knowing it is more of the nature of Wisdom than that which is desirable on account of its results, and the superior science is more of the nature of Wisdom than the ancillary; for the wise man must not be ordered but must order, and he must not obey another, but the less wise must obey him.

Such and so many are the notions, then, which we have about Wisdom and the wise. Now of these characteristics that of knowing all things must belong to him who has in the highest degree universal knowledge; for he knows in a sense all the instances that fall under the universal. And these things, the most universal, are on the whole the hardest for men to know; for they are farthest from the senses. And the most exact of the sciences are those which deal most with first principles; for those which involve fewer principles are more exact than those which involve additional principles, e.g. arithmetic than geometry. But the science which investigates causes is also instructive, in a higher degree, for the people who instruct us are those who tell the causes of each thing. And understanding and knowledge pursued for their own sake are found most in the knowledge of that which is most knowable (for he who chooses to know for the sake of knowing will choose most readily that which is most truly knowledge, and such is the knowledge of that which is most knowable); and the first principles and the causes are most knowable; for by reason of these, and from these, all other things come to be known, and not these by means of the things subordinate to them. And the science which knows to what end each thing must be done is the most authoritative of the sciences, and more authoritative than any ancillary science; and this end is the good of that thing, and in general the supreme good in the whole of nature. Judged by all the tests we have mentioned, then, the name in question falls to the same science; this must be a science that investigates the first principles and causes; for the good, i.e. the end, is one of the causes.

Hence also the possession of it might be justly regarded as beyond human power; for in many ways human nature is in bondage, so that according to Simonides 'God alone can have this privilege', and it is unfitting that man should not be content to seek the knowledge that is suited to him. If, then, there is something in what the poets say, and jealousy is natural to the divine power, it would probably occur in this case above all, and all who excelled in this knowledge would be unfortunate. But the divine power cannot be jealous (nay, according to the proverb, 'bards tell a lie'), nor should any other science be thought more honourable than one of this sort. For the most divine science is also most honourable; and this science alone must be, in two ways, most divine. For the science which it would be most meet for God to have is a divine science, and so is any science that deals with divine objects; and this science alone has both these qualities; for God is thought to be among the causes of all things and to be a first principle, and such a science either God alone can have, or God above all others. All the sciences, indeed, are more necessary than this, but none is better....Some think that even the ancients who lived long before the present generation, and first framed accounts of the gods, had a similar view of nature; for they made Ocean and Tethys the parents of creation, and described the oath of the gods as being by water, to which they give the name of Styx; for what is oldest is most honourable, and the most honourable thing is that by which one swears. It may perhaps be uncertain whether this opinion about nature is primitive and ancient, but Thales at any rate is said to have declared himself thus about the first cause. Hippo no one would think fit to include among these thinkers, because of the paltriness of his thought."

In c.350 BC Aristotle also wrote a fascinating book 'On the Soul,' all of which is relevant here of course but it is too long to quote it in full, although here are a few parts to give you the flavour of it.

"The view we have just been examining, in company with most theories about the soul, involves the following absurdity: they all join the soul to a body, or place it in a body, without adding any specification of the reason of their union, or of the bodily conditions required for it. Yet such explanation can scarcely be omitted; for some community of nature is presupposed by the fact that the one acts and the other is acted upon, the one moves and the other is moved; interaction always implies a special nature in the two interagents. All, however, that these thinkers do is to describe the specific characteristics of the soul; they do not try to determine anything about the body which is to contain it, as if it were possible, as in the Pythagorean myths, that any soul could be clothed upon with any body – an absurd view, for each body seems to have a form and shape of its own. It is as absurd as to say that the art of carpentry could embody itself in flutes; each art must use its tools, each soul its body.

There is yet another theory about soul, which has commended itself to many as no less probable than any of those we have hitherto mentioned, and has rendered public account of itself in the court of popular discussion. Its supporters say that the soul is a kind of harmony, for (a) harmony is a blend or composition of contraries, and (b) the body is compounded out of contraries. Harmony, however, is a certain proportion or composition of the constituents blended, and soul can be neither the one nor the other of these. Further, the power of originating movement cannot belong to a harmony, while almost all concur in regarding this as a principal attribute of soul. It is more appropriate to call health (or generally one of the good states of the body) a harmony than to predicate it of the soul. The absurdity becomes most apparent when we try to attribute the active and passive affections of the soul to a harmony; the necessary readjustment of their conceptions is difficult. Further, in using the word 'harmony' we have one or other of two cases in our mind; the most proper sense is in relation to spatial magnitudes which have motion and position, where harmony means the disposition and cohesion of their parts in such a manner as to prevent the introduction into the whole of anything homogeneous with it, and the secondary sense, derived from the former, is that in which it means the ratio between the constituents so blended; in neither of these senses is it plausible to predicate it of soul. That soul is a harmony in the sense of the mode of composition of the parts of the body is a view easily refutable; for there are many composite parts and those variously compounded; of what bodily part is mind or the sensitive or the appetitive faculty the mode of composition? And what is the mode of composition which constitutes each of them? It is equally absurd to identify the soul with the ratio of the mixture; for the mixture which makes flesh has a different ratio between the elements from that which makes bone. The consequence of this view will therefore be that distributed throughout the whole body there will be many souls, since every one of the bodily parts is a different mixture of the elements, and the ratio of mixture is in each case a harmony, i.e. a soul.

From Empedocles at any rate we might demand an answer to the following question for he says that each of the parts of the body is what it is in virtue of a ratio between the elements: is the soul identical with this ratio, or is it not rather something over and above this which is formed in the parts? Is love the cause of any and every mixture, or only of those that are in the right ratio? Is love this ratio itself, or is love something over and above this? Such are the problems raised by this account. But, on the other hand, if the soul is different from the mixture, why does it disappear at one and the same moment with that relation between the elements which constitutes flesh or the other parts of the animal body? Further, if the soul is not identical with the ratio of mixture, and it is consequently not the case that each of the parts has a soul, what is that which perishes when the soul quits the body?

That the soul cannot either be a harmony, or be moved in a circle, is clear from what we have said. Yet that it can be moved incidentally is, as we said above, possible, and even that in a sense it can move itself, i.e. in the sense that the vehicle in which it is can be moved, and moved by it; in no other sense can the soul be moved in space.

More legitimate doubts might remain as to its movement in view of the following facts. We speak of the soul as being pained or pleased, being bold or fearful, being angry, perceiving, thinking. All these are regarded as modes of movement, and hence it might be inferred that the soul is moved. This, however, does not necessarily follow. We may admit to the full that being pained or pleased, or thinking, are movements (each of them a 'being moved'), and that the movement is originated by the soul. For example we may regard anger or fear as such and such movements of the heart, and thinking as such and such another movement of that organ, or of some other; these modifications may arise either from changes of place in certain parts or from qualitative alterations (the special nature of the parts and the special modes of their changes being for our present purpose irrelevant). Yet to say that it is the soul which is angry is as inexact as it would be to say that it is the soul that weaves webs or builds houses. It is doubtless better to avoid saying that the soul pities or learns or thinks and rather to say that it is the man who does this with his soul. What we mean is not that the movement is in the soul, but that sometimes it terminates in the soul and sometimes starts from it, sensation e.g. coming from without inwards, and reminiscence starting from the soul and terminating with the movements, actual or residual, in the sense organs.

The case of mind is different; it seems to be an independent substance implanted within the soul and to be incapable of being destroyed. If it could be destroyed at all, it would be under the blunting influence of old age. What really happens in respect of mind in old age is, however, exactly parallel to what happens in the case of the sense organs; if the old man could recover the proper kind of eye, he would see just as well as the young man. The incapacity of old age is due to an affection not of the soul but of its vehicle, as occurs in drunkenness or disease. Thus it is that in old age the activity of mind or intellectual apprehension declines only through the decay of some other inward part; mind itself is impassible. Thinking, loving, and hating are affections not of mind, but of that which has mind, so far as it has it. That is why, when this vehicle decays, memory and love cease; they were activities not of mind, but of the composite which has perished; mind is, no doubt, something more divine and impassible. That the soul cannot be moved is therefore clear from what we have said, and if it cannot be moved at all, manifestly it cannot be moved by itself."

(*Physics*, book ii, pt 8, available at: http://classics.mit.edu/Aristotle/physics.2.ii.html ; the second quote is from http://classics.mit.edu/Aristotle/nicomachaen.mb.txt ; the third from http://classics.mit.edu/Aristotle/heavens.1.i.html ; the fourth from:
http://classics.mit.edu/Aristotle/parts_animals.4.iv.html ;
the second last quote is from:
 http://classics.mit.edu/Aristotle/metaphysics.mb.txt ; and the last from http://classics.mit.edu/Aristotle/soul.1.i.html .)

Book of Wisdom (written c.200-100 BC)

The teleogical argument was mentioned at an early date by the anonymous author of the Book of Wisdom, one of the books of the Old Testament, which was written in Greek in Alexandria c.200-100 BC.

"But all men are vain, in whom there is not the knowledge of God: and who by these good things that are seen, could not understand him that is, neither by attending to the works have acknowledged who was the workman: But have imagined either the fire, or the wind, or the swift air, or the circle of the stars, or the great water, or the sun and moon, to be the gods that rule the world. With whose beauty, if they, being delighted, took them to be gods: let them know how much the Lord of them is more beautiful than they: for the first author of beauty made all those things. Or if they admired their power, and their effects, let them understand by them, that he that made them, is mightier than they: For by the greatness of the beauty, and of the creature, the creator of them may be seen, so as to be known thereby. But yet as to these they are less to be blamed. For they perhaps err, seeking God, and desirous to find him. For being conversant among his works, they search: and they are persuaded that the things are good which are seen. But then again they are not to be pardoned. For if they were able to know so much as to make a judgment of the world: how did they not more easily find out the Lord thereof?"

(Book of Wisdom 13:1-9.)

Marcus Tullius Cicero (106-43 BC),

the great Roman politician and writer, often considered the father of oratory, goes into considerable detail on this subject and he finds it absurd not to accept the presence of a divine hand in the Universe.

"But if the structure of the world in all its parts is such that it could not have been better whether in point of utility or beauty, let us consider whether this is the result of chance, or whether on the contrary the parts of the world are in such a condition that they could not possibly have cohered together if they were not controlled by intelligence and by divine providence. If then the products of nature are better than those of art, and if art produces nothing without reason, nature too cannot be deemed to be without reason. When you see a statue or a painting, you recognize the exercise of art; when you observe from a distance the course of a ship, you do not hesitate to assume that its motion is guided by reason and by art; when you look at a sun-dial or a water-clock, you infer that it tells the time by art and not by chance; how then can it be consistent to suppose that the world, which includes both the works of art in question, the craftsmen who made them, and everything else besides, can be devoid of purpose and of reason? Suppose a traveller to carry into Scythia or Britain the orrery recently constructed by our friend Posidonius, which at each revolution reproduces the same motions of the sun, the moon and the five planets that take place in the heavens every twenty-four hours, would any single native doubt that this orrery was the work of a rational being? These thinkers however raise doubts about the world itself from which all things arise and have their being, and debate whether it is the product of chance or necessity of some sort, or of divine reason and intelligence; they think more highly of the achievement of Archimedes in making a model of the revolutions of the firmament than of that of nature in creating them, although the perfection of the original shows a craftsmanship many times as great as does the counterfeit.

...

So it would have been the proper course for the philosophers, if it so happened that the first sight of the world perplexed them, afterwards when they had seen its definite and regular motions, and all its phenomena controlled by fixed system and unchanging uniformity, to infer the presence not merely of an inhabitant of this celestial and divine abode, but also of a ruler and governor, the architect as it were of this mighty and monumental structure.

But as it is they appear to me to have no suspicion even of the marvels of the celestial and terrestrial creation. For in the first place the earth, which is situated in the centre of the world, is surrounded on all sides by this living and respirable substance named the air. 'Air' is a Greek word, but yet it has by this time been accepted in use by our race, and in fact passes current as Latin. The air in turn is embraced by the immeasurable aether, which consists of the most elevated portions of fire...From aether then arise the innumerable fires of the heavenly bodies, chief of which is the sun, who illumines all things with most brilliant light, and is many times greater and vaster than the whole earth; and after him the other stars of unmeasured magnitudes. And these vast and numerous fires not merely do no harm to the earth and to terrestrial things, but are actually beneficial, though with the qualification that were their positions altered, the earth would inevitably be burnt up by such enormous volumes of heat when uncontrolled and untempered.

At this point must I not marvel that there should be anyone who can persuade himself that there are certain solid and indivisible particles of matter borne along by the force of gravity, and that the fortuitous collision of those particles produces this elaborate and beautiful world? I cannot understand why he who considers it possible for this to have occurred should not also think that, if a countless number of copies of the one-and-twenty letters of the alphabet, made of gold or what you will, were thrown together into some receptacle and then shaken out on to the ground, it would be possible that they should produce the Annals of Ennius, all ready for the reader. I doubt whether chance could possibly succeed in producing even a single verse! Yet according to the assertion of your friends, that out of particles of matter not endowed with heat, nor with any 'quality' (the Greek term poiotes), nor with sense, but colliding together at haphazard and by chance, the world has emerged complete, or rather a countless number of worlds are some of them being born and some perishing at every moment of time yet if the clash of atoms can create a world, why can it not produce a colonnade, a temple, a house, a city, which are less and indeed much less difficult things to make? The fact is, they indulge in such random babbling about the world that for my part I cannot think that they have ever looked up at this marvellously beautiful sky which is my next topic.

...

Who would not deny the name of human being to a man who, on seeing the regular motions of the heaven and the fixed order of the stars and the accurate interconnexion and interrelation of all things, can deny that these things possess any rational design, and can maintain that phenomena, the wisdom of whose ordering transcends the capacity of our wisdom to understand it, take place by chance? When we see something moved by machinery, like an orrery or clock or many other such things, we do not doubt that these contrivances are the work of reason; when therefore we behold the whole compass of the heaven moving with revolutions of marvellous velocity and executing with perfect regularity the annual changes of the seasons with absolute safety and security for all things, how can we doubt that all this is effected not merely by reason, but by a reason that is transcendent and divine?

...

Moreover the gods have often appeared to men in person, as in the cases which I have mentioned above, so testifying that they care both for communities and for individuals. And the same is proved by the portents of future occurrences that are vouchsafed to men sometimes when they are asleep and sometimes when they are awake...Therefore no great man ever existed who did not enjoy some portion of divine inspiration. Nor yet is this argument to be disproved by pointing to cases where a man's cornfields or vineyards have been damaged by a storm, or an accident has robbed him of some commodity of value, and inferring that the victim of one of these misfortunes is the object of god's hatred or neglect. The gods attend to great matters; they neglect small ones."

(*De Natura Deorum*, ii, xxxiv-xxxviii, and lxvi, available at: http://ia600302.us.archive.org/27/items/denaturadeorumac00ciceuoft/denaturadeorumac00ciceuoft.pdf .)

Lucius Annaeus **Seneca**, the younger (4-65 AD),

was one of the great philosophers of the heyday of Imperial Rome, the greatest of the Stoics.

"Now God, who is the Father of us all, has placed ready to our hands those things which he intended for our own good; he did not wait for any search on our part, and he gave them to us voluntarily. But that which would be injurious, he buried deep in the earth. We can complain of nothing but ourselves; for we have brought to light the materials for our destruction, against the will of Nature, who hid them from us. We have bound over our souls to pleasure, whose service is the source of all evil; we have surrendered ourselves to self-seeking and reputation, and to other aims which are equally idle and useless. What, then, do I now encourage you to do? Nothing new – we are not trying to find cures for new evils – but this first of all: namely, to see clearly for yourself what is necessary and what is superfluous. What is necessary will meet you every where; what is superfluous has always to be hunted-out – and with great endeavour.

...

If any one gave you a few acres, you would say that you had received a benefit; can you deny that the boundless extent of the earth is a benefit? If any one gave you money, and filled your chest, since you think that so important, you would call that a benefit. God has buried countless mines in the earth, has poured out from the earth countless rivers, rolling sands of gold; He has concealed in every place huge masses of silver, copper and iron, and has bestowed upon you the means of discovering them, placing upon the surface of the earth signs of the treasures hidden below; and yet do you say that you have received no benefit? If a house were given you, bright with marble, its roof beautifully painted with colours and gilding, you would call it no small benefit. God has built for you a huge mansion that fears no fire or ruin, in which you see no flimsy veneers, thinner than the very saw with which they are cut, but vast blocks of most precious stone, all composed of those various and different substances whose paltriest fragments you admire so much; he has built a roof which glitters in one fashion by day, and in another by night; and yet do you say that you have received no benefit? When you so greatly prize what you possess, do you act the part of an ungrateful man, and think that there is no one to whom you are indebted for them? Whence comes the breath which you draw? the light by which you arrange and perform all the actions of your life? the blood by whose circulation your vital warmth is maintained? those meats which excite your palate by their delicate flavour after your hunger is appeased? those provocatives which rouse you when wearied with pleasure? that repose in which you are rotting and mouldering? Will you not, if you are grateful, say—

'Tis to a god that this repose I owe,
For him I worship, as a god below.
Oft on his altar shall my firstlings bleed,
See, by his bounty here with rustic reed
I play the airs I love the livelong day,
The while my oxen round about me stray.'

The true God is he who has placed, not a few oxen, but all the herds on their pastures throughout the world; who furnishes food to the flocks wherever they wander; who has ordained the alternation of summer and winter pasturage, and has taught us not merely to play upon a reed, and to reduce to some order a rustic and artless song, but who has invented so many arts and varieties of voice, so many notes to make music, some with our own breath, some with instruments. You cannot call our inventions our own any more than you call our growth our own, or the various bodily functions which correspond to each stage of our lives; at one time comes the loss of childhood's teeth, at another, when our age is advancing and growing into robuster manhood, puberty and the last wisdom-tooth marks the end of our youth. "We have implanted in us the seeds of all ages, of all arts, and God our master brings forth our intellects from obscurity."

"Nature," says my opponent, "gives me all this." Do you not perceive when you say this that you merely speak of God under another name? for what is nature but God and divine reason, which pervades the universe and all its parts? You may address the author of our world by as many different titles as you please; you may rightly call him Jupiter, Best and Greatest, and the Thunderer, or the Stayer, so called, not because, as the historians tell us, he stayed the flight of the Roman army in answer to the prayer of Romulus, but because all things continue in their stay through his goodness. If you were to call this same personage Fate, you would not lie; for since fate is nothing more than a connected chain of causes, he is the first cause of all upon which all the rest depend. You will also be right in applying to him any names that you please which express supernatural strength and power: he may have as many titles as he has attributes.

...

Whither-soever you turn yourself you will see him meeting you: nothing is void of him, he himself fills his own work. Therefore, most ungrateful of mortals, it is in vain that you declare yourself indebted, not to God, but to nature, because there can be no God without nature, nor any nature without God; they are both the same thing, differing only in their functions. If you were to say that you owe to Annaeus or to Lucius what you received from Seneca, you would not change your creditor, but only his name, because he remains the same man whether you use his first, second, or third name. So whether you speak of nature, fate, or fortune, these are all names of the same God, using his power in different ways. So likewise justice, honesty, discretion, courage, frugality, are all the good qualities of one and the same mind; if you are pleased with any one of these, you are pleased with that mind."

(Epistles, *On True and False Riches*, vol III, 110, available at: http://www.stoics.com/seneca_epistles_book_3.html#%E2%80%98CX1 , and the second and subsequent quotes are from *On Benefits*, book 4, vi-viii, available at: http://www.gutenberg.org/files/3794/3794-h/3794-h.htm .)

St Paul (c.5 - c.67 AD),

here writing, probably in Corinth, at some time between c.55-58 AD, in a letter being sent to the Christian community at Rome.

"For the invisible things of him [God] from the creation of the world are clearly seen, being understood by the things that are made. His eternal power also and divinity: so that they are inexcusable. Because that, when they knew God, they have not glorified him as God or given thanks: but became vain in their thoughts. And their foolish heart was darkened. For, professing themselves to be wise, they became fools."
(Romans 1:16-25)

Lucius Mestrius **Plutarch** (c.46-120 AD),

was a Greek writer who became one of the great historians of Roman history.

"To men the heavenly bodies that are so visible did give the knowledge of the deity; when they contemplated that they are the causes of so great an harmony, that they regulate day and night, winter and summer, by their rising and setting, and likewise considered those things which by their influences in the earth do receive a being and do likewise fructify. It was manifest to men that the Heaven was the father of those things, and the Earth the mother; that the Heaven was the father is clear, since from the heavens there is the pouring down of waters, which have their spermatic faculty; the Earth the mother, because she receives them and brings forth.

...

If you traverse the earth, you may find cities without walls, or literature, or laws, or fixed habitation, or coin. But a city destitute of temples and gods – a city that employeth not prayers or oracles, that offereth not sacrifice to obtain blessings and avert evil, no one has ever seen, or ever shall see...Nay, I am of opinion, that a city might sooner be built without any ground to fix it on, than a commonweal be constituted altogether void of any religion and opinion of the gods,—or being constituted, be preserved. But this, which is the foundation and ground of all laws.."

(The first quote is from *Essays and Miscellanies*, book I, chapter VI, available at:
http://www.gutenberg.org/files/3052/3052-h/3052-h.htm#2HCH0004 ,
and the second quote from *Contra Coloten* C.XXXI, partly from John A O'Brien, *Truths Men Live By* (New York, 1949), p.80, and partly from the latter website.)

Plotinus (205-270 AD),

born and raised in Egypt although he did most of his work in Rome and Italy, was the great 'neo-Platonist' who popularised Plato's philosophy during the declining years of the Roman Empire. Although not a Christian he elaborates here on why chance and materialism cannot possibly explain the origin of the Universe and life.

'"Atoms" or "elements" – it is in either case an absurdity, an impossibility, to hand over the universe and its contents to material entities, and out of the disorderly swirl thus occasioned to call order, reasoning, and the governing soul into being; but the atomic origin is, if we may use the phrase, the most impossible.

A good deal of truth has resulted from the discussion of this subject; but, even to admit such principles does not compel us to admit universal compulsion or any kind of "fate."

Suppose the atoms to exist:

These atoms are to move, one downwards – admitting a down and an up – another slant-wise, all at haphazard, in a confused conflict. Nothing here is orderly; order has not come into being, though the outcome, this Universe, when it achieves existence, is all order; and thus prediction and divination are utterly impossible, whether by the laws of the science – what science can operate where there is no order? – or by divine possession and inspiration, which no less require that the future be something regulated.

Material entities exposed to all this onslaught may very well be under compulsion to yield to whatsoever the atoms may bring: but would anyone pretend that the acts and states of a soul or mind could be explained by any atomic movements? How can we imagine that the onslaught of an atom, striking downwards or dashing in from any direction, could force the soul to definite and necessary reasonings or impulses or into any reasonings, impulses or thoughts at all, necessary or otherwise? And what of the soul's resistance to bodily states? What movement of atoms could compel one man to be a geometrician, set another studying arithmetic or astronomy, lead a third to the philosophic life? In a word, if we must go, like soulless bodies, wherever bodies push and drive us, there is an end to our personal act and to our very existence as living beings.

The School that erects other material forces into universal causes is met by the same reasoning: we say that while these can warm us and chill us, and destroy weaker forms of existence, they can be causes of nothing that is done in the sphere of mind or soul: all this must be traceable to quite another kind of Principle.

...

To make the existence and coherent structure of this Universe depend upon automatic activity and upon chance is against all good sense.

Such a notion could be entertained only where there is neither intelligence nor even ordinary perception; and reason enough has been urged against it, though none is really necessary."

(*Third enneads*,
   : http://classics.mit.edu/Plotinus/enneads.3.third.html .)

Sir **Francis Bacon** (1561-1626)

was a somewhat cynical, and not overly honest, politician and philosopher from Jacobean England who nonetheless wrote some very influential works which developed further 'The Scientific Method,' sometimes known after him as the 'Baconian Method'.

"I had rather believe all the fables in the Legend, and the Talmud, and the Alcoran, than that this universal frame is without a mind. And therefore, God never wrought miracle, to convince atheism, because his ordinary works convince it. It is true, that a little philosophy inclineth man's mind to atheism; but depth in philosophy bringeth men's minds about to religion. For while the mind of man looketh upon second causes scattered, it may sometimes rest in them, and go no further; but when it beholdeth the chain of them, confederate and linked together, it must needs fly to Providence and Deity. Nay, even that school which is most accused of atheism doth most demonstrate religion; that is, the school of Leucippus and Democritus and Epicurus. For it is a thousand times more credible, that four mutable elements, and one immutable fifth essence, duly and eternally placed, need no

God, than that an army of infinite small portions, or seeds unplaced, should have produced this order and beauty, without a divine marshal.

The Scripture saith, "The fool hath said in his heart, there is no God;" it is not said, "The fool hath thought in his heart;" so as he rather saith it, by rote to himself, as that he would have, than that he can thoroughly believe it, or be persuaded of it. For none deny, there is a God, but those, for whom it maketh [footnote: "To whose (seeming) advantage it is; the wish being father to the thought."] that there were no God. It appeareth in nothing more, that atheism is rather in the lip, than in the heart of man, than by this; that atheists will ever be talking of that their opinion, as if they fainted in it, within themselves, and would be glad to be strengthened, by the consent of others. Nay more, you shall have atheists strive to get disciples, as it fareth with other sects. And, which is most of all, you shall have of them, that will suffer for atheism, and not recant; whereas if they did truly think, that there were no such thing as God, why should they trouble themselves?

Epicurus is charged, that he did but dissemble for his credit's sake, when he affirmed there were blessed natures, but such as enjoyed themselves, without having respect to the government of the world. Wherein they say he did temporize; though in secret, he thought there was no God. But certainly he is traduced; for his words are noble and divine: Non deos vulgi negare profanum; sed vulgi opiniones diis applicare profanum ['It is not profane to deny the existence of the Deities of the vulgar: but to apply to the Divinities the received notions of the vulgar is profane.']. Plato could have said no more. And although he had the confidence, to deny the administration, he had not the power, to deny the nature.

The Indians of the West, have names for their particular gods, though they have no name for God: as if the heathens should have had the names Jupiter, Apollo, Mars, etc., but not the word Deus [God]; which shows that even those barbarous people have the notion, though they have not the latitude and extent of it. So that against atheists, the very savages take part, with the very subtlest philosophers.

The contemplative atheist is rare: a Diagoras, a Bion, a Lucian perhaps, and some others; and yet they seem to be more than they are; for that all that impugn a received religion, or superstition, are by the adverse part branded with the name of atheists. But the great atheists, indeed are hypocrites; which are ever handling holy things, but without feeling; so as they must needs be cauterized in the end.

The causes of atheism are: divisions in religion, if they be many; for any one main division, addeth zeal to both sides; but many divisions introduce atheism. Another is, scandal of priests; when it is come to that which St. Bernard saith, non est jam dicere, ut populus sic sacerdos; quia nec sic populus ut sacerdos. ['It is not for us now to say, 'Like priest like people,' for the people are not even so bad as the priest.'] A third is, custom of profane scoffing in holy matters; which doth, by little and little, deface the reverence of religion. And lastly, learned times, specially with peace and prosperity; for troubles and adversities do more bow men's minds to religion.

They that deny a God, destroy man's nobility; for certainly man is of kin to the beasts, by his body; and, if he be not of kin to God, by his spirit, he is a base and ignoble creature. It destroys likewise magnanimity, and the raising of human nature; for take an example of a dog, and mark what a generosity and courage he will put on, when he finds himself maintained by a man; who to him is instead of a God, or melior natura ['superior nature']; which courage is manifestly such, as that creature, without that confidence of a better nature than his own, could never attain. So man, when he resteth and assureth himself, upon divine protection and favour, gathered a force and faith, which human nature in itself could not obtain. Therefore, as atheism is in all respects hateful, so in this, that it depriveth human nature of the means to exalt itself, above human frailty. As it is in particular persons, so it is in nations. Never was there such a state for magnanimity as Rome. Of this state hear what Cicero saith:

'Quam volumus licet, patres conscripti, nos amemus, tamen nec numero Hispanos, nec robore Gallos, nec calliditate Poenos, nec artibus Graecos, nec denique hoc ipso hujus gentis et terrae domestico nativoque sensu Italos ipsos et Latinos; sed pietate, ad religione, atque hac una sapientia, quod deorum immortalium numine omnia regi gubernarique perspeximus, omnes gentes nationesque superavimus.'

['We may admire ourselves, conscript fathers, as much as we please; still, neither by numbers did we vanquish the Spaniards, nor by bodily strength the Gauls, nor by cunning the Carthaginians, nor through the arts the Greeks, nor, in fine, by the inborn and native good sense of this our nation, and this our race and soil, the Italians and Latins themselves; but through our devotion and our religious feeling, and this, the sole true wisdom, the having perceived that all things are regulated and governed by the providence of the immortal Gods, have we subdued all races and nations.']"

(Francis Bacon, *On Atheism*, No.16 in, *The Essays of Lord Bacon* (Philadelphia, c.1900), p.88-94.)

Johannes Kepler (1571-1630),

was a German mathematician and key figure in the scientific revolution of those days who discovered the three laws of planetary motion.

"Eventually Bodin compares the kingdom which he has described with the actual world, showing how God the creator has embellished this work of his by joining the ratios of equal and of similar in one concerted harmony. I agree with his purpose, as much as anyone; and what he or the preceding philosophers have not even touched on, which concerns the most accurate harmonic tempering of certain motions, I supply in the books which follow, and bring to light by the clearest demonstrations....there is this mixture of the equal and similar from the chief parts of the world, from the Sun which is the mover, the sphere which marks the position of the fixed stars, and the intermediate part, which is allotted to the moving bodies. For equality has been established in the parts of matter, so that there is just as much of it in the Sun as in the circle of the outermost sphere, or in the intermediate space. But arithmetic equality is due to matter, as to the people. On the otherhand there is geometrical similarity of proportion in the density of the three bodies; and again there is another between the diameters of the Sun which is the mover, the region of the moving bodies, and the furthest unmoving sphere which marks their place...All of which are arranged by God the supreme Regent for a good end, and the most complete harmony of all things. To Him every creature that can beathe brings the most fitting sacrifices of praise with unceasing exercise of piety; and I myself indeed, if it should seem good to Him that I should not die but shall live, shall in the following books declare the works of the Lord.

...

I feel carried away and possessed by an unutterable rapture over the divine spectacle of heavenly harmony... I write a book for the present time, or for posterity. It is all the same to me. It may wait a hundred years for its readers, as God has also waited six thousand years for an onlooker.

...

We see how God, like a human architect, approached the founding of the world according to order and rule and measured everything in such a manner."

(Johannes Kepler, translated by E.J. Aiton, A.M. Duncan and J.V. Field, *The Harmony of the World* (Philadelphia, 1997), p.278-280, the second quote from Steven G. Krantz and Brian E. Blank, *Calculus: Multivariable* (Hoboken, 2006), p.126, and the last quote from J. H. Tiner, *Johannes* Kepler–Giant of Faith and Science (Milford, 1977), p. 193.)

Sir **William Harvey** (1578-1657),

was of course a giant in the history of medicine, particularly for his work on the heart and the circulation of blood:

"We acknowledge God, the Supreme and Omnipotent Creator, to be present in the production of all animals, and to point, as it were, with a finger to His existence in His works.

All things are indeed contrived and ordered with singular providence, divine wisdom, and most admirable and incomprehensible skill. And to none can these attributes be referred save to the Almighty."

(William Harvey, *Anatomical Exercises on the Generation of Animals* (Toronto, 1989), p.443.)

René Descartes (1596-1650),

was a French soldier who became one of the greatest philosophers and mathematicians of all time. He wrote a lot about God throughout his works and was motivated to write about him partly, it seems, because he received some revelations from what he called the 'Spirit of Truth.' In any case he settled on maybe three proofs:

 a) the Cosmological Argument, which is scattered here and there throughout his Meditations;

 b) the argument from the existence of human consciousness of the divine, or of an infinite or all perfect being, and this was one of his favourite arguments that he elaborated on at length, as can be seen in the long quote from him in the main part of this text infra;

 c) surprisingly he opted for a type of Ontological Argument, but with many more subtleties than is usually given.

Since this argument is not described elsewhere in this work I thought I might describe it here. There are some old Greek philosophers that seem to touch upon this type of proof but usually it is attributed to St Anselm (1033-1109). He was a Norman monk who became Archbishop of Canterbury in 1093 *and who composed this basic proof:*

i) Try to imagine in your mind the most powerful and greatest being you can.

ii) Well the most powerful being must be something that exists, after all if you had powerful being A that didn't exist and you compared it to being B that did exist then which would you say is the most powerful? Surely the most powerful one is the one that really exists?

iii) And that 'being,' the most powerful being you can conceive of, is what we call God, and therefore he exists.

But this basic proof has not been popular at all among serious Christian scholars, especially since St Thomas Aquinas rejected it in the thirteenth century. Nonetheless the fame of some philosophers who did feel that it had some validity, like Descartes and Leibniz, would cause you to pause before dismissing it completely, at least not every derivation of it.

To get back to Descartes, you can see here some deductions common to the Cosmological Argument although mostly it refers to the 'perfect being' proof.

"If one concentrates carefully, all this is quite evident by the natural light. But when I relax my concentration, and my mental vision is blurred by the images of things I perceive by the senses, I lose sight of the reasons why my idea of more perfect being has to come from a being that really is more perfect. So I want to push on with my enquiry, now asking a new question: If the more perfect being didn't' exist, could I exist? My hope is that the answer to this will yield a new proof of the existence of a perfect being—a proof that it will be easier for me to keep in mind even when I relax my concentration. Well, if God didn't exist, from what would I derive my existence? It would have to come from myself, or from my parents, or from some other beings less perfect than God (a being more perfect than God, or even one as perfect, is unthinkable).

...

Perhaps this being is not God, though. Perhaps I was produced by causes less perfect than God, such as my parents. No; for as I have said before, it is quite clear that there must be at least as much reality or perfection in the cause as in the effect. And therefore, given that I am a thinking thing and have within me some idea of God, the cause of me—whatever it is—must itself be a thinking thing and must have the idea of all the perfections that I attribute to God. What is the cause of this cause of me? If it is the cause of its own existence, then it is God; for if it has the power of existing through its own strength, then undoubtedly it also has the power of actually possessing all the perfections of which it has an idea—that is, all the perfections that I conceive to be in God. If on the other hand it gets its existence from another cause, then the question arises all over again regarding this further cause: Does it get its existence from itself or from another cause? Eventually we must reach the ultimate cause, and this will be God. It is clear enough that this sequence of causes of causes can't run back to infinity, especially since I am dealing with the cause that not only produced me in the past but also preserves me at the present moment.

One might think this:

Several partial causes contributed to my creation; I received the idea of one of the perfections that I attribute to God from one cause, and the idea of another from another. Each perfection is to be found somewhere in the universe, but no one thing has them all.

That can't be right, because God's simplicity—that is, the unity or inseparability of all his attributes—is one of the most important of the perfections that I understand him to have. The idea of his perfections as united in a single substance couldn't have been placed in me by any cause that didn't also provide me with the ideas of the perfections themselves; for no cause could have made me understand that the perfections are united without at the same time showing me what they are."

(Rene Descartes, Third Meditation, in *Meditations on First Philosophy*, first published as *Meditationes de prima philosophia* (Paris, 1641), available at:
http://www.earlymoderntexts.com/pdfbits/dm2.pdf , p.15.)

Blaise Pascal (1623-1662),

eclipsed only by Descartes in the pantheon of great mathematicians, physicists and philosophers of France in the 17th century, and indeed of all time. He invented the first calculator, was central to the origins of the theory of probability but also was always very interested in theology. He had experienced the divine in some incidents around him and was desperate to communicate this to others (including, as a somewhat optimistic attempt, his 'wager', whereby a person should try to live like a Christian even if one doesn't completely believe it all, so covering your bets when you reach the pearly gates!) as comes across from these poignant words:

"What advantage is it to us to hear a man saying that he has thrown off the yoke; that he does not think there is any God who watches over his actions; that he considers himself as the sole judge of his conduct, and that he is accountable to none but himself? Does he imagine that we shall hereafter repose special confidence in him, and expect from him consolation, advice, succour, in the exigencies of life? Do such men imagine that it is any matter of delight to us to hear that they hold that our soul is but a little vapour or smoke, and that they can tell us this in an assured and self-sufficient tone of voice? Is this, then, a thing to say with gaiety? Is it not rather a thing to be said with tears, as the saddest thing in the world?"

Here he is trying to encourage his readers to at least try out Catholicism and its strictures for a while, even if they don't really believe in it yet.

"But learn, at least, your inability to believe, since reason brings you to it, and yet you cannot believe; try then to convince yourself, not by the augmentation of proofs of the existence of God, but by the diminution of your own passions. You would have recourse to faith, but you know not the way: you wish to be cured of infidelity, and you ask for the remedy: learn it from those who have been bound like yourself, and who would wager now all their goods; these know the road that you wish to follow, and are cured of a disease that you wish to be cured of. Follow their course, then, from its beginning; it consisted in doing all things as if they believed in them, in using holy water, in having masses said, etc. Naturally this will make you believe and stupefy you at the same time.

– But this is what I fear. –

And why? what have you to lose?

But to show you that this leads to it, this will diminish the passions, which are your great obstacles, etc.

Now, what harm will come to you in taking this course? You would be faithful, virtuous, humble, grateful, beneficent, a sincere friend, truthful. Truly, you would not be given up to infectious pleasures, to false glory, or false joys; but would you not have other pleasures?

I say to you that you will gain by it in this life; and that at each step you take in this direction, you will see so much of the certainty of gain, and so much of the nothingness of what you hazard, that you will acknowledge in the end that you have wagered for something certain, infinite, for which you have given nothing.

Oh! this discourse transports me, delights me, etc.

If this discourse pleases you and appears to you strong, know that it is made by a man who has put himself on his knees, before and after, to pray that Being, who is infinite and without parts, and to whom he entirely submits himself, that he would also subject you to himself for your good and his glory; and that thus power accords with this weakness....I would very soon abandon these pleasures, they say, if I had faith. And I answer: You would very soon have faith, if you had abandoned these pleasures. Now, it is for you to begin. If I could, I would give you faith. I cannot do it; and, consequently I cannot prove the truth of what you say. But you may easily quit your pleasures, and experience whether what I say is true...Now, if the passions do not hold us, a week and a hundred years are the same.

The metaphysical proofs of God are so remote from the reasoning of men, and so complicated, that they make but little impression; and even were this to serve some persons, it would be only during the instant of their seeing the demonstration, and an hour afterwards they would fear they had been deceived.

Quod curiositate cognoverint superbia amiserunt.

This is what produces the knowledge of God, which is deduced without Jesus Christ, which is to communicate without mediator, with the God whom we have known without mediator. Whilst those who have known God by a mediator know their misery.

Jesus Christ is the object of all, and the centre whither all tends. Whoever knows him knows the reason of all things.

Those who go astray, go astray only because they do not see one of these two things. We can then indeed know God without knowing our misery, and our misery without knowing God; but we cannot know Jesus Christ without knowing both God and our misery.

And this is why I will not undertake here to prove by natural reasons, either the existence of God, the Trinity, or the immortality of the soul, or any thing else of this nature; not only because I should not feel myself strong enough to find in nature wherewith to convince hardened atheists, but also because this knowledge, without Jesus Christ, is useless and barren. Even were a man persuaded that the proportions of numbers are truths immaterial, eternal, and dependent on a primary truth in which they subsist, and which we call God, I should not find him much advanced towards his salvation ...For we must not mistake ourselves, we are automaton as much as mind; and hence it comes that the instrument by which persuasion is made is not the only demonstration. How few things are demonstrated! Proofs convince only the mind. Custom makes our strongest and hardest proofs; it influences the automaton, which carries along the mind without its being aware of it. Who has demonstrated that there will be a tomorrow, and that we shall die? and what is more believed? It is custom, then, that persuades us of these things; it is custom that makes so many Christians, it is custom that makes Turks, pagans, trades, soldiers etc. In fine, we must have recourse to custom when once the mind has seen where the truth is, in order to drench and dye ourselves in this belief, which escapes us at every hour: for to have the proofs always present would be impossible. We must acquire a more easy belief, which is that of habit, which, without violence, without art, without argument, makes us believe things, and inclines all our powers to this belief, so that our soul falls into it naturally. When we believe only from the force of conviction, and the automaton is inclined to believe the contrary, it is not enough. Both our powers must be made to believe: the mind, by reason, which suffices to have examined but once; and the automaton, by custom, which does not permit it to incline to the contrary. Inclina cor meum Deus."

Pascal was, as pointed out, a very respected figure in France, considered a great master of French prose alongwith everything else, and has remained so since – e.g. there is now also a computer language called after him, alongwith the SI unit for pressure and 'Pascal's law' in hydrostatics –, for his tremendous intelligence and indeed integrity in all he did, so it might interest you to realise that he himself personally had a vision from God, after which he wrote this short 'Memorial'.

"The year of grace 1654,

Monday, 23 November, feast of St. Clement, pope and martyr, and others in the martyrology.
Vigil of St. Chrysogonus, martyr, and others.
From about half past ten at night until about half past

midnight,

FIRE.

GOD of Abraham, GOD of Isaac, GOD of Jacob
not of the philosophers and of the learned.
Certitude. Certitude. Feeling. Joy. Peace.
GOD of Jesus Christ.
My God and your God.
Your GOD will be my God.
Forgetfulness of the world and of everything, except GOD.
He is only found by the ways taught in the Gospel.
Grandeur of the human soul.
Righteous Father, the world has not known you, but I have known you.
Joy, joy, joy, tears of joy.
I have departed from him:
They have forsaken me, the fount of living water.
My God, will you leave me?
Let me not be separated from him forever.
This is eternal life, that they know you, the one true God, and the one that you sent, Jesus Christ.
Jesus Christ.
Jesus Christ.
I left him; I fled him, renounced, crucified.
Let me never be separated from him.
He is only kept securely by the ways taught in the Gospel:
Renunciation, total and sweet.
Complete submission to Jesus Christ and to my director.
Eternally in joy for a day's exercise on the earth.
May I not forget your words. Amen."
(First quote from *The Edinburgh Review* (1847) vol 85, p.203; second quote from: O. W. Wight, *The thoughts, letters and opuscules of Blaise* Pascal (New York, 1869), p.254-259; and final quote from:
http://www.users.csbsju.edu/~eknuth/pascal.html .)

John Ray (1627-1705),

known as the Father of Natural History, and wrote numerous works on that subject, was also successively a lecturer in Greek, Mathematics and College Steward of Cambridge University, and wrote a whole book proving the existence of Intelligent Design.

"First, the Belief of a Deity being the Foundation of all Religion, (Religion being nothing but a devout Worshipping of God, or an Inclination of Mind to serve and worship Him) "for he that cometh to God, must believe that he is" [Hebrews 11:6], it is a Matter of the highest concernment, to be firmly settled and established in a full Persuasion of this main Point: Now this must be demonstrated by Arguments drawn from the Light of Nature, and Works of the Creation: For as all other Sciences, so Divinity proves not, but supposes its Subjects, taking it for granted that by Natural Light, Men are sufficiently convinced of the Being of a Deity. There are indeed supernatural Demonstrations of this fundamental Truth, but not common to all Persons or Times, and so liable to Cavil and Exception by Atheistical Persons, as inward Illuminations of Mind, a Spirit of Prophecy and Foretelling future Contingents, illustrious Miracles, and the like. But these Proofs taken from Effects, and Operations, exposed to every Man's view, not to be denied or questioned by any, are most effectual to convince all that deny or doubt of it. Neither are they only convictive of the greatest and subtlest Adversaries, but intelligible also to the meanest Capacities: For you may hear illiterate Persons of the lowest Rank of the Commonalty affirming, That they need no Proof of the Being of a God, for that every Pile of Grass, or Ear of Corn, sufficiently proves that: For, say they, all the Men of the World cannot make such a thing as one of these; and if they cannot do it, who can, or did make it but God? To tell them, that it made itself, or sprung up by Chance, would be as ridiculous as to tell the greatest Philosopher so."

(John Ray, *The Wisdom of God manifested in the Works of Creation* (London, the first edition is from 1691 and this is from the 1717 edition) preface, available at:
http://www.jri.org.uk/ray/wisdom/index.htm .)

Robert Boyle (1627-1691),

generally considered the 'Father of Chemistry,' born in Lismore Co. Waterford the youngest son of the Earl of Cork, and the author of Boyle's Law of course, was a keen student of this kind of philosophy.

"I can scarcely forbear (as unwilling as I am to digress) to represent to you on the present occasion a few considerations, which may assist you, if not to lessen the arrogance of such persons [atheists], at least to keep yourself from thinking their evidence as great as their confidence is wont to be.

...

I shall next take notice that philosophers who scorn to ascribe anything to God do often deceive themselves in thinking they have sufficiently satisfied our enquiries, when they have given us the nearest and most immediate causes of some things; whereas oftentimes the assignment of those causes is but the manifesting that such and such effects may be deduced from the more catholic affections of things, though these be not unfrequently as abstruse as the phenomena explicated by them, as having only their effects more obvious, not their nature better understood: as when, for instance, an account is demanded of that strange supposed sympathy betwixt quicksilver and gold, in that we find that, whereas all other bodies swim upon quicksilver, it will readily swallow up gold and hide it in its bosom...the cause of this effect be thus plausibly assigned, by deducing it from so known and obvious an affectation of bodies as gravity, which every man is apt to think he sufficiently understands, yet will not this put a satisfactory period to a severe enquirer's curiosity, who will perchance be apt to allege that, though the effects of gravity indeed be very obvious, yet the cause and nature of it are as obscure as those of almost any phenomenon it can be brought to explicate, and that therefore he that desires no further account desists too soon from his enquiries, and acquiesces long before he comes to his journey's end...And sure, Pyrophilus, there are divers effects in nature, of which, though the immediate cause may be plausibly assigned, yet if we further enquire into the causes of those causes, and desist not from ascending in the scale of causes till we are arrived at the top of it, we shall perhaps find the more catholic and primary causes of things to be either certain primitive, general, and fixed laws of nature (or rules of action and passion among the parcels of the universal matter); or else the shape, size, motion, and other primary affections of the smallest parts of matter, and of their first coalitions or clusters, especially those endowed with seminal faculties or properties; or (to dispatch) the admirable conspiring of the several parts of the universe to the production of particular effects – of all which it will be difficult to give a satisfactory account without acknowledging an intelligent Author or Disposer of things.

...

They [early Greek philosophers like Anaxagoras and Thales] discerned and acknowledged the necessity of a wise and powerful agent to dispose and fashion this rude matter, and contrive it into so goodly a structure as we behold, without imagining with Epicurus that chance should turn a chaos into a world. And really it is much more unlikely that so many admirable creatures that constitute this one exquisite and stupendous fabric of the world should be made by the casual confluence of falling atoms, jostling or knocking one another in the immense vacuity, than that in a printer's working-house a multitude of small letters, being thrown upon the ground, should fall disposed into such an order as clearly to exhibit the history of the Creation of the world described in the 3 or 4 first chapters of Genesis, of which history it may be doubted whether chance may ever be able to dispose the fallen letters in the words of one line.

...
Let us give a further and direct answer to the proposed objection [the objection being that just because a thing is complex, like the operations of a gun, it doesn't follow that it has to have any spiritual or supernatural agent], by representing that, although, as things are now established in the world, an atomist were able to explain the phenomena we meet with by supposing the parts of matter to be of such sizes, and such shapes, and to be moved after such a manner, as is agreeable to the nature of the particular phenomenon to be thereby exhibited, yet it would not thence necessarily follow that, at the first production of the world, there was no need of a most powerful and intelligent Being, to dispose that *chaos* or confused heap of numberless atoms into the world, to establish the universal and conspiring harmony of things, and especially to connect those atoms into those various seminal contextures upon which most of the more abstruse operations and elaborate productions of nature appear to depend. For many things may be performed by matter variously figured and moved, which yet would never be performed by it if it had been still left to itself, without being, at first at least, fashioned after such a manner and put into such a motion by an intelligent agent: as the quill that a philosopher writes with, being dipped in ink, and then moved after such and such a manner upon white paper, all which are corporeal things or their motions, may very well trace an excellent and rational discourse, but the quill would never have been moved after the requisite manner upon the paper had not its motion been guided and regulated by the understanding of the writer. Or rather, yet once more to resume our former example of the Strasbourg clock, though a skilful artist, admitted to examine and consider it both without and within, may very well discern that such wheels, springs, weights, and other pieces of which the engine consists, being set together in such a coaptation, are sufficient to produce such and such motions and such other effects as that clock is celebrated for, yet, the more he discerns the aptness and sufficiency of the parts to produce the effects emergent from them, the less he will be apt to suspect that so curious an engine was produced by any casual concurrence of the parts it consists of, and not rather by the skill

of an intelligent and ingenious contriver; or that the wheels and other parts were of this or that size, or this or that determinate shape, for any other reason than because it pleased the artificer to make them so: though the reason that moved the artificer to employ such figures and quantities sooner than others may well be supposed to have been that the nature of his design made him think them very proper and commodious for its accomplishment, if not better than any other suited to the several exigencies of it.

...

And it would as well be incredible that an innumerable multitude of insensible particles, as that a lesser number of bigger parcels of matter, should either conspire to constitute or fortuitously jostle themselves into so admirable and harmonious a fabric as the universe, or as the body of man; and consequently it is not credible that they should constitute either, unless as their motions were (at least, in order to their seminal contextures and primary coalitions) regulated and guided by an intelligent contriver and orderer of things."

(Robert Boyle, *An Essay containing a requisite digression, concerning those that would exclude the Deity from intermeddling with matter*, an essay in Robert Boyle, *Some Considerations Touching the Usefulness of Experimental Natural Philosophy* (Oxford, 1663), quoted in M. A. Stewart edit., *Selected Philosophical Papers of* Robert Boyle (Manchester, 1979), p.155; 156-157; 166; 173-4; 175.)

John Locke (1632-1704),

a well known English philosopher, known as the 'Father of Liberalism' partly because his writings are sometimes considered the intellectual backbone of the Whig and later Liberal party in British politics, is considered one of a famous troika of philosophers (including the Scottish Hume and the Irish Berkeley) who are thought to be the most important thinkers presaging the heyday of the British Empire and even in forming the US constitution.

"Our faculties for discovery of the qualities and powers of substances suited to our state. The infinite wise Contriver of us, and all things about us, hath fitted our senses, faculties, and organs, to the conveniences of life, and the business we have to do here. We are able, by our senses, to know and distinguish things: and to examine them so far as to apply them to our uses, and several ways to accommodate the exigencies of this life. We have insight enough into their admirable contrivances and wonderful effects, to admire and magnify the wisdom, power, and goodness of their Author. Such a knowledge as this, which is suited to our present condition, we want not faculties to attain.

But it appears not that God intended we should have a perfect, clear, and adequate knowledge of them: that perhaps is not in the comprehension of any finite being. We are furnished with faculties (dull and weak as they are) to discover enough in the creatures to lead us to the knowledge of the Creator, and the knowledge of our duty; and we are fitted well enough with abilities to provide for the conveniences of living: these are our business in this world. But were our senses altered, and made much quicker and acuter, the appearance and outward scheme of things would have quite another face to us; and, I am apt to think, would be inconsistent with our being, or at least well-being, in this part of the universe which we inhabit. He that considers how little our constitution is able to bear a remove into parts of this air, not much higher than that we commonly breath in, will have reason to be satisfied, that in this globe of earth allotted for our mansion, the all-wise Architect has suited our organs, and the bodies that are to affect them, one to another. If our sense of hearing were but a thousand times quicker than it is, how would a perpetual noise distract us. And we should in the quietest retirement be less able to sleep or meditate than in the middle of a sea-fight.

...

Of our Knowledge of the Existence of a God

1. We are capable of knowing certainly that there is a God. Though God has given us no innate ideas of himself; though he has stamped no original characters on our minds, wherein we may read his being; yet having furnished us with those faculties our minds are endowed with, he hath not left himself without witness: since we have sense, perception, and reason, and cannot want a clear proof of him, as long as we carry ourselves about us. Nor can we justly complain of our ignorance in this great point; since he has so plentifully provided us with the means to discover and know him; so far as is necessary to the end of our being, and the great concernment of our happiness. But, though this be the most obvious truth that reason discovers, and though its evidence be (if I mistake not) equal to mathematical certainty: yet it requires thought and attention; and the mind must apply itself to a regular deduction of it from some part of our intuitive knowledge, or else

we shall be as uncertain and ignorant of this as of other propositions, which are in themselves capable of clear demonstration. To show, therefore, that we are capable of knowing, i.e., being certain that there is a God, and how we may come by this certainty, I think we need go no further than ourselves, and that undoubted knowledge we have of our own existence.

2. For man knows that he himself exists. I think it is beyond question, that man has a clear idea of his own being; he knows certainly he exists, and that he is something. He that can doubt whether he be anything or no, I speak not to; no more than I would argue with pure nothing, or endeavour to convince nonentity that it were something. If any one pretends to be so sceptical as to deny his own existence, (for really to doubt of it is manifestly impossible,) let him for me enjoy his beloved happiness of being nothing, until hunger or some other pain convince him of the contrary. This, then, I think I may take for a truth, which every one's certain knowledge assures him of, beyond the liberty of doubting, viz., that he is something that actually exists.

3. He knows also that nothing cannot produce a being; therefore something must have existed from eternity. In the next place, man knows, by an intuitive certainty, that bare nothing can no more produce any real being, than it can be equal to two right angles. If a man knows not that nonentity, or the absence of all being, cannot be equal to two right angles, it is impossible he should know any demonstration in Euclid. If, therefore, we know there is some real being, and that nonentity cannot produce any real being, it is an evident demonstration, that from eternity there has been something; since what was not from eternity had a beginning; and what had a beginning must be produced by something else.

4. And that eternal Being must be most powerful. Next, it is evident, that what had its being and beginning from another, must also have all that which is in and belongs to its being from another too. All the powers it has must be owing to and received from the same source. This eternal source, then, of all being must also be the source and original of all power; and so this eternal

Being must be also the most powerful.

5. And most knowing. Again, a man finds in himself perception and knowledge. We have then got one step further; and we are certain now that there is not only some being, but some knowing, intelligent being in the world. There was a time, then, when there was no knowing being, and when knowledge began to be; or else there has been also a knowing being from eternity. If it be said, there was a time when no being had any knowledge, when that eternal being was void of all understanding; I reply, that then it was impossible there should ever have been any knowledge: it being as impossible that things wholly void of knowledge, and operating blindly, and without any perception, should produce a knowing being, as it is impossible that a triangle should make itself three angles bigger than two right ones. For it is as repugnant to the idea of senseless matter, that it should put into itself sense, perception, and knowledge, as it is repugnant to the idea of a triangle, that it should put into itself greater angles than two right ones.

6. And therefore God. Thus, from the consideration of ourselves, and what we infallibly find in our own constitutions, our reason leads us to the knowledge of this certain and evident truth, -- That there is an eternal, most powerful, and most knowing Being; which whether any one will please to call God, it matters not. The thing is evident; and from this idea duly considered, will easily be deduced all those other attributes, which we ought to ascribe to this eternal Being. If, nevertheless, any one should be found so senselessly arrogant, as to suppose man alone knowing and wise, but yet the product of mere ignorance and chance; and that all the rest of the universe acted only by that blind haphazard; I shall leave with him that very rational and emphatical rebuke of Tully [Cicero] (I. ii. De Leg.), to be considered at his leisure: "What can be more sillily arrogant and misbecoming, than for a man to think that he has a mind and understanding in him, but yet in all the universe beside there is no such thing? Or that those things, which with the utmost stretch of his reason he can scarce comprehend, should be moved and managed without any reason at all?" Quid est enim verius, quam neminem esse oportere tam stulte arrogantem, ut in se mentem et

rationem putet inesse, in caelo mundoque non putet? Aut ea quae vix summa ingenii ratione comprehendat, nulla ratione moveri putet? [The Latin corresponding to the previous quote in English.]

From what has been said, it is plain to me we have a more certain knowledge of the existence of a God, than of anything our senses have not immediately discovered to us. Nay, I presume I may say, that we more certainly know that there is a God, than that there is anything else without us. When I say we know, I mean there is such a knowledge within our reach which we cannot miss, if we will but apply our minds to that, as we do to several other inquiries.

7. Our idea of a most perfect Being, not the sole proof of a God. How far the idea of a most perfect being, which a man may frame in his mind, does or does not prove the existence of a God, I will not here examine. For in the different make of men's tempers and application of their thoughts, some arguments prevail more on one, and some on another, for the confirmation of the same truth. But yet, I think, this I may say, that it is an ill way of establishing this truth, and silencing atheists, to lay the whole stress of so important a point as this upon that sole foundation: and take some men's having that idea of God in their minds, (for it is evident some men have none, and some worse than none, and the most very different,) for the only proof of a Deity; and out of an over fondness of that darling invention, cashier, or at least endeavour to invalidate all other arguments; and forbid us to hearken to those proofs, as being weak or fallacious, which our own existence, and the sensible parts of the universe offer so clearly and cogently to our thoughts, that I deem it impossible for a considering man to withstand them. For I judge it as certain and clear a truth as can anywhere be delivered, that "the invisible things of God are clearly seen from the creation of the world, being understood by the things that are made, even his eternal power and Godhead." [quote from St Paul] Though our own being furnishes us, as I have shown, with an evident and incontestable proof of a Deity; and I believe nobody can avoid the cogency of it, who will but as carefully attend to it, as to any other demonstration of so many parts: yet this being so fundamental a truth, and of that consequence, that all religion and genuine

morality depend thereon, I doubt not but I shall be forgiven by my reader if I go over some parts of this argument again, and enlarge a little more upon them.

8. Recapitulation--something from eternity. There is no truth more evident than that something must be from eternity. I never yet heard of any one so unreasonable, or that could suppose so manifest a contradiction, as a time wherein there was perfectly nothing. This being of all absurdities the greatest, to imagine that pure nothing, the perfect negation and absence of all beings, should ever produce any real existence.

It being, then, unavoidable for all rational creatures to conclude, that something has existed from eternity; let us next see what kind of thing that must be.

9. Two sorts of beings, cogitative and incogitative. There are but two sorts of beings in the world that man knows or conceives.

First, such as are purely material, without sense, perception, or thought, as the clippings of our beards, and parings of our nails.

Secondly, sensible, thinking, perceiving beings, such as we find ourselves to be. Which, if you please, we will hereafter call cogitative and incogitative beings; which to our present purpose, if for nothing else, are perhaps better terms than material and immaterial.

10. Incogitative being cannot produce a cogitative being. If, then, there must be something eternal, let us see what sort of being it must be. And to that it is very obvious to reason, that it must necessarily be a cogitative being. For it is as impossible to conceive that ever bare incogitative matter should produce a thinking intelligent being, as that nothing should of itself produce matter. Let us suppose any parcel of matter eternal, great or small, we shall find it, in itself, able to produce nothing. For example: let us suppose the matter of the next pebble we meet with eternal, closely united, and the parts firmly at rest together; if there were no other being in the world, must it not eternally remain so, a dead inactive lump? Is it possible to conceive it can add motion to itself, being purely matter, or produce anything? Matter, then, by its own strength, cannot produce in itself so much as motion: the motion it has must also be from eternity, or else be produced, and added to matter by some other being more powerful than matter;

matter, as is evident, having not power to produce motion in itself. But let us suppose motion eternal too: yet matter, incogitative matter and motion, whatever changes it might produce of figure and bulk, could never produce thought: knowledge will still be as far beyond the power of motion and matter to produce, as matter is beyond the power of nothing or nonentity to produce. And I appeal to every one's own thoughts, whether he cannot as easily conceive matter produced by nothing, as thought to be produced by pure matter, when, before, there was no such thing as thought or an intelligent being existing? Divide matter into as many parts as you will, (which we are apt to imagine a sort of spiritualizing, or making a thinking thing of it,) vary the figure and motion of it as much as you please--a globe, cube, cone, prism, cylinder, etc., whose diameters are but 100,000th part of a gry, will operate no otherwise upon other bodies of proportionable bulk, than those of an inch or foot diameter; and you may as rationally expect to produce sense, thought, and knowledge, by putting together, in a certain figure and motion, gross particles of matter, as by those that are the very minutest that do anywhere exist. They knock, impel, and resist one another, just as the greater do; and that is all they can do. So that, if we will suppose nothing first or eternal, matter can never begin to be: if we suppose bare matter without motion, eternal, motion can never begin to be: if we suppose only matter and motion first, or eternal, thought can never begin to be. For it is impossible to conceive that matter, either with or without motion, could have, originally, in and from itself, sense, perception, and knowledge; as is evident from hence, that then sense, perception, and knowledge, must be a property eternally inseparable from matter and every particle of it. Not to add, that, though our general or specific conception of matter makes us speak of it as one thing, yet really all matter is not one individual thing, neither is there any such thing existing as one material being, or one single body that we know or can conceive. And therefore, if matter were the eternal first cogitative being, there would not be one eternal, infinite, cogitative being, but an infinite number of eternal, finite, cogitative beings, independent one of another, of limited force, and distinct thoughts, which could never produce that order, harmony, and beauty which are to be found in nature. Since, therefore, whatsoever is the first eternal being must necessarily be cogitative; and whatsoever is first of all things must necessarily contain in it, and actually have, at least, all the perfections that can ever after exist; nor can it ever give to another any perfection that it hath not either actually in itself, or, at least, in a higher degree; it necessarily follows, that the first eternal being cannot be matter.

...

Objection: "Creation out of nothing." But you will say, Is it not impossible to admit of the making anything out of nothing, since we cannot possibly conceive it? I answer, No. Because it is not reasonable to deny the power of an infinite being, because we cannot comprehend its operations. We do not deny other effects upon this ground, because we cannot possibly conceive the manner of their production. We cannot conceive how anything but impulse of body can move body; and yet that is not a reason sufficient to make us deny it possible, against the constant experience we have of it in ourselves, in all our voluntary motions; which are produced in us only by the free action or thought of our own minds, and are not, nor can be, the effects of the impulse or determination of the motion of blind matter in or upon our own bodies; for then it could not be in our power or choice to alter it. For example: my right hand writes, whilst my left hand is still: What causes rest in one, and motion in the other? Nothing but my will, – a thought of my mind; my thought only changing, the right hand rests, and the left hand moves. This is matter of fact, which cannot be denied: explain this and make it intelligible, and then the next step will be to understand creation. For the giving a new determination to the motion of the animal spirits (which some make use of to explain voluntary motion) clears not the difficulty one jot. To alter the determination of motion, being in this case no easier nor less, than to give motion itself: since the new determination given to the animal spirits must be either immediately by thought, or by some other body put in their way by thought which was not in their way before, and so must owe its motion to thought: either of which leaves voluntary motion as unintelligible as it was before. In the meantime, it is an overvaluing ourselves to reduce all to the narrow measure of our capacities, and to conclude all things impossible to be done, whose manner of doing exceeds our comprehension. This is to make our comprehension infinite, or God finite, when what He can do is limited to what we can conceive of it. If you do not understand the operations of your own finite mind, that thinking thing within you, do not deem it strange that you cannot comprehend the operations of that eternal infinite Mind, who made and governs all things, and whom the heaven of heavens cannot contain."

(John Locke, *An Essay Concerning Human Understanding* (London, 1690), book II chap XXIII, no.12, and book 4, chapter 10, available: http://socserv2.mcmaster.ca/~econ/ugcm/3ll3/locke/Essay.htm .)

Gottfreid Wilhelm Leibniz (1646-1716),

a famous German mathematician and philosopher, who, among many other things, refined the binary number system and developed calculus, at the same time, but independently of, Newton.

"God is absolutely perfect, for perfection is nothing but amount of positive reality, in the strict sense, leaving out of account the limits or bounds in things which are limited. And where there are no bounds, that is to say in God, perfection is absolutely infinite.

It follows also that created beings derive their perfections from the influence of God, but that their imperfections come from their own nature, which is incapable of being without limits. For it is in this that they differ from God."

(Gottfreid Wilhelm Leibniz, *The Monadology and Other Philosophical Writings* (Oxford, 1898), no.41-42.)

Sir **Isaac Newton** (1643-1727),

the discoverer of gravity and obviously the great English physicist and mathematician etc etc, had no doubt at all as to where it, gravity, and the design of the Universe must have came from.

"The six primary Planets are revolv'd about the Sun, in circles concentric with the Sun, and with motions directed towards the same parts and almost in the same plane. Ten Moons are revolv'd about the Earth, Jupiter and Saturn, in circles concentric with them, with the same direction of motion, and nearly in the planes of the orbits of those Planets. But it is not to be conceived that mere mechanical causes could give birth to so many regular motions: since the Comets range over all parts of the heavens, in very eccentric orbits. For by that kind of motion they pass easily through the orbs of the Planets, and with great rapidity; and in their aphelions, where they move the slowest, and are detain'd the longest, they recede to the greatest distances from each other, and thence suffer the least disturbance from their mutual attractions.

This most beautiful System of the Sun, Planets and Comets, could only proceed from the counsel and dominion of an intelligent and powerful being. And if the fixed Stars are the centers of other like systems, these being form'd by the like wise counsel, must be all subject to the dominion of One; especially, since the light of the fixed Stars is of the same nature with the light of the Sun, and from every system light passes into all the other systems. And lest the systems of the fixed Stars should, by their gravity, fall on each other mutually, he hath placed those Systems at immense distances one from another.

...

We know him only by his most wise and excellent contrivances of things, and final causes; we admire him for his perfections; but we reverence and adore him on account of his dominion. For we adore him as his servants; and a God without dominion, providence, and final causes, is nothing else but Fate and Nature. Blind metaphysical necessity, which is certainly the same always and every where, could produce no variety of things. All that diversity of natural things which we find, suited to different times and places, could arise from nothing but the ideas and will of a Being necessarily existing.

He went into this in a bit more detail in a letter to Richard Bentley of the 11th of Feb 1693.

The Hypothesis of deriving the frame of the world by mechanical principles from matter evenly spread through the heavens being inconsistent with my system, I had considered it very little before your letters put me upon it, & therefore trouble you with a line or two more about it if this come not too late for your use. In my former I [represented] that the diurnal rotations of the Planets could not be derived from gravity but required a divin[e] power to impress them. And though gravity might give the Planets a motion of descent towards the Sun either directly or with some little obliquity, yet the transverse motions by which they revolve in their several orbs required the divine Arm to impress them according to the tangents of their orbs I would now add that the Hypothesis of matters being at first evenly spread through the heavens is, in my opinion, inconsistent with the Hypothesis of innate gravity without a supernatural power to reconcile them, & therefore it infers a Deity. For if there be innate gravity its impossible now for the matter of the earth & all the Planets & stars to fly up from them & become evenly spread throughout all the heavens without a supernatural power. & certainly that which can never be hereafter without a supernatural power could never be heretofore without the same power.

And finally one more quote from his works.

Whence is it that Nature doth nothing in vain; and whence arises all that Order and Beauty which we see in the World? To what end are Comets, and whence is it that Planets move all one and the same way in Orbs concentrick, while Comets move all manner of ways in Orbs very excentrick, and what hinders the fix'd Stars from falling upon one another? How came the Bodies of Animals to be contrived with so much Art, and for what ends were their several Parts? Was the Eye contrived without Skill in Opticks, and the Ear without Knowledge of Sounds? How do the Motions of the Body follow from the Will, and whence is the Instinct in Animals? Is not the Sensory of Animals that place to which the sensitive Substance is present, and into which the sensible Species of Things are carried through the Nerves and Brain, that there they may be perceived by their immediate presence to that Substance? And these things being rightly dispatch'd, does it not appear from Phænomena that there is a Being incorporeal, living, intelligent, omnipresent, who in infinite Space, as it were in his Sensory, sees the things themselves intimately, and throughly perceives them, and comprehends them wholly by their immediate presence to himself."

(Sir Isaac Newton, *The Mathematical Principles of Natural Philosophy* (London, 1729), p.388-391, available at: http://www.newtonproject.sussex.ac.uk/view/extract/normalized/NATP00056/start=par3&end=par4%29 , and the second quote, from the 1693 letter, is from the manuscript 189.R.4.47, f. 6, Trinity College Library, Cambridge, UK, available at: http://www.newtonproject.sussex.ac.uk/view/texts/normalized/TH

EM00256 , and finally the last quote is from Sir Isaac Newton, *Opticks: Or, A Treatise of the Reflections, Refractions, Inflexions and Colours of Light. The Second Edition, with Additions* (London: 1718), p.344-5, available at:
 http://www.newtonproject.sussex.ac.uk/view/texts/normalized/NATP00051 .)

Dr **Jonathan Swift**

was obviously the great Irish writer and satirist, author of *Gulliver's Travels* etc etc.

"Philosophers say, that man is a microcosm, or little world, resembling in miniature every part of the great: and, in my opinion, the body natural may be compared to the body politic: and if this be so, how can the epicurean's opinion be true, that the universe was formed by a fortuitous concourse of atoms: which I will no more believe, than that the accidental jumbling of the letters of the alphabet, could fall by chance into a most ingenious and learned treatise of philosophy. 'Risum teneatis amici?' (Horace) This false opinion must needs create many more: it is like an error in the first concoction, which cannot be corrected in the second; the foundation is weak, and whatever superstructure you raise upon it, must of necessity fall to the ground. Thus men are led from one error to another, until with Ixion they embrace a cloud instead of Juno; or like the dog in the fable, lose the substance in gaping at the shadow.

...

But to return from this digression: I think it as clear as any demonstration of Euclid, that Nature does nothing in vain; if we were able to dive into her secret recesses, we should find that the smallest blade of grass, or most contemptible weed, has its particular use: but she is chiefly admirable in her minutest compositions, the least and most contemptible insect most discovers the art of nature, if I may so call it, though nature, which delights in variety, will always triumph over art, and as the poet observes, 'Naturam expellas furca licet, usque recurret' (Horace).

But the various opinions of philosophers have scattered through the world as many plagues of the mind as Pandora's box did those of the body; only with this difference, that they have not left hope at the bottom. And if truth be not fled with Astrea, she is certainly as hidden as the source of Nile, and can be found only in Utopia. Not that I would reflect on those wise sages, which would be a sort of ingratitude; and he that calls a man ungrateful, sums up all the evil that a man can be guilty of, 'Ingratum si dixeris omnia dicis.' But what I blame the philosophers for (though some may think it a paradox) is chiefly their pride; nothing less than an ipse dixit and you must pin your faith on their sleeve.

...

I may perhaps be censured for my free opinions by those carping Momuses whom authors worship, as the Indians do the devil, for fear. They will endeavour to give my reputation as many wounds as the man in the almanac but I value it not and perhaps like flies they may buzz so often about the candle till they burn their wings. They must pardon me if I venture to give them this advice, not to rail at what they cannot understand: it does but discover that self-tormenting passion of envy..."

(Dr Jonathan Swift, *A Tritical Essay upon the Faculties of the Mind*, published in *Miscellanies in prose and verse* (London, 1711).)

Abraham de Moivre (1667-1754),

a French Huguenot refugee in London whose mastery of mathematics and astronomy was such that Newton himself deferred to him, saying: "Go to Mr. de Moivre; he knows these things better than I do." As well as being a Fellow of the Royal Society in London he was a member of the Royal Academies of Science in Paris and Berlin, and was particularly an expert on probability, writing only the second important book in history on the topic, which laid the foundation of much of our modern understanding of this field of mathematics. 'de Moivre's formula', which links complex numbers and trigonometry, is called after him.

"As, upon the Supposition of a certain determinate Law according to which any Event is to happen, we demonstrate that the Ratio of Happenings will continually approach to that Law, as the Experiments or Observations are multiplied: so, conversely, if from numberless Observations we find the Ratio of the Events to converge to a determinate quantity, as to the Ratio of P to Q; then we conclude that this Ratio expresses the determinate Law according to which the Event is to happen.

For let that Law be expressed not by the Ratio P:Q, but by some other, as R:S; then would the Ratio of the Events converge to this last, not to the former: which contradicts our Hypothesis. And the like, or greater, Absurdity follows, if we should suppose the Event not to happen according to any Law, but in a manner altogether desultory and uncertain; for then the Events would converge to no fixt Ratio at all.

Again, as it is thus demonstrable that there are, in the constitution of things, certain Laws according to which Events happen, it is no less evident from Observation, that those Laws serve to wise, useful and beneficent purposes; to preserve the steadfast Order of the Universe, to propagate the several Species of Beings, and furnish to the sentient Kind such degrees of happiness as are suited to their State.

But such Laws, as well as the original Design and Purpose of their Establishment, must all be from without –, the Inertia of matter, and the nature of all created Beings, rendering it impossible that any thing should modify its own essence, or give to itself, or to any thing else, an original determination or propensity. And hence, if we blind not ourselves with metaphysical dust, we shall be led, by a short and obvious way, to the acknowledgment of the great Maker and Governour of all: Himself all-wise, all-powerful and good.

Mr. Nicolas Bernoulli, a very learned and good Man, by not connecting the latter part of our reasoning with the first, was led to discard and even to vilify this Argument from Final Causes, so much insisted on by our best Writers; particularly in the Instance of the nearly equal numbers of male and female Births, adduced by that excellent Person the late Dr. Arbuthnot, in Phil Trans No°. 328.

Mr. Bernoulli collects from Tables of Observations continued for 82 years, that is from A. D. 1629 to 1711, that the number of Births in London was, at a medium, about 14000 yearly: and likewise, that the number of Males to that of Females, or the facility of their production, is nearly as 18 to 17. But he thinks it the greatest weakness to draw any Argument from this against the Influence of Chance in the production of the two Sexes. For, says he,

"Let 14000 Dice, each having 35 faces, 18 white and 17 black, be thrown up, and it is great Odds that the numbers of white and black faces shall come as near, or nearer, to each other, as the numbers of Boys and Girls do in the Tables."

To which the short answer is this: "Dr. Arbuthnot never said, that supposing the facility of the production of a Male to that of the production of a female to be already fixt to nearly the Ratio of equality, or to that of 18 to 17; he was amazed that the Ratio of the numbers of Males and Females born should, for many years, keep within such narrow bounds:" the only Proposition against which Mr. Bernoulli's reasoning has any force.

But he might have said, and we do still insist, that

"as, from the Observations, we can, with Mr. Bernoulli, infer the facilities of production of the two Sexes to be nearly in a Ratio of equality; so from this Ratio once discovered, and *manifestly serving to a wise purpose*, we conclude the Ratio itself, or if you will the Form of the Die, to be an Effect of Intelligence and Design."

As if we were shewn a number of Dice, each with 18 white and 17 black faces, which is Mr. Bernoulli's supposition, we should not doubt but that those Dice had been made by some Artist; and that their form was not owing to Chance, but was adapted to the particular purpose he had in View.

Thus much was necessary to take off any impression that the authority of so great a name might make to the prejudice of our argument. Which, after all, being level to the lowest understanding, and falling in with the common sense of mankind, needed no formal Demonstration, but for the scholastic subtleties with which it may be perplexed; and for the abuse of certain words and phrases; which sometimes are imagined to have a meaning merely because they are often uttered.

Chance, as we understand it, supposes the Existence of things, and their general known Properties: that a number of Dice, for instance, being thrown, each of them shall settle upon one or other of its Bases. After which, the Probability of an assigned

Chance, that is of some particular disposition of the Dice, becomes as proper a subject of Investigation as any other quantity or Ratio can be.

But Chance, in atheistical writings or discourse, is a sound utterly insignificant: It imports no determination to any mode of Existence; nor indeed to Existence itself, more than to non-existence; it can neither be defined nor understood: nor can any Proposition concerning it be either affirmed or denied, excepting this one, "That it is a mere word."

The like may be said of some other words in frequent use; as fate, necessity, nature, a course of nature in contradistinction to the Divine energy: all which, as used on certain occasions, are mere sounds: and yet, by artful management, they serve to sound specious conclusions: which however, as soon as the latent fallacy of the Term is detected, appear to be no less absurd in themselves, than they commonly are hurtful to society."

(Abraham de Moivre, *The Doctrine of Chances* (London, 1756), p.251-253.)

George Berkeley (1685-1753),

received his MA from Trinity in 1707 and went on to become the most famous Irish philosopher of the period – one of his works on 'time', De Motu, is thought to herald the work of Einstein to a remarkable degree – and also the Church of Ireland Bishop of Cloyne, for whom Berkeley College in the US is called after, and puts this question in the form of a dialogue between himself, Euphranor, and a free-thinker, i.e. atheist, called Alciphron.

"5. Euphranor – The soul of man actuates but a small body, an insignificant particle, in respect of the great masses of nature, the elements, and heavenly bodies, and the system of the world. And the wisdom that appears in those motions, which are the effect of human reason, is incomparably less that that which discovers itself, in the structure and use of organised natural bodies, animal or vegetable. A man, with his hand, can make no machine so admirable as the hand itself; nor can any of those motions by which we trace out human reason approach the skill and contrivance of those wonderful motions of the heart, and brain, and other vital parts, which do not depend on the will of man.

Alciphron – All this is true.

Euphranor – Doth it not follow then, that from natural motions, independent of man's will, may be inferred both power and wisdom, incomparably greater than that of the human soul?

Alciphron – It should seem so.

Euphranor – Further, is there not, in natural productions and effects, a visible unity of counsel and design? Are not the rules affixed and immoveable? Do not the same laws of motion obtain throughout? The same in China and here, the same two thousand years ago, and at this day?

Alciphron – All this I do not deny.

Euphranor – Is there not also a connexion or relation between animals and vegetables, between both and the elements, between the elements and heavenly bodies; so that, from their mutual respects, influences, subordinations, and uses, they may be collected to be parts of one whole, conspiring to one and the same end, and fulfilling the same design?

Alciphron – Supposing all this to be true.

Euphranor – Will it not then follow that this vastly great, or infinite, power and wisdom must be supposed in one and the same agent, spirit, or mind; and that we have, at least, as clear, full, and immediate certainty of the being of this infinitely wise and powerful Spirit, as of any one human soul whatsoever besides our own?"

(George Berkeley, *Alciphron* (Newhaven, 1803, but first published in 1732), Dialogue IV section 5.)

François-Marie Arouet, well known as **Voltaire** (1694-1778),

was certainly the best known philosopher from the 'Enlightenment' era in pre-revolutionary France.

"It is perfectly evident to my mind that there exists a necessary, eternal, supreme, and intelligent being. This is no matter of faith, but of reason

...

Modern Atheists.—Arguments of the Worshippers of God.

We are intelligent beings, and intelligent beings cannot have been formed by a blind, brute, insensible being; there is certainly some difference between a clod and the ideas of Newton. Newton's intelligence, then, came from some other intelligence.

When we see a fine machine, we say there is a good machinist, and that he has an excellent understanding. The world is assuredly an admirable machine; therefore there is in the world, somewhere or other, an admirable intelligence. This argument is old, but is not therefore the worse.

All animated bodies are composed of levers and pulleys, which act according to the laws of mechanics; of liquors, which are kept in perpetual circulation by the laws of hydrostatics; and the reflection that all these beings have sentiment which has no relation to their organization, fills us with wonder.

The motions of the stars, that of our little earth round the sun—all are operated according to the laws of the profoundest mathematics. How could it be that Plato, who knew not one of these laws—the eloquent but chimerical Plato, who said that the foundation of the earth was an equilateral triangle, and that of water a right-angled triangle—the strange Plato, who said there could be but five worlds, because there were but five regular bodies—how, I say, was it that Plato, who was not even acquainted with spherical trigonometry, had nevertheless so fine a genius, so happy an instinct, as to call God the Eternal Geometrician—to feel that there exists a forming Intelligence? Spinoza himself confesses it. It is impossible to controvert this truth, which surrounds us and presses us on all sides.

Argument of the Atheists.

I have, however, known refractory individuals, who have said that there is no forming intelligence, and that motion alone has formed all that we see and all that we are. They say boldly that the combination of this universe was possible because it exists; therefore it was possible for motion of itself to arrange it. Take four planets only—Mars, Venus, Mercury, and the Earth; let us consider them solely in the situations in which they now are; and let us see how many probabilities we have that motion will bring them again to those respective places. There are but twenty-four chances in this combination; that is, it is only twenty-four to one that these planets will not be found in the same situations with respect to one another. To these four globes add that of Jupiter; and it is then only a hundred and twenty to one that Jupiter, Mars, Venus, Mercury, and our globe will not be placed in the same positions in which we now see them.

Lastly, add Saturn; and there will then be only seven hundred and twenty chances to one against putting these planets in their present arrangement, according to their given distances. It is, then, demonstrated that once, at least, in seven hundred and twenty cases, chance might place these planets in their present order.

Then take all the secondary planets, all their motions, all the beings that vegetate, live, feel, think, act, on all these globes; you have only to increase the number of chances; multiply this number to all eternity—to what our weakness calls infinity—there will still be an unit in favor of the formation of the world, such as it is, by motion alone; therefore it is possible that, in all eternity, the motion of matter alone has produced the universe as it exists. Nay, this combination must, in eternity, of necessity happen. Thus, say they, not only it is possible that the world is as it is by motion alone, but it was impossible that it should not be so after infinite combinations.

Answer.

All this supposition seems to me to be prodigiously chimerical, for two reasons: the first is, that in this universe there are intelligent beings, and you cannot prove it possible for motion alone to produce understanding. The second is, that, by your own confession, the chances are infinity to unity, that an intelligent forming cause produced the universe. Standing alone against infinity, a unit makes but a poor figure.

Again Spinoza himself admits this intelligence; it is the basis of his system. You have not read him, but you must read him. Why would you go further than he, and, through a foolish pride, plunge into the abyss where Spinoza dared not to descend? Are you not aware of the extreme folly of saying that it is owing to a blind cause that the square of the revolution of one planet is always to the squares of the others as the cube of its distance is to the cubes of the distances of the others from the common centre? Either the planets are great geometricians, or the Eternal Geometrician has arranged the planets.

But where is the Eternal Geometrician? Is He in one place, or in all places, without occupying space? I know not. Has He arranged all things of His own substance? I know not. Is He immense, without quantity and without quality? I know not. All I know is, that we must adore Him and be just.

New Objection of a Modern Atheist.

Can it be said that the conformation of animals is according to their necessities? What are those necessities? Self-preservation and propagation. Now, is it astonishing that, of the infinite combinations produced by chance, those only have survived which had organs adapted for their nourishment and the continuation of their species? Must not all others necessarily have perished?

Answer.

This argument, taken from Lucretius, is sufficiently refuted by the sensation given to animals and the intelligence given to man. How, as has just been said in the preceding paragraph, should combinations produced by chance produce this sensation and this intelligence? Yes, doubtless, the members of animals are made for all their necessities with an incomprehensible art, and you have not the boldness to deny it. You do not mention it. You feel that you can say nothing in answer to this great argument which Nature brings against you. The disposition of the wing of a fly, or of the feelers of a snail, is sufficient to confound you.

An Objection of Maupertuis.

The natural philosophers of modern times have done nothing more than extend these pretended arguments; this they have sometimes done even to minuteness and indecency. They have found God in the folds of a rhinoceros's hide; they might, with equal reason, have denied His existence on account of the tortoise's shell.

Answer.

What reasoning! The tortoise and the rhinoceros, and all the different species, prove alike in their infinite varieties the same cause, the same design, the same end, which are preservation, generation, and death. Unity is found in this immense variety; the hide and the shell bear equal testimony. What! deny God, because a shell is not like a skin! And journalists have lavished upon this coxcombry praises which they have withheld from Newton and Locke, both worshippers of the Divinity from thorough examination and conviction!

Another of Maupertuis's Objections.

Of what service are beauty and fitness in the construction of a serpent? Perhaps, you say, it has uses of which we are ignorant. Let us then, at least, be silent, and not admire an animal which we know only by the mischief it does.

Answer.

Be you silent, also, since you know no more of its utility than myself; or acknowledge that, in reptiles, everything is admirably proportioned. Some of them are venomous; you have been so too. The only subject at present under consideration is the prodigious art which has formed serpents, quadrupeds, birds, fishes, and bipeds. This art is evident enough. You ask, Why is not the serpent harmless? And why have you not been harmless? Why have you been a persecutor? which, in a philosopher, is the greatest of crimes. This is quite another question; it is that of physical and moral evil. It has long been asked, Why are there so many serpents, and so many wicked men worse than serpents? If flies could reason, they would complain to God of the existence of spiders; but they would, at the same time, acknowledge what Minerva confessed to Arachne in the fable, that they arrange their webs in a wonderful manner.

We cannot, then, do otherwise than acknowledge an ineffable Intelligence, which Spinoza himself admitted. We must own that it is displayed as much in the meanest insect as in the planets. And with regard to moral and physical evil, what can be done or said? Let us console ourselves by the enjoyment of physical and moral good, and adore the Eternal Being, who has ordained the one and permitted the other.

One word more on this topic. Atheism is the vice of some intelligent men, and superstition is the vice of fools. And what is the vice of knaves?—Hypocrisy.

...

It is, it seems to me, to stop one's eyes and understanding to maintain that there is no design in nature; and if there is design, there is an intelligent cause, there exists a God.

Some point us to the irregularities of our globe, the volcanoes, the plains of moving sand, some small mountains swallowed up in the ocean, others raised by earthquakes, etc. But does it follow from the naves of your chariot wheel taking fire, that your chariot was not made expressly for the purpose of conveying you from one place to another?

The chains of mountains which crown both hemispheres, and more than six hundred rivers which flow from the foot of these rocks towards the sea; the various streams that swell these rivers in their courses, after fertilizing the fields through which they pass; the innumerable fountains which spring from the same source, which supply necessary refreshment, and growth, and beauty to animal and vegetable life; all this appears no more to result from a fortuitous concourse and an obliquity of atoms, than the retina which receives the rays of light, or the crystalline humor which refracts it, or the drum of the ear which admits sound, or the circulation of the blood in our veins, the systole and diastole of the heart, the regulating principle of the machine of life.

It would appear that a man must be supposed to have lost his senses before he can deny that stomachs are made for digestion, eyes to see, and ears to hear.

On the other hand, a man must have a singular partiality for final causes, to assert that stone was made for building houses, and that silkworms are produced in China that we may wear satins in Europe.

But, it is urged, if God has evidently done one thing by design, he has then done all things by design. It is ridiculous to admit Providence in the one case and to deny it in the others. Everything that is done was foreseen, was arranged. There is no arrangement without an object, no effect without a cause; all, therefore, is equally the result, the product of the final cause; it is, therefore, as correct to say that noses were made to bear spectacles, and fingers to be adorned with rings, as to say that the ears were formed to hear sounds, the eyes to receive light.

All that this objection amounts to, in my opinion, is that everything is the result, nearer or more remote, of a general final cause; that everything is the consequence of eternal laws. When the effects are invariably the same in all times and places, and when these uniform effects are independent of the beings to which they attach, then there is visibly a final cause.

All animals have eyes and see; all have ears and hear; all have mouths with which they eat; stomachs, or something similar, by which they digest their food; all have suitable means for expelling the fæces; all have the organs requisite for the continuation of their species; and these natural gifts perform their regular course and process without any application or intermixture of art. Here are final causes clearly established; and to deny a truth so universal would be a perversion of the faculty of reason.

But stones, in all times and places, do not constitute the materials of buildings. All noses do not bear spectacles; all fingers do not carry a ring; all legs are not covered with silk stockings. A silkworm, therefore, is not made to cover my legs, exactly as your mouth is made for eating, and another part of your person for the "garderobe." There are, therefore, we see, immediate effects produced from final causes, and effects of a very numerous description, which are remote productions from those causes.

Everything belonging to nature is uniform, immutable, and the immediate work of its author.

...

one must be blind not to be dazzled by this spectacle [of nature] ... one must be stupid not to recognize the author of it.

...

There is something; therefore there is something eternal; for nothing is produced from nothing. Here is a certain truth on which the mind reposes. Every work which shows us means and an end, announces a workman: then this universe, composed of springs, of means, each of which has its end, discovers a most mighty, a most intelligent workman. Here is a probability approaching the greatest certainty."

(http://www.sveinbjorn.org/voltaire_d_holbach_and_the_design_argument , but the first long quote is from his 1764 *Philosophical Dictionary* vol III pt 1 under 'Atheist', available at: http://oll.libertyfund.org/index.php?option=com_staticxt&staticfile=show.php%3Ftitle=352&layout=html#chapter_53827 , and the second long quote above is also from his *Philosophical Dictionary*, this time vol V pt 3, under 'Final Causes', available at: http://oll.libertyfund.org/index.php?option=com_staticxt&staticfile=show.php%3Ftitle=354&layout=html#chapter_58972 .)

Jean-Jacques Rousseau (1712-1778),

from Geneva originally, was of course the other famous philosopher, alongwith Voltaire, of pre-Revolutionary France:

"Whether matter is eternal or created, whether its origin is passive or not, it is still certain that the whole is one, and that it proclaims a single intelligence; for I see nothing that is not part of the same ordered system, nothing which does not co-operate to the same end, namely, the conservation of all within the established order. This being who wills and can perform his will, this being active through his own power, this being, whoever he may be, who moves the universe and orders all things, is what I call God. To this name I add the ideas of intelligence, power, will, which I have brought together, and that of kindness which is their necessary consequence.

...

It is not in my power to believe that passive and dead matter can have brought forth living and feeling beings, that blind chance has brought forth intelligent beings, *that* that which does not think has brought forth thinking beings. I believe, therefore, that the world is governed by a wise and powerful Will; I see it or rather I feel it, and it is a great thing to know this.

...

Conscience! Conscience! Divine instinct, immortal voice from heaven; sure guide for a creature ignorant and finite indeed, yet intelligent and free; infallible judge of good and evil, making man like to God! In thee consists the excellence of man's nature and the morality of his actions; apart from thee, I find nothing in myself to raise me above the beasts – nothing but the sad privilege of wandering from one error to another, by the help of an unbridled understanding and a reason which knows no principle."

(Jean-Jacques Rousseau, *Emile* (London, 1911), book IV.)

David Hume (1711-1776),

a famous Scot, alongwith Locke is one of the most influential of the British philosophers of the 18th century. He tended to take an extreme sceptical view of most things including causes and effects, often not satisfied that an observable effect which 'is' necessarily 'ought', as opposed to 'might' say, have been the result of a given cause. It seems to this observer that his increasing popularity in the 21st century is because so many people list him as an atheist, but actually nothing could be further from the truth, although he was frequently critical of some religions he was in fact very convinced by the Intelligent Design argument:

"The whole frame of nature bespeaks an intelligent author; and no rational enquirer can, after serious reflection, suspend his belief a moment with regard to the primary principles of genuine Theism and Religion . . .

Were men led into the apprehension of invisible, intelligent power by a contemplation of the works of nature, they could never possibly entertain any conception but of one single being, who bestowed existence and order on this vast machine, and adjusted all its parts, according to one regular plan or connected system . . .

All things of the universe are evidently of a piece. Every thing is adjusted to every thing. One design prevails throughout the whole. And this uniformity leads the mind to acknowledge one author.

...

Wherever I see Order, I infer from Experience that there, there hath been Design and Contrivance. And the same Principle which leads me into this Inference, when I contemplate a Building, regular and beautiful in its whole Frame and Structure; the same Principle obliges me to infer an infinitely perfect Architect, from the infinite Art and Contrivance which is display'd in the whole Fabrick of the Universe.

...

The whole frame of nature bespeaks an intelligent Author; and no rational enquirer can, after serious reflection, suspend his belief a moment with regard to the primary principles of genuine Theism and Religion.

...

The order of the universe proves an omnipotent Mind."

(David Hume, ed by H E Root, *The Natural History of Religion* (London, 1956), p.21 and 26, the second quote from David Hume, *A Letter From a Gentleman to His Friend in Edinburgh* in his *An Enquiry Concerning Human Understanding* (Indianapolis, 1977), p.120; the third from David Hume, ed by H E Root, *The Natural History of Religion* (London, 1956), p.21; and the last from David Hume, *A Treatise of Human Nature* (Oxford, 1978), 633n.)"

Carl Linnaeus (1707-1778),

was a famous Swedish botanist from whom we get the great classifications in biology like 'homo sapiens' etc,:

"Those who visit museums of natural productions, generally pass them over with a careless eye, and immediately take the liberty of giving a decided opinion upon them. The indefatigable collectors of these things sometimes have the fate of being reckoned monsters; many people wonder at their great but useless labours, and those who judge most tenderly, exclaim, that such things serve to amuse persons of great leisure, but are of no real use to the community. It shall therefore be the business of this discourse to examine the design and end of such collections.

The knowledge of one's self is the first step towards wisdom: this was the favorite precept of the wise Solon, and was written in letters of gold on the entrance of the temple of Diana.

A man surely cannot be said to have attained this self-knowledge, unless he has at least made himself acquainted with his origin, and the duties that are incumbent upon him.

Men and all animals increase and multiply in such a manner, that however few at first, their numbers are continually and gradually increasing. If we trace them backwards, from a greater to a lesser number, we at length arrive at one original pair. Now mankind, as well as all other creatures, being formed with such exquisite and wonderful skill, that human wisdom is utterly insufficient to imitate the most simple fibre, vein, or nerve, much less a finger, or other contriving or executive organ; it is perfectly evident, that all these things must originally have been made by an omnipotent and omniscient Being; for "he who formed the ear, shall he not hear? and he who made the eye, shall he not see?"

Moreover, if we consider the generation of Animals, we find that each produces an offspring after its own kind, as well as Plants, Tœnias, and Corallines; that all are propagated by their branches, by buds, or by seed; and that from each proceeds a germ of the same nature with its parent; so that all living things, plants, animals, and even mankind themselves, form one "chain, of universal Being," from the beginning to the end of the world: in this sense truly may it be said, that there is nothing new under the sun.

If we next turn our thoughts to the place we inhabit, we find ourselves situated on a vast globe of land and water, which must necessarily owe its origin to the same Almighty Being; for it is altogether made up of wonders, and displays such a degree of contrivance and perfection, as mortals can neither describe nor comprehend. This globe may therefore be considered as a museum, furnished with the works of the Supreme Creator, disposed in three grand classes."

(Carl Linnaeus, *Reflections on the Study of Nature* (London, 1785), p.1-4.)

Immanuel Kant (1724-1804)

a German writer, from modern day Kalingrad, who was a really big figure in the history of modern philosophy and as such his comments here, while brief, are nonetheless important.

"God is the only ruler of the world. He governs as a monarch, but not as a despot; for He wills to have His commands observed out of love, and not out of servile fear. Like a father, He orders what is good for us, and does not command out of mere arbitrariness, like a tyrant. God even demands of us that we reflect on the reason for His commandments, and He insists on our observing them because He wants first to make us worthy of happiness and then participate in it. God's will is benevolence, and His purpose is what is best.

...

There is an all-comprehending nature (in space and time) in

which reason coordinates all physical relations into unity. There is a universally ruling operative cause with freedom in rational beings, and, [given] with the latter, a categorical imperative which connects them all, and, with that, in turn, an all-embracing, morally commanding, original being – a God.

The phenomona from the moving forces of moral-practical reason, insofar as they are a priori with respect to men in relation to one another, are the ideas of right – *moral practical reason. Categorical imperative which our reason expresses through the divine. Freedom under laws, duties as divine commands. There is a God.*

Metaphysics has to do with sense-objects and their system, insofar as the latter is knowable a priori, analytically (cogitabile, cognoscibile). *Aenesidemus inwardly determining. Thence the transition to the synthetic a priori principles takes place through concepts (not through representation of intuition) which contain a priori the formal element of the connection of the manifold (ampliatively) and coordinate a whole of sensible representations in one system (not empirically, through experience, but according to rational principles for the sake of the possibility of experience) which, subjectively, amounts to only that which can be thought [through] reason. [The latter also] contains ideas of right [which lead] toward the concept of a highest moral being under which all world-beings stand – God. Which cannot be the dabile (intuition) but only the cogitabile (thinkable) – the moral-practical. There is a God: for there is in moral practical reason a categorical imperative, which extends to all rational world-beings and through which all world-beings are united. *Eleutherology, which contains freedom under laws (moral-practical reasons) according to maxims.

The concept of God is the idea which man, as a moral being, forms of the highest moral being in relation according to principles of right, insofar as he, according to the categorical imperative, regards all duties as commands of this being."

(Immanuel Kant, *Lectures on Philosophical Theology* (Ithaca, 1978), p.156, and the second quote from his last work, translated by Eckart Forster and Michael Rosen, *Opus Postumum* (Cambridge, 1993), p.198-199.)

Alessandro Volta (1745-1827),

from Como in Italy, invented the battery in 1800 and for whom voltage is called after.

"In this faith [in the Catholic religion] I recognise a pure gift of God, a supernatural grace; but I have not neglected those human means which confirm belief, and overthrow the doubts which at times arise. I studied attentively the grounds and basis of religion, the works of apologists and assailants, the reasons for and against, and I can say that the result of such study is to clothe religion with such a degree of probability, even for the merely natural reason, that every spirit unperverted by sin and passion, every naturally noble spirit must love and accept it."

(Karl Alois Kneller, translated from the German by Thomas Kettle MP, *Christianity and the leaders of modern science* (London, 1911), p.118, quoting a letter written from Milan on the 6th of Jan 1815.)

Andre-Marie Ampere (1775-1836),

was a Frenchman from whom we get the 'Amp' in electricity.

"We can see only the works of the Creator but through them we rise to a knowledge of the Creator Himself. Just as the real movements of the stars are hidden by their apparent movements, and yet it is by observation of the one that we determine the other: so God is in some sort hidden by His works, and yet it is through them that we discern Him and catch a hint of the Divine attributes.

One of the most striking evidences of the existence of God is the wonderful harmony by which the universe is preserved and living beings are furnished in their organization with everything necessary to life, multiplication, and the enjoyment of all their powers, physical and intellectual."

(Karl Alois Kneller, translated from the German by Thomas Kettle MP, *Christianity and the leaders of modern science* (London, 1911), p.118, quoting from *Essai sur la philosophie des sciences* II, Paris 1843, 24 f.)

John Stuart Mill (1806-1873),

was a well known British philosopher, economist, civil servant and MP who emphasised the liberties of the individual and communities as opposed to increasing the power of the state.

"Whatever ground there is to believe in an Author of nature is derived from the appearances of the universe. The argument from design is grounded wholly on our experience of the appearances of the universe. It is, therefore, a far more important argument for theism than any other.

The order of nature exhibits certain qualities that are found to be characteristic of such things as are made by an intelligent mind for a purpose. We are entitled from this great similarity in the effects to infer similarity in the cause, and to believe that things which it is beyond the power of man to make, but which resemble the works of man in all but power, must also have been made by Intelligence armed with a power greater than human.

...

The parts of which the eye is composed, and the arrangement of these parts, resemble one another in this very remarkable respect, that they all conduce to enabling the animal to see. These parts and their arrangement being as they are, the animal sees.

Now sight, being a fact which follows the putting together of the parts of the eye, can only be connected with the production of the eye as a final cause, not an efficient cause; since all efficient causes precede their effects. But a final cause is a purpose, and at once marks the origin of the eye as proceeding from an Intelligent Will." .

(Alburey Castell, *An Introduction to Modern Philosophy* (New York, 1988), p.181-182.)

Professor **George Boole** (1815-1864),

was the first Professor of Mathematics at UCC, famous for his invention of Boolean logic, i.e. the 'AND' and 'OR' statements in search engines and similar 'gates' in electronics, who, because of the importance of this logic in the binary world of computers, is now sometimes called the founder of the field of computer science.

"To infer the existence of an intelligent cause from the teeming evidences of surrounding design, to rise to the conception of a moral Governor of the world, from the study of the constitution and the moral provisions of our own nature; these, though but the feeble steps of an understanding limited in its faculties and its materials of knowledge, are of more avail than the ambitious attempt to arrive at a certainty unattainable on the ground of natural religion. And as these were the most ancient, so are they still the most solid foundations, Revelation being set apart, of the belief that the course of this world is not abandoned to chance and inexorable fate."

(George Boole, *An Investigation of the Laws of Thought* (London, 1854), p.218, available at: http://www.archive.org/stream/investigationofl00boolrich/investigationofl00boolrich_djvu.txt .)

Professor **Michael Faraday** (1791-1867),

was *"born at Newington Butts [London] on Sept. 22nd 1791 of a poor family of Irish origin,"* and we are told that *"his inventions of electromagnetic rotary devices formed the foundation of electric motor technology, and it was largely due to his efforts that electricity became viable for use in technology."* The 'farad' and the Faraday Constant are named after him.

"Our philosophy, feeble as it is, gives us to see in every particle of matter, a centre of force reaching to an infinite distance, binding worlds and suns together, and unchangeable in its permanency. Around this same particle we see grouped the powers of all the various phenomena of nature: the heat, the cold, the wind, the storm, the awful conflagration, the vivid lightning flash, the stability of the rock and the mountain, the grand mobility of the ocean, with its mighty tidal wave sweeping round the globe in its diurnal journey, the dancing of the stream and the torrent; the glorious cloud, the soft dew, the rain dropping fastness, the harmonious working of all these forces in nature, until at last the molecule rises up in accordance with the mighty purpose ordained for it, and plays its part in the gift of life itself. And therefore our philosophy, whilst it shows us these things, should lead us to think of Him who hath wrought them; for it is said by an authority far above even that which these works present, that 'the invisible things of Him from the creation of the world are clearly seen, being understood by the things that are made, even His eternal power and Godhead.' "

(Karl Alois Kneller, translated from the German by the Irish MP Thomas Kettle, *Christianity and the leaders of modern science* (London, 1911), p.127, quoting Dr Bence Jones, *The Life and Letters of Faraday* (London, 1870) vol ii, p.224-5.)

Charles Babbage (1791-1871),

from 1828-1839 was Lucasian Professor of Mathematics at Cambridge and famous for a number of inventions, like the 'cow catcher' attached to old railway engines, but of course he is particularly well known as the first inventor of a type of computer, the 'difference engine', and as such he is often known as the 'father of the computer'. In fact he tells us repeatedly that it was his 'computer' – its functions were similar to a modern day programmable calculator, able to calculate any algebraic equation, which is incredible of course for the 1830s – which inspired him to write this work on what he felt was the way that natural laws are managed by God. He begins here by passionately refuting the idea that the scientist or mathematician is in any way hostile to theism.

"If, by "rising above his mathematics and physics," it is meant, that inquiry into the relation of man to his Maker, is of more importance to his welfare than those other subjects, then it is a proposition which scarcely requires to be asserted, because it has never been denied. Even the atheist, who has arrived, by reasoning, at his desolate conclusion, would not fail to admit its truth, by attending to any new argument which might be proposed against his creed. But if it is meant, that there is a "higher region" of evidence than that of "mathematical proof and physical consequence," then it is in my opinion utterly and completely erroneous; and as I am confident this erroneous light will be that in which the statement will be understood by many, I think it necessary to state distinctly what appears to me the relative position of the subjects in discussion.

First, The truths of pure mathematics are necessary truths; they are of such a nature, that to suppose the reverse, involves a contradiction.

Secondly, The laws of nature, on which physical reasonings are founded, although some of them are considered as necessary truths, depend, in many instances, on the testimony of our senses. These derive their highest confirmation from the aid of pure mathematics, by which innumerable consequences, previously unobserved, are proved to result from them.

Thirdly, The truths of natural religion rest also on the testimony of our external senses, but united with that internal consciousness of intention or design which we experience in our own breast, and from which we infer similar powers in other beings. Many of the facts on which the conclusions of natural religion are founded, derive their chief importance from the aid supplied by the united power of the two former classes, and the amount and value of this support will be enlarged with the advance of those sciences. Fourthly, Revealed religion rests on human testimony; and on that alone. Its first and greatest support arises from natural religion. I have endeavoured in one chapter of the present volume to show, that, notwithstanding the weakening effect of transmission upon testimony, a time may arrive when, by the progress of knowledge, internal evidence of the truth of revelation may start into existence with all the force that can be derived from the testimony of the senses.

The first class of truths then (those of Pure Mathematics) appears to rest on necessity. The second, (the Laws of Nature,) on necessity and our external senses. The third, (those of Natural Religion,) on our external senses and internal consciousness. The last, (those of Revelation,) on human testimony. If they admit of any classification, as subjects having a common resemblance, or as possessing different degrees of evidence, I have placed them in the only order which, in my opinion, is consistent with truth; convinced that it is more injurious to religion to overrate, than to undervalue the cogency of the evidence on which it rests.

...

Feeling convinced that the truths of Natural Religion rest on foundations far stronger than those of any human testimony; that they are impressed in indelible characters, by almighty power, on every fragment of the material world...

...

Simple as the law of gravity now appears, and beautifully in accordance with all the observations of past and of present times, consider what it has cost of intellectual study. Copernicus, Galileo, Kepler, Euler, Lagrange, Laplace, all the great names which have exalted the character of man, by carrying out trains of reasoning unparalleled in every other science; these, and a host of others, each of whom might have been the Newton of another field, have all laboured to work out, the consequences which resulted from that single law which he discovered. All that the human mind has produced—the brightest in genius, the most persevering in application, has been lavished on the details of the law of gravity.

Had that law been other than it is—had it been, for example, the inverse cube of the distance, it would still have required an equal expense of genius and of labour to have worked out its details. But, between the laws represented by the inverse square, and the inverse cube of the distance, there are interposed an infinite number of other laws, each of which might have been the basis of a system requiring the most extensive knowledge to trace out its consequences. Again, between every law which can be expressed by whole numbers, whether it be direct or inverse, an infinity of others can still be interposed. All these might be combined by two, by three, or in any other groups, and new systems might be imagined, submitted to such combinations. Thus, another infinity of laws, of a far higher order – in fact, of an infinitely higher order – might again be added to the list. And this might still be increased by all the other combinations, of which such laws admit, besides that by addition, to which we have already alluded, thus forming an infinity itself of so high an order, that it is difficult to conceive. Man has, as yet, no proof of the impossibility of the existence of any of these laws. Each might, for any reason we can assign, be the basis of a creation different from our own.

It is at this point that skill and knowledge re-enter the argument, and banish for ever the dominion of chance. The Being who called into existence this creation, of which we are parts, must have chosen the present form, the present laws, in preference to the infinitely infinite variety which he might have willed into existence. He must have known and foreseen all, even the remotest consequences of every one of those laws, to have penetrated but a little way into one of which has exhausted the intellect of our whole species.

If such is the view we must take of the knowledge of the Creator, when contemplating the laws of inanimate matter – laws into whose consequences it has cost us such accumulated labour to penetrate – what language can we speak, when we consider that the laws which connect matter with animal life may be as infinitely varied as those which regulate material existence?

...

Before entering on the main argument of the last Chapter, it may be remarked, that the plainest and most natural view of the language employed by the sacred historian [Moses transmitting to us the Book of Genesis] is, that his expressions ought to be received by us in the sense in which they were understood by the people to whom he addressed himself. If, when speaking of the creation, instead of using the terms light and water, he had spoken of the former as a wave, and of the latter as the union of two invisible airs, he would assuredly have been perfectly unintelligible to his countrymen:– at the distance of above three thousand years his writings would just have begun to be comprehended; and possibly three thousand years hence those views may be as inapplicable to the then existing state of human knowledge as they would have been when the first chapter of Genesis was written. Those, however, who attempt to disprove the facts presented by observation, by placing them in opposition to revelation, have mistaken the very groundwork of the question. The revelation of Moses itself rests, and must necessarily rest, on testimony [meaning that it is not necessarily entirely the word of God anyway, it went through human hands and rests on his testimony]. Moses, the author of the oldest of the sacred books, lived about fifteen hundred years before the Christian era, or about three thousand three hundred years ago. The oldest manuscripts of the Pentateuch at present known, appear to have been written about 900 years ago. These were copied from others of older date, and those again might probably, if their history were known, be traced up through a few transcripts to the original author; but no part of this history is revelation; it is testimony. Although the matter which the book contains was revealed to Moses, the fact that what we now receive as revelation is the same with that originally communicated revelation, is entirely dependent on testimony."

(Charles Babbage, *The ninth Bridgewater Treatise*: *On the Power, Wisdom and Goodness of God, as manifested in the Creation* (London, 1837), p.v-vii, x-xvi, quote starting at 'Simple' from p.57-60, next quote is p.72-75, available at: http://www.victorianweb.org/victorian/science/science_texts/bridgewater/intro.htm , and subsequent pages.)

Sir William Rowan Hamilton (1805-1865),

the famous Irish mathematician – and godson of the United Irishman Archibald Hamilton Rowan, confusingly not a close relative –, astronomer and physicist, the discoverer of 'Hamilton's Principal Function' and the author of a general theory of dynamics, is important for both maths and physics because he discovered, and named, quaternions, which is a kind of special algebra of complex numbers that is becoming increasingly popular in computer science, in maths, and Hamiltonians, describing the energy of mechanical systems, in physics. He wrote this on the question of God and the laws of physics.

"I am glad you agree with me in having a leaning to Idealism, and in liking Berkeley. It has long been a fundamental article of my philosophic faith, derived perhaps from Berkeley, but adopted before I yet knew him, except from unfriendly reports, that one Supreme Spirit excites perceptions in dependent minds, according to a covenant or plan, of which the terms or conditions are what we call the Laws of Nature. These terms or conditions it is the business of physical science to discover; and since we cannot know them after the manner of Divine Intuition, to express them at least in language congenial to the necessities and aspirations of our own inward being. Power, Space, and Time appear to me to constitute the elements of this language. Power, acting by law in Space and Time, is the ideal base of an ideal world, into which it is the problem of physical science to refine the phenomenal world, that so we may behold as one, and under the forma of our own understanding, what had seemed to be manifold and foreign; and may express our passive perceptions, and their connexions with our acts and with each other, not as mere facts remembered, but as laws conceived and reasoned on. But Space and Time themselves, and Power as localised in them, have, as I willingly admit, only a relative and subjective existence. In seeking for absolute objective reality I can find no rest but in God: though, in a lower sense, reality may be attributed to all act and passion of mind, and especially to the Will, as obeying or opposing the conscience. The views of Berkeley and Kant appear to me to agree, in many important respects, with the foregoing view and with each other. Indeed I think that Kant did not differ so much from Berkeley as he believed, though the two schemes are certainly distinguishable. Whoever compares the passage in which Kant refutes the vulgar distinction between the Rainbow as an appearance, and the Rain as a reality, with Berkeley's explanation (in the Third Dialogue) of the kind of knowledge gained by a microscope, will observe a very close analogy, the difference being, chiefly, that while Berkeley habitually, and perhaps dogmatically (though I think truly), refers our perceptions to the immediate operation of God, Kant, with perhaps not less of dogmatism, refers them to some *Things in themselves*, which he confesses and contends must be for ever totally unknown."

(Writing to H F C Logan, from the observatory at Dunsink, on the 27th of June 1834, printed in Robert Perceval Graves, *Life of Sir William* Rowan Hamilton (Dublin, 1885) vol ii, p.87-88, available at:
http://www.archive.org/stream/lifeofsirwilliam02gravuoft/lifcofsir william02gravuoft_djvu.txt .)

Charles Darwin (1809-1882),

obviously the author of 'Origin of Species' and hence the originator of the theory of evolution, which actually draws quite a bit on the theories of his grandfather, Dr Erasmus Darwin, said this in his Autobiography.

"Another source of conviction in the existance of God connected with the reason and not the feelings, impresses me as having much more weight. This follows from the extreme difficulty or rather impossibility of conceiving this immense and wonderful universe, including man with his capability of looking far backwards and far into futurity, as the result of blind chance or necessity. When thus reflecting I feel compelled to look at a first cause having an intelligent mind in some degree analogous to that of man; and I deserve to be called a theist."

(Charles Darwin, edited by Nora Barlow, *The Autobiography of Charles Darwin* (London, 1958), p.92-3, available at http://www.update.uu.se/~fbendz/library/cd_relig.htm .)

James Prescott Joule (1818-1889),

was the English brewer who discovered the First Law of Thermodynamics, and for whom the unit of energy is called after.

"Indeed the phenomena of nature, whether mechanical, chemical, or vital, consist almost entirely in a continual conversion of attraction through space, living force, and heat into one another. Thus it is that order is maintained in the universe – nothing is deranged, nothing ever lost, but the entire machinery, complicated as it is, works smoothly and harmoniously. And though, as in the awful vision of Ezekiel, "wheel may be in the middle of wheel," and everything may appear complicated and involved in the apparent confusion and intricacy of an almost endless variety of causes, effects, conversions, and arrangements, yet is the most perfect regularity preserved – the whole being governed by the sovereign will of God."

(James Joule, *The Scientific Papers of James Prescott Joule* (London, 1963), p.273.)

Louis Pasteur (1822-1895),

surely requires no introduction with the process of Pasteurisation called after him etc etc.

"Posterity will one day laugh at the foolishness of modern materialistic philosophers. The more I study nature, the more I stand amazed at the work of the Creator. I pray while I am engaged at my work in the laboratory."
(*The Literary Digest* of the 18th of October 1902.)

Ernst Werner von Siemens (1816-1892),

has given his name to a unit of electrical conductance, was the founder of the famous Siemens firm and is sometimes considered the founding father of electrical engineering in Germany.

"The deeper we penetrate into the harmonious and immutable order of nature, and unveil her hidden forces, the more modestly do we come to think of the little compass of our knowledge, and the more intense is our admiration of the supreme ordering Wisdom which pervades the whole created world."
(Karl Alois Kneller, translated from the German by Thomas Kettle MP, *Christianity and the leaders of modern science* (London, 1911), p.144, quoting from Hovestadt in *Natur und Offenbarung* XXXIX, (Munster, 1893), p.170.)

Sir William Thomson (1824-1907), Lord **Kelvin**,

born in Belfast but is mostly associated with the University of Glasgow, was the first scientist elevated to the House of Lords, as Baron Kelvin, and obviously under that name a unit of temperature is called after him.

"Sir John Herschel, in expressing a favourable judgement on the hypothesis of zoological evolution (with, however, some reservation in respect to the origin of man) objected to the doctrine of natural selection that it was too like the Laputan method of making books, and that it did not sufficiently take into account a continually guiding and controlling intelligence. This seems to me a most valuable and instructive criticism. I feel profoundly convinced that the argument of design has been greatly too much lost sight of in recent zoological speculations. Reactions against the frivolities of teleology, such as are to be found not rarely in the notes of the learned commentators on Paley's Natural Theology, have, I believe, a temporary effect in turning attention from the solid and irrefragable argument so well put forward in that excellent old book. But overpoweringly strong proofs of intelligent and benevolent design lie all round us; and if ever perplexities, whether metaphysical or scientific, turn us away from them for a time, they come back upon us with irresistible force, showing to us through Nature the influence of a free will, and teaching us that living beings depend on one ever-acting

Creator and Ruler.

Speaking this time in a speech paraphrased in 'The Times' in May 1903:

Science positively affirmed creative power. Science made everyone feel a miracle in himself. It was not in dead matter that they lived and moved and had their being, but in the creating and directive power which science compelled them to accept as an article of belief. They could not escape from that when they studied the physics and dynamics of living and dead matter all around. Modern biologists were coming once more to a firm acceptance of something, and that was a vital principle. They had an unknown object put before them in science. In thinking of that subject they were all agnostics. They only knew God in His works, but they were absolutely forced by science to admit and to believe with absolute confidence in a directive power – in an influence other than physical, dynamical, electrical forces. Cicero had denied that they could have come into existence by a fortuitous concourse of atoms. There was nothing between absolute scientific belief in creative power, and the acceptance of the theory of a fortuitous concourse of atoms. Was there, he asked, anything so absurd as to believe that a number of atoms by falling together of their own accord could make a crystal, a sprig of moss, a microbe, a living animal? People thought that given millions of years, these might come to pass, but they could not think that a million of millions of millions of years could give them unaided a beautiful world like ours. They had a spiritual influence, and in science a knowledge that there was that influence, in the world around them. He admired the healthy, breezy atmosphere of free thought in Professor Henslow's lecture. Let no one, he urged, be afraid of true freedom. They could be free in their thought, in their criticisms, and with freedom of thought they were bound to come to the conclusion that science was not antagonistic to religion, but a help for religion.

In a letter to the paper a short time later Lord Kelvin wished to delete the word 'crystal' in the above and says that:

...while, 'fortuitous concourse of atoms' is not an inappropriate description of the formation of a crystal, it is utterly absurd in respect to the coming into existence, or the growth, or the continuation of the molecular combinations presented in the bodies of living things. Here scientific thought is compelled to accept the idea of creative power. Forty years ago I asked Liebig, walking somewhere in the country, if he believed that the grass and flowers which we saw around us grew by mere chemical forces. He answered, 'No, no more than I could believe that a book of botany describing them could grow by mere chemical forces.' Every action of human free will is a miracle to physical and chemical and mathematical science.

This later comment was added in by Lord Kelvin to a copy of this speech that he printed in June 1903:

Do not be afraid of being free-thinkers! If you think strongly enough, you will be forced by science to the belief in God, which is the foundation of all religion. You will find science not antagonistic but helpful to religion."

(The first quote is from William Thomson, *Address of Sir William Thomson...meeting of the British Association for the Advancement of Science held in Edinburgh in August 1871* (London, 1871), p.cv, and the later quotes from Karl Alois Kneller, translated from the German by Thomas Kettle, *Christianity and the leaders of modern science* (London, 1911), p.38.)

Thomas Alva Edison (1847-1931),

arguably the greatest applier of science to practical products in history, like the phonograph, motion picture camera, and the electric light bulb, was considered the third most prolific inventor in history.

"No person can be brought into close contact with the mysteries of nature or make a study of chemistry or of the laws of growth without being convinced that behind It all there is a supreme Intelligence. I do not mean to say a supreme law, for that implies no consciousness, but a supreme mind operating through unchangeable laws. I am convinced of that, and I think that I could – perhaps I may some time – demonstrate the existence of such an intelligence through the operation of these mysterious laws with the certainty of a demonstration in mathematics."
(*New York Tribune*, 17th of February 1907, available at: http://www.oldnewsads.com/Old-News-Articles-on-Thomas-Edison.html .)

Dr **John Scott Haldane** (1860-1936),

from a famous Scottish family of scientists, jointly discovered the 'bends' phenomenon among divers, and helped design the oxygen chamber that aids them, also invented many other things including a lamp used by miners and the gas mask. This account is very interesting because the reason why he rejected the 'mechanistic theory' of life, basically evolution and natural selection, is because he saw that the germ of life, in heredity, would have to be too complicated to have arisen by chance. If you read his book he is saying that the complexity of this germ must be enormous, since it contains all the instructions necessary for the cells to function etc etc, which means in fact that he argued against evolution on the basis of the complexity of DNA long before the structure of DNA had actually being discovered! Another reason he gave against a purely 'mechanistic' theory of biology was the argument that this could not give you the 'will' in human consciousness, a familiar refrain of modern day philosophers, which serves to show how much ahead of his time he was in his knowledge of human physiology.

"As a physiologist I can see no use for the hypothesis that life, as a whole, is a mechanical process. This theory does not help me in my work; and indeed I think it now hinders very seriously the progress of physiology. I should as soon go back to the mythology of our Saxon forefathers as to the mechanistic physiology.

Although the mechanistic theory of life will soon become a matter of past history...[goes on to say that it is nonetheless useful to use 'mechanistic' tools and methods in laboratory settings.]

...

The mechanists have contended that the misty sphere [the origin of life as seen by 'vitalists', who basically believed that God was responsible] is only the mist of our ignorance of the physical and chemical conditions, and that year by year this mist is being gradually dispelled by the advance of physiological investigation. We have seen already that this is a complete illusion. The advance of investigation has only served to make the misty sphere more evident; and not only does it exist, but there is not the remotest chance, as we have just seen, that physical or chemical investigation will ever dispel the mist. The phenomena of life are of such a nature that no physical or chemical explanation of them is remotely conceivable.

...

The main outstanding fact is that the mechanistic account of the universe breaks down completely in connection with the phenomena of life. Whether it is not also insufficient in connection with phenomena outside what we at present regard as life is a further question which need not be discussed at present. When any hypothesis fails to correspond with facts it is the hypothesis which needs reconsideration."

(John Scott Haldane *Mechanism, Life, and Personality* (London, 1913), p.60-61, 64-65.)

Professor **Louis Trenchard More** (1870-1944),

Professor of Physics and Dean of the graduate school at the University of Cincinnati, makes here a telling admission about how 'faith based' the theory of evolution is.

"The more one studies paleontology, the more certain one becomes that evolution is based on faith alone; exactly the same sort of faith which is necessary to have when one encounters the great mysteries of religion…. The only alternative is the doctrine of special creation, which may be true, but is irrational."

(Louis T More, *The Dogma of Evolution* (Princeton, 1925), p.160.)

Professor **Albert Einstein** (1879-1955),

German born of Jewish descent, was awarded a PhD from the University of Zurich in 1905, received the 1921 Nobel prize for physics, and was certainly the first, and arguably the greatest, of the modern day scientist superstars.

"I am not an atheist, and I don't think I can call myself a pantheist...We see the universe marvelously arranged and obeying certain laws, but only dimly understand these laws. Our limited minds grasp the mysterious force that moves the constellations.

...

Certain it is that a conviction, akin to religious feeling, of the rationality or intelligibility of the world lies behind all scientific work of a higher order... This firm belief, a belief bound up with deep feeling, in a superior mind that reveals itself in the world of experience, represents my conception of God.

...

Everyone who is seriously engaged in the pursuit of science becomes convinced that the laws of nature manifest the existence of a spirit vastly superior to that of men, and one in the face of which we with our modest powers must feel humble.

...

My religiosity consists of a humble admiration of the infinitely superior spirit who reveals himself in the slight details we are able to perceive with our frail and feeble minds. That deeply emotional conviction of the presence of a superior reasoning power, which is revealed in the incomprehensible universe, forms my idea of God.

...

"You accept the historical existence of Jesus?"

Unquestionably! No one can read the Gospels without feeling the actual prescence of Jesus. His personality pulsates in every word. No myth is filled with such life."

(The quotes are respectively from: Max Jammer, *Einstein and Religion: physics and theology* (Princeton, 1999), p44; Albert Einstein, *Ideas and Opinions* (London, 1956), p255; Jammer, *Einstein and Religion,* op.cit. p.93; Albert Einstein, *The New Quotable Einstein* (Princeton, 2005), p195-6; and the last quote is from G S Viereck, "What Life means to Einstein", *Saturday Evening Post,* 26 October 1929.)

Guglielmo Marconi (1874-1937),

was of course the great Italian inventor of the radio, and the winner of the Nobel Prize in physics in 1909, etc etc.

"The more I work with the powers of Nature, the more I feel God's benevolence to man; the closer I am to the great truth that everything is dependent on the Eternal Creator and Sustainer; the more I feel that the so-called science, I am occupied with, is nothing but an expression of the Supreme Will, which aims at bringing people closer to each other in order to help them better understand and improve themselves.

...

I believe it would be a great tragedy if men were to lose their faith in prayer. Without the help of prayer I might perhaps have failed where I have succeeded. In allowing me to attain what I have done, God has made of me merely an instrument of His own will, for the revelation of His own Divine power."

(The first quote from Maria Cristina Marconi, *Mio Marito Guglielmo* (Milan, 1995), p.244, and the second quote from Rev Dr Leslie Rumble *Another Thousand Radio Replies* (Minnesota, 1942) vol 3, p.20-21.)

Dr **Thomas Dwight** (1843-1911),

was appointed Professor of Anatomy at Harvard Medical School in 1883.

"We have now the remarkable spectacle that just when many scientific men are agreed that there is no part of the Darwinian system that is of any great influence, and that, as a whole, the theory is not only unproved, but impossible, the ignorant, half-educated masses have acquired the idea that it is to be accepted as a fundamental fact."

(Dr Thomas Dwight, *Thoughts of a Catholic Anatomist* (New York, 1911), p.6.)

Professor **Arthur Compton** (1892-1962),

a PhD from Princeton in 1916 he was awarded the Nobel Prize for Physics, for his discovery of the 'Compton effect', in 1927.

"If religion is to be acceptable to science it is important to examine the hypothesis of an Intelligence working in nature. The discussion of the evidences for an intelligent God is as old as philosophy itself.

The argument on the basis of design, though trite, has never been adequately refuted. On the contrary, as we learn more about our world, the probability of its having resulted by chance processes becomes more and more remote, so that few indeed are the scientific men of today who will defend an atheistic attitude."

(Arthur H Compton, *The Freedom of Man* (New Haven, 1935), p.73.)

Sir **Joseph J Thompson** (1856-1940),

the British discoverer of the electron who also won the Nobel Prize in Physics in 1906.

"As we conquer peak after peak we see in front of us regions full of interest and beauty, but we do not see our goal, we do not see the horizon; in the distance tower still higher peaks, which will yield to those who ascend them still wider prospects, and deepen the feeling, the truth of which is emphasized by every advance in science, that 'Great are the Works of the Lord'."
(*Nature* 26th of August 1909, vol 81, p.257.)

Dr **Robert A Millikan** (1868-1953),

was a Noble Laureate for Physics in 1923, was put on a US stamp in 1982, had been President of Caltech in Pasadena from 1921-45, and wrote this in 1927 talking about the laws of physics.

"know a God not of caprice and whim, such as were all the gods of the ancient world, but a god who works through law
...
a nature of orderliness, and a nature capable of being known; a nature, too, whose functioning might be predicted, a nature which could be relied upon; a nature, also, of possibly unlimited forces, capable of being discovered, and then of being harnessed for the benefit of mankind."

Addressing the American Chemical Society in 1937:

"everyone who reflects believes in God" [and that it is pathetic] "that many scientists are trying to prove the doctrine of evolution, which no scientist can do.
...
But I wish to go a step farther, for someone asks, 'Where does the idea of God come in? Isn't it a part of religion?'.

Yes, I think it is, and I should like to reply in three different ways to the question here raised.

My first answer is taken directly from Holy Writ and reads: 'No man hath seen God at any time. If a man says I love God and hateth his brother he is a liar: for he that loveth not his brother whom he hath seen, how can he love God whom he hath not seen?' In other words, one's attitude toward God is revealed by and reflected in his attitude toward his brother men.

My second answer is taken from Dean Shailer Mathews, head of the Baptist Divinity School of the University of Chicago. To the inquiry, 'Do you believe in God?' he replied, 'That, my friend, is a question which requires an education rather than an answer.'

My third form of reply is my own and reads: Thousands of years ago Job saw the futility of finite man's attempting to define God when he cried, 'Can man with searching find out God?'. Similarly, wise men ever since have always looked in amazement at the wonderful orderliness of nature and then recognized their own ignorance and finiteness and have been content to stand in silence and in reverence before the Being who is immanent in Nature, repeating with the psalmist, 'The fool hath said in his heart, there is no God.'

...

Just how we fit into the plans of the Great Architect and how much he has assigned us to do we do not know.

Fit in we certainly do somehow, else we would not have a sense of our own responsibility. A purely materialistic philosophy is to me the height of unintelligence.

It is our sense of responsibility for playing our part to the best of our ability that makes us Godlike."

(Robert A Millikan, *Evolution in Science and Religion* (New Haven, 1927), p.39-40, and the second quote from R Millikan, Robert Millikan's address to the American Chemical Society Meeting, *The Commentator*, June 1937, available at: http://creation.com/images/pdfs/tj/j24_1/j24_1_88-91.pdf , the second last quote is from Robert A Millikan, *The Autobiography of Robert A Millikan* (New York, 1950), p.286-287, and the last quote from ibid p.277-8.)

Professor **Ludwig Wittgenstein** (1889-1951),

an Austrian professor of philosophy at Cambridge (1939-1947), who, although not as well known as some philosophers, particularly during his lifetime, is now considered one of the greatest, if not the greatest, modern philosopher. He was nothing if not eccentric and almost all of what we understand of his philosophy comes from his voluminous notebooks discovered after his death, he published virtually nothing when alive. He clearly believed in C S Lewis' idea that humans seem to aspire to the divine or supernatural.

"If something is good it is also divine. In a strange way this sums up my ethics. Only the supernatural can express the Supernatural.
...
Christianity is indeed the only sure way to happiness.
...
Christianity is not a doctrine; I mean, not a theory about what has happened and will happen with the human soul, but a description of an actual occurrence in human life. For 'consciousness of sin' is an actual occurrence, and so are despair and salvation through faith.
...
I have had a letter from an old friend in Austria, a priest. In it he says he hopes my work will go well, if it should be God's will. Now that is all I want: if it should be God's will. Bach wrote on the title page of his *Orgelbuechlein*, 'To the glory of the most high God, and that my neighbour may be benefited thereby.' That is what I would have liked to say about my work."

(The first quote is from Norman Malcolm, *Wittgenstein: A*

Religious Point of View? (London, 1993), p.16; second quote from Ray Monk, *Ludwig Wittgenstein: The Duty of Genius* (London, 1991), p.122, third quote from Norman Malcolm, *Wittgenstein: A Religious Point of View?* (London, 1993), p.16; and the last quote from Rush Rhees ed., *Ludwig Wittgenstein: Personal Recollections* (Oxford, 1981), p.181-182.)

Dr **Werner Heisenberg** (1901-1976),

awarded a PhD in Physics in the University of Munich in 1923, won the Nobel Prize for Physics in 1932 "for the creation of Quantum Mechanics," and in 1927 published a book on 'the principle of uncertainty,' or indeterminacy, which now bears his name.

"The first gulp from the glass of natural sciences will turn you into an atheist, but at the bottom of the glass God is waiting for you.

...

Where no guiding ideals are left to point the way, the scale of values disappears and with it the meaning of our deeds and sufferings, and at the end can lie only negation and despair.

Religion is therefore the foundation of ethics, and ethics the presupposition of life."

(Ulrich Hildebrand, "Das Universum – Hinweis auf Gott?", published in *Ethos* no.10, October 1988, and the second quote from Werner Heisenburg, *Across the Frontiers* (New York, 1974), p.219.)

Professor **Max Planck** (1858-1947),

the founder of quantum theory and as such a very big name in science, and Nobel Prize winner in Physics in 1918, wrote this in 1937.

"...the whole nature...is governed by certain laws, which are independent of the existence of thinking humanity, but which nevertheless...admit formulation which corresponds to a purposeful behavior. This then represents a rational world order, to which nature and mankind is subject,...Really rich results of scientific research, however, entitle our belief in...steady deepening of our outlooks into the reign of almighty reason ruling over the nature.

...

The religion and science meet, on the contrary, in the question about the existence and essence of the supreme power governing the world, and here the answers they both furnish, are at least to a certain extent mutually comparable. They are in no way, as we have seen, in contradiction, but they agree in that firstly, there exists a reasonable world order independent from man and secondly, the essence of this order is never knowable directly, but only indirectly, or it can be only intuitively guessed. Religion uses to this effect its own specific symbols, exact sciences use measurements based on sensual perceptions. In this sense nothing prevents us – and our instinct of knowledge, demanding a unified world view, even requires it – to identify the world order of natural sciences with the god of religion. According to this, the deity, which believing man strives to approach using his visual symbols, is in its essence identical with the power of natural laws, about which the researching man learns to a certain extent with the help of sensual experiences."

This is from a later, 1944, speech.

"As a man who has devoted his whole life to the most clear headed science, to the study of matter, I can tell you as a result of my research about atoms this much: There is no matter as such. All matter originates and exists only by virtue of a force which brings the particle of an atom to vibration and holds this most minute solar system of the atom together. We must assume behind this force the existence of a conscious and intelligent mind. This mind is the matrix of all matter."

(The 1937 quote is from
http://www.angelfire.com/folk/infidel/MaxPlanck.html ,
quoting his lecture entitled: *Religion and Science* (Leipzig, 1958, but first delivered in 1937), p.25-27; and the 1944 speech is from Max Planck, *Das Wesen der Materie* [The Nature of Matter], speech at Florence, Italy, 1944, from Archiv zur Geschichte der Max-Planck-Gesellschaft, Abt. Va, Rep. 11 Planck, Nr. 1797.)

Dr **William Robin Thompson** (1887-1972),

an entomologist – the study of insects – who received a DSc in 1921 in Zoology from the University of Paris and a PhD in philosophy at St Maximin College in 1924, became the editor of 'The Canadian Entomologist' from 1947 to 1958 and the author of some 150 scientific papers, and also Director of the Commonwealth Institute of Biological Control in Ottawa (1928-1958).

"The argumentation used by evolutionists, said de Quatrefages, makes the discussion of their ideas extremely difficult. Personal convictions, simple possibilities, are presented as if they were proofs, or at least valid arguments in favour of the theory. As an example de Quatrefages cited Darwin's explanation of the manner in which the titmouse might become transformed into the nutcracker, by the accumulation of small changes in structure and instinct owing to the effect of natural selection; and then proceeded to show that it is just as easy to transform the nutcracker into the titmouse. The demonstration can be modified without difficulty to fit any conceivable case. It is without scientific value, since it cannot be verified; but since the imagination has free rein, it is easy to convey the impression that a concrete example of real transmutation has been given. This is the more appealing because of the extreme fundamental simplicity of the Darwinian explanation. The reader may be completely ignorant of biological processes yet he feels that he really understands and in a sense dominates the machinery by which the marvellous variety of living forms has been produced.

This was certainly a major reason for the success of the Origin. Another is the elusive character of the Darwinian argument.

...

The chronological succession of the fossils is also open to doubt, for it appears generally speaking, that the age of the rocks is not determined by their intrinsic characteristics but by the fossils they contain while the succession of the fossils is determined by the succession of the strata. ...it does appear to me, in the first place, that Darwin in the Origin was not able to produce paleontological evidence sufficient to prove his views but that the evidence he did produce was adverse to them; and I may note that the position is not notably different to-day. The modern Darwinian paleontologists are obliged, just like their predecessors and like Darwin, to water down the facts with subsidiary hypotheses which, however plausible, are in the nature of things unverifiable

...

I do not contest the fact that the advent of the evolutionary idea, due mainly to the Origin, very greatly stimulated biological research. But it appears to me that owing precisely to the nature of the stimulus, a great deal of this work was directed into unprofitable channels or devoted to the pursuit of will-o'- the-wisps. I am not the only biologist of this opinion. Darwin's conviction that evolution is the result of natural selection, acting on small fortuitous variations, says Guyenot, was to delay the progress of investigations on evolution by half a century. Really fruitful researches on heredity did not begin until the rediscovery in 1900 of the fundamental work of Mendel, published in 1865 and owing nothing to the work of Darwin.

...

The success of Darwinism was accompanied by a decline in scientific integrity. This is already evident in the reckless statements of Haeckel and in the shifting, devious and histrionic argumentation of T. H. Huxley.

...

As we know, there is a great divergence of opinion among biologists, not only about the causes of evolution but even about the actual process. This divergence exists because the evidence is unsatisfactory and does not permit any certain conclusion. It is therefore right and proper to draw the attention of the non-scientific public to the disagreements about evolution. But some recent remarks of evolutionists show that they think this unreasonable. This situation, where scientific men rally to the defence of a doctrine they are unable to define scientifically, much less demonstrate with scientific rigour, attempting to maintain its credit with the public by the suppression of criticism and the elimination of difficulties, is abnormal and undesirable in science.

...

The concept of organic Evolution is very highly prized by biologists, for many of whom it is an object of genuinely religious devotion, because they regard it as a supreme integrative principle. This is probably the reason why the severe methodological criticism employed in other departments of biology has not yet been brought to bear against evolutionary speculation."

(W R Thompson's introduction to Charles Darwin, *Origin of Species* (London, 1967), p.xi, xvii-xiv, xx, ibid, xxii, and W R Thompson, *Science and Common Sense* (London, 1937), p.229.; and also there are long quotes of his available here: http://creationevolutiondesign.blogspot.com/2006/08/quote-of-day-wr-thompsons-critique-of.html , and here: http://bevets.com/equotest.htm .)

Dr **Theodore Newton Tahmisian**

received his BA from Fresno State College and PhD from the State University of Iowa, was an Associate Biologist and Group leader of the Biological and Medical Research Division of Argonne National Laboratory (which actually grew out of the Manhattan project, and so some of his work was performed 'under the auspices of the Atomic Energy Commission') in Illinois, and had numerous important research papers of his published from 1942-71 (as can be seen here: http://www.ncbi.nlm.nih.gov/pubmed?term=%22TAHMISIAN %20TN%22[Author]). Incidentally he was pictured in Life magazine on the 21st Mar 1955 (as seen above) in relation to his work on the effects of radiation on grasshoppers.

"Scientists who go about teaching that evolution is a fact of life are great con men. In explaining evolution, we do not have one iota of fact – it is a tangled mishmash of guessing games and figure jaggling. . . ."
(*Fresno Bee*, 20th of August, 1959, available at http://amarillo.com/stories/092399/opi_letters.shtml .)

Dr **James Bryant Conant** (1893-1978),

received a PhD in Chemistry in 1917, was President of Harvard University (1933-1953) and US ambassador to Germany (1955-57),:

"Therefore, a grotesque account of a period some thousands of years ago is taken seriously though it be built by piling special assumptions on special assumptions, ad hoc hypothesis [invented for a purpose] on ad hoc hypothesis, and tearing apart the fabric of science whenever it appears convenient. The result is a fantasia which is neither history nor science."

(Dr James Conant, *Science and Common Sense* (New Haven, 1961), p.278.)

Wernher von Braun (1912-1977),

the quintessential German rocket scientist, got his doctorate in physics from the University of Berlin in 1934 etc etc, and was certainly the most famous person involved in the science of sending humans into space, writing in a 1963 newspaper article:

"The two most powerful forces shaping our civilization today are science and religion.

Through science man strives to learn more of the mysteries of creation. Through religion he seeks to know the creator.

Neither operates independently. It is as difficult for me to understand a scientist who does not acknowledge the presence of a superior rationality behind the existence of the universe as it is to comprehend a theologian who would deny the advances of science. Far from being independent or opposing forces, science and religion are sisters. Both seek a better world. While science seeks control over the forces of nature around us, religion controls the forces of nature within us.

As we learn more and more about nature, we become more deeply impressed and humbled by its orderliness and unerring perfection. Our expanding knowledge of the laws of the universe have enabled us to send men out of their natural environment into the strange new environment of space, and return them safely to earth.

...

Finite man cannot comprehend an omnipresent, omniscient, omnipotent, and infinite God. Any effort to visualize God, to reduce him to our comprehension, to describe him in our language, beggars his greatness.

I find it best through faith to accept God as an intelligent will, perfect in goodness, revealing himself in the world of experience more fully down through the ages, as man's capacity for understanding grows.

...

The knowledge that man can choose between good and evil should draw him closer to his creator. Next, the realization should dawn that his survival here and hereafter depends on his adherence to the spiritual rather than the scientific.

...

The ethical guidelines of religion are the bonds that can hold our civilization together. Without them man can never attain that cherished goal of lasting peace with himself, his God, and his fellowman."

And in a letter of 1972, answering a direct question on Intelligent Design, he wrote the following.

"For me, the idea of a creation is not conceivable without evoking the necessity of design. One cannot be exposed to the law and order of the universe without concluding that there must be design and purpose behind it all. In the world round us, we can behold the obvious manifestations of an ordered, structured plan or design. We can see the will of the species to live and propagate. And we are humbled by the powerful forces at work on a galactic scale, and the purposeful orderliness of nature that endows a tiny and ungainly seed with the ability to develop into a beautiful flower. The better we understand the intricacies of the universe and all harbors, the more reason we have found to marvel at the inherent design upon which it is based.

While the admission of a design for the universe ultimately raises the question of a Designer (a subject outside of science), the scientific method does not allow us to exclude data which lead to the conclusion that the universe, life and man are based on design. To be forced to believe only one conclusion—that everything in the universe happened by chance—would violate the very objectivity of science itself.

Certainly there are those who argue that the universe evolved out of a random process, but what random process could produce the brain of a man or the system of the human eye?

Some people say that science has been unable to prove the existence of a Designer. They admit that many of the miracles in the world around us are hard to understand, and they do not deny that the universe, as modern science sees it, is indeed a far more wondrous thing than the creation medieval man could perceive. But they still maintain that since science has provided us with so many answers the day will soon arrive when we will be able to understand even the creation of the fundamental laws of nature without a Divine intent. They challenge science to prove the existence of God. But must we really light a candle to see the sun?

Many men who are intelligent and of good faith say they cannot visualize a Designer. Well, can a physicist visualize an electron? The electron is materially inconceivable and yet it is so perfectly known through its effects that we use it to illuminate our cities, guide our airlines through the night skies and take the most accurate measurements. What strange rationale makes some physicists accept the inconceivable electrons as real while refusing to accept the reality of a Designer on the ground that they cannot conceive Him? I am afraid that, although they really do not understand the electron either, they are ready to accept it because they managed to produce a rather clumsy mechanical model of it borrowed from rather limited experience in other fields, but they would not know how to begin building a model of God.

I have discussed the aspect of a Designer at some length because it might be that the primary resistance to acknowledging the "Case for Design" as a viable scientific alternative to the current "Case for Chance" lies in the inconceivability, in some scientists' minds, of a Designer. The inconceivability of some ultimate issue (which will always lie outside scientific resolution) should not be allowed to rule out any theory that explains the interrelationship of observed data and is useful for prediction.

We in NASA were often asked what the real reason was for the amazing string of successes we had with our Apollo flights to the Moon. I think the only honest answer we could give was that we tried to never overlook anything. It is in that same sense of scientific honesty that I endorse the presentation of alternative theories for the origin of the universe, life and man in the science classroom. It would be an error to overlook the possibility that the universe was planned rather than happened by chance."

(*American Weekly*, 10th of Feb 1963, available at: http://creationsafaris.com/wgcs_4vonbraun.htm , and the 1972 letter was to Vernon L Grose, in relation to the California Board of Education, of the 14th of Sept 1972, reproduced in Vernon L Grose, *Science but not Scientists*(Bloomington, 2006), p.637.)

Dr **Leonard Harrison Matthews** (1901-1986),

was the Scientific Director of the Zoological Society of London from 1951 to 1966.

"The fact of evolution is the backbone of biology, and biology is thus in the peculiar position of being a science founded on an unproved theory – is it then a science or faith? Belief in the theory of evolution is thus exactly parallel to belief in special creation – both are concepts which believers know to be true but neither up to the present has been capable of proof."

(The Introduction to Charles Darwin, *Origin of Species* (London, 1971), p.x, xi.)

Sir **John Eccles** (1903-1997),

an Australian who won the 1963 Nobel Prize in Medicine, for his ongoing work on electrophysiology, a field he basically invented, was inter alia Professor of Physiology at Oxford University.

"There has been a regrettable tendency of many scientists to claim that science is so powerful and all pervasive that in the not too distant future it will provide an explanation in principle for all phenomena in the world of nature, including man, even of human consciousness in all its manifestations. In our recent book Popper has labelled this claim as promissory materialism, which is extravagant and unfulfillable.

Yet on account of the high regard for science, it has great persuasive power with the intelligent laity because it is advocated unthinkingly by the great mass of scientists who have not critically evaluated the dangers of this false and arrogant claim.

In 1994 he wrote further about this 'promissory materialism'.

I regard this theory as being without foundation. The more we discover scientifically about the brain the more clearly do we distinguish between the brain events and the mental phenomena and the more wonderful do the mental phenomena become.

Promissory materialism is simply a superstition held by dogmatic materialists. It has all the features of a Messianic prophecy, with the promise of a future freed of all problems – a kind of Nirvana for our unfortunate successors.

Writing in 1990 letter to Erika Erdmann:

You refer to protection of our Earth as the most urgent goal at present. I disagree. It is to save mankind from materialist degradation. It comes in the media, in the consumer society, in overriding quest for power and money, in the degradation of our values (that used to be thought as based on love, truth, and beauty), and in the disintegration of the human family.

This is from his 1979 book, 'Human Mystery':

I repudiate philosophies and political systems which recognize human beings as mere things with a material existence of value only as cogs in the great bureaucratic machine of the state, which thus becomes a slave state. The terrible and cynical slaveries depicted in Orwell's *'1984'* are engulfing more and more of our planet.

Is there yet time to rebuild a philosophy and a religion that can give us a renewed faith in this great spiritual adventure, which for each of us is a human life lived in freedom and dignity?"

(John C Eccles, *The Human Mystery* (Berlin, 1979), p.1, the second quote from John Eccles, *How the Self Controls Its Brain* (Berlin, 1994), the second last from his letter of the 19th Dec 1990 to Erika Erdmann, and the last quote from John C Eccles, *The Human Mystery* (Berlin, 1979), p.237.)

Professor **Richard Smalley** (1943-2005),

a scientist that the US Senate referred to as the 'Father of Nanotechnology', was awarded the Nobel Prize in Chemistry in 1996 and here is referring to two books written by the astrophysicist Dr Hugh Ross and the biochemist Dr Fazale Rana:

"Evolution has just been dealt its death blow. After reading *'Origins of Life'*, with my background in chemistry and physics, it is clear evolution could not have occurred. The new book, *'Who Was Adam?'*, is the silver bullet that puts the evolutionary model to death."

(*Creation Scientists Applaud PA Judge's Ruling Against 'Intelligent Design'* (Pasadena, 2005).)

Alexander Solzhenitsyn (1918-2008),

although his background was actually in physics, he graduated in physics and mathematics from Rostov State University in 1941 and later taught physics, nonetheless won great fame of course as a writer and in that capacity won the Nobel Prize in 1970. He is widely seen as one of the great intellectuals of the 20th century and is much revered in Russia.

"Imperceptibly, through decades of gradual erosion, the meaning of life in the West has ceased to be seen as anything more lofty than the 'pursuit of happiness,' a goal that has even been solemnly guaranteed by constitutions. The concepts of good and evil have been ridiculed for several centuries; banished from common use, they have been replaced by political or class considerations of short lived value.

The West is ineluctably slipping toward the abyss. Western societies are losing more and more of their religious essence as they thoughtlessly yield up their younger generation to atheism. If a blasphemous film about Jesus is shown throughout the United States, reputedly one of the most religious countries in the world, or a major newspaper publishes a shameless caricature of the Virgin Mary, what further evidence of godlessness does one need?

...

Our life consists not in the pursuit of material success but in the quest for worthy spiritual growth. Our entire earthly existence is but a transitional stage in the movement toward something higher, and we must not stumble and fall, nor must we linger fruitlessly on one rung of the ladder. Material laws alone do not explain our life or give it direction. The laws of physics and physiology will never reveal the indisputable manner in which the Creator constantly, day in and day out, participates in the life of each of us, unfailingly granting us the energy of existence; when this assistance leaves us, we die. And in the life of our entire planet, the Divine Spirit surely moves with no less force: this we must grasp in our dark and terrible hour."

(From his speech, *Men have forgotten God*, given on the 10th of May 1983 at Buckingham Palace.)

Jean Paul Sartre (1905-1980),

the famous modern French philosopher who won the Nobel Prize for Literature in 1964, was no fan of the theist position most of his life of course but he changed his mind dramatically towards the end.

"I do not feel that I am the product of chance, a speck of dust in the universe, but someone who was expected, prepared, prefigured. In short, a being whom only a Creator could put here; and this idea of a creating hand refers to God."

(In a dialogue with Pierre Victor in *Nouvel Observateur*, with the full dialogue in the issues of March 10th, 17th, and 24th, 1980.)

Malcolm Muggeridge (1903-1990),

a famous journalist often on BBC etc, was among many other things in MI6 at one point.

"I myself am convinced that the theory of evolution, especially the extent to which it's been applied, will be one of the great jokes in the history books in the future. Posterity will marvel that so very flimsy and dubious an hypothesis could be accepted with the incredible credulity that it has. I think I spoke to you before about this age as one of the most credulous in history, and I would include evolution as an example.

I'm very happy to say I live near a place called Piltdown. I like to drive there because it gives me a special glow. You probably know that a skull was discovered there and no less than five hundred doctoral theses were written on the subject and then it was discovered that the skull was a practical joke by a worthy dentist in Hastings who'd hurriedly put a few bones together, not even from the same animal, and buried them and stirred up all this business. So I'm not a great man for bones."

(From his Pascal Lecture given to the University of Waterloo in Canada in 1978 and published in Malcolm Muggeridge, *The End of Christendom* (Grand Rapids, 1980), p.59, and partly quoted in: *The Journal of the American Scientific Affiliation*: vols 32-33 (1980), p.123.)

Professor **Michael George Pitman** (1933-2000) OBE,

received a PhD from Cambridge in 1959, and was Professor of Biology at the University of Sydney (1966-1983) and chief scientist of Australia (1992-1996).

"There is a consistency of information in the genetic book, a point beyond which it cannot be misprinted. In biological terms, there is a limit past which the 'elasticity' of a genome cannot be 'stretched'. Rather than transmute into another type of organism, the mutant 'snaps' (aborts, is sterile or cannot survive) or 'recoils' back towards the form of the wild-type.

Do we, therefore, ever see mutations going about the business of producing new structures for selection to work on? No nascent organ has ever been observed emerging, though their origin in pre-functional form is basic to evolutionary theory. Some should be visible today, occurring in organisms at various stages up to integration of a functional new system, but we don't see them: there is no sign at all of this kind of radical novelty. Neither observation nor controlled experiment has shown natural selection manipulating mutations so as to produce a new gene, hormone, enzyme system or organ."

(Michael Pitman, *Adam and evolution: a scientific critique of neo-Darwinism* (London, 1984), p.68.)

Professor **Søren Løvtrup** (1922-),

received his doctorate at Copenhagen University in 1953, and was Professor of Zoology at the University of Umea in Sweden (1965-87).

"Micromutations do occur, but the theory that these alone can account for evolutionary change is either falsified, or else it is an unfalsifiable, hence metaphysical theory.

I suppose that nobody will deny that it is a great misfortune if an entire branch of science becomes addicted to a false theory. But this is what has happened in biology: for a long time now people discuss evolutionary problems in a peculiar 'Darwinian' vocabulary – 'adaptation', 'selection pressure,' 'natural selection,' etc. – thereby believing that they contribute to the explanation of natural events. They do not, and the sooner this is discovered, the sooner we shall be able to make real progress in our understanding of evolution. I believe that one day the Darwinian myth will be ranked the greatest deceit in the history of science. When this happens many people will pose the question: How did this happen? The present text surveys some of the answers which have been given, but there is no reason to believe that we have yet reached the final one. There will be a lot of work to do for coming generations of historians of biology."

(Søren Løvtrup, *Darwinism: The Refutation of a Myth* (London, 1987), p. 422.)

Professor **Ernst Chain** (1906-1979),

awarded a PhD in the University of Berlin in 1930 but fled Germany sometime later, is of Jewish extraction and worked on developing our understanding of penicillin for which he won a Nobel Prize in Medicine in 1945. In 1961-73 he was Professor of Biochemistry at Imperial College London and also became chairman of the World Health Organisation.

"I consider the power to believe to be one of the great divine gifts to man through which he is allowed in some inexplicable manner to come near to the mysteries of the Universe without understanding them. The capability to believe is as characteristic and as essential a property of the human mind as is its power of logical reasoning, and far from being incompatible with the scientific approach, it complements it and helps the human mind to integrate the world into an ethical and meaningful whole.

There are many ways in which people are made aware of their power to believe in the supremacy of Divine guidance and power: through music or visual art, some event or experience decisively influencing their life, looking through a microscope or telescope, or just by looking at the miraculous manifestations or purposefulness of Nature.

...

Only one theory has been advanced to make an attempt to understand the development of life – the Darwin-Wallace theory of evolution. And a very feeble attempt it is, based on such flimsy assumptions, mainly of morphological-anatomical nature that it can hardly be called a theory.

...

To postulate, as the positivists of the end of the 19th century and their followers here have done, that the development and survival of the fittest is entirely a consequence of chance mutations, or even that nature carries out experiments by trial and error through mutations in order to create living systems better fitted to survive, seems to me a hypothesis based on no evidence and irreconcilable with the facts.

This hypothesis wilfully neglects the principle of teleological purpose which stares the biologist in the face wherever he looks, whether he be engaged in the study of different organs in one organism, or even of different subcellular compartments in relation to each other in a single cell, or whether he studies the interrelation and interactions of various species.

These classical evolutionary theories are a gross oversimplification of an immensely complex and intricate mass of facts, and it amazes me that they were swallowed so uncritically and readily, and for such a long time, by so many scientists without a murmur of protest."

(Ronald W. Clark, *The Life of* Ernst Chain: Penicillin and Beyond (London, 1985), p.143, cited in Tihomir Dimitrov, *50 Nobel Laureates and Other Great Scientists Who Believe in God* (1995-2008), p.37-38, available at http://nobelist.tripod.com/sitebuildercontent/sitebuilderfiles/50-nobelists.pdf , and the last quote from E. Chain, "Social Responsibility and the Scientist in Modern Western Society," in *Perspectives in Biology and Medicine*, Spring 1971, Vol. 14, No. 3, p.367.)

Professor **Antony Hewish** (1924-),

is a British radio astronomer who won the Nobel Prize for Physics in 1974.

"I believe in God. It makes no sense to me to assume that the Universe and our existence is just a cosmic accident, that life emerged due to random physical processes in an environment which simply happened to have the right properties.

...

I think both science and religion are necessary to understand our relation to the Universe. In principle, Science tells us how everything works, although there are many unsolved problems and I guess there always will be. But science raises questions that it can never answer. Why did the big bang eventually lead to conscious beings who question the purpose of life and the existence of the Universe? This is where religion is necessary.

...

God certainly seems to be a rational Creator. That the entire terrestrial world is made from electrons, protons and neutrons and that a vacuum is filled with virtual particles demands incredible rationality.

...

You've got to have something other than just scientific laws. More science is not going to answer all the questions that we ask."

(In a 2002 letter to the author Tihomir Dimitrov, of the elaborately documented book called, *50 Nobel Laureates and Other Great Scientists Who Believe in God* (1995-2008), p.29-30, from which I received this and many other references, available online at http://nobelists.net/ .)

Sir **Fred Hoyle** (1915-2001),

arguably the greatest English mathematician and astronomer of the 20th century, who worked mainly in Cambridge during his long career in academia. In his autobiography he talks about his altered views on atheism – which came about from observing the sense of order in the laws of physics – although he still wasn't fond of what he called religious fundamentalism.

"Today we have the extremes of atheistic and fundamentalist views, and it is, in my opinion, a case of a plague on all their houses. The atheistic view that the Universe just happens to be here without purpose and yet with exquisite logical structure appears to me to be obtuse...

...

Once we see, however, that the probability of life originating at random is so utterly minuscule as to make the random concept absurd, it becomes sensible to think that the favourable properties of physics, on which life depends, are in every respect deliberate...It is, therefore, almost inevitable that our own measure of intelligence must reflect higher intelligence – even to the extreme idealized limit of God.

...

The notion that not only the biopolymers but the operating programme of a living cell could be arrived at by chance in a primordial organic soup here on Earth is evidently nonsense of a high order.

...

We owe our existence to another intelligence which created a structure for life as part of a deliberate plan.

Hoyle made some very important contributions to what is now the overall Big Bang theory (actually he gave the theory its name, during a BBC radio broadcast in 1949, but intended it as a kind of ironic criticism!), particularly on the question of nucleosynthesis in stars. An atheist up to that time, the following realisation left him "greatly shaken," and seeking some kind of intelligent design to the universe.

Would you not say to yourself, "Some super-calculating intellect must have designed the properties of the carbon atom, otherwise the chance of my finding such an atom through the blind forces of nature would be utterly minuscule." Of course you would... A common sense interpretation of the facts suggests that a superintellect has monkeyed with physics, as well as with chemistry and biology, and that there are no blind forces worth speaking about in nature. The numbers one calculates from the facts seem to me so overwhelming as to put this conclusion almost beyond question.

Here he gives a little more detail as to why he thinks that the random creation of the first life is mathematically impossible.

... enzymes are a large class of molecule that for the most part runs across the whole of biology, without there being any hint of their mode of origin....Enzymes are polypeptides (proteins).... their function....is determined by the particular sequence of amino acids in the polypeptide structure...There are...twenty distinct amino acids...and these simply must be in the correct position in the polypeptide structure...The chance of obtaining a suitable backbone can hardly be greater than one part in 1015, and the chance of obtaining the appropriate active site can hardly be greater than one part in 105...The two small probabilities...have to be multiplied, when they yield a chance of one part in 1020 of obtaining the required enzyme in a functioning form....there are about two thousand enzymes, and the chance of obtaining them all in a random trial is only one part in (1020)2000 = 1040,000, an outrageously small probability...this simple calculation wipes the idea entirely out of court."

(Sir Fred Hoyle, *Home is where the wind blows: chapters from a cosmologist's life* (Oxford, 1997), p.421, the second quote is from the *Guardian* newspaper in 2001, available at: http://www.guardian.co.uk/education/2001/aug/23/highereducatio n.peopleinscience , the third quote is from Sir Fred Hoyle, 'The Big Bang in Astronomy', in the *New Scientist* 19th Nov 1981, p.527:
http://books.google.ie/books?
id=riW31Fy4kpkC&printsec=frontcover&lr=&rview=1#v=onepa ge&q&f=false ,
the fourth series of quotes from:
http://www.answers.com/topic/fred-hoyle , the second last quote is from Fred Hoyle, *The Universe: Past and Present Reflections,* Engineering and Science, November, 1981. pp. 8–12, and the final quote is from Sir Fred Hoyle and Chandra Wickramasinghe, *Evolution from Space* (London, 1981), p.19-21.)

Dr **Dean H Kenyon**,

who received his PhD in 1965 from Stanford, is a Professor of Biology at San Francisco State University.

"It is my conviction that if any professional biologist will take adequate time to examine carefully the assumptions upon which the macroevolutionary doctrine rests, and the observational and laboratory evidence that bears on the problem of origins, he/she will conclude that there are substantial reasons for doubting the truth of this doctrine. Moreover, I believe that a scientifically sound creationist view of origins is not only possible, but is to be preferred over the evolutionary view."

(In a 1984 affidavit prepared for the Edwards v. Aguillard court case, available at: http://www.talkorigins.org/faqs/edwards-v-aguillard/kenyon.html .)

Dr **Kenneth J Hsu** (1929-),

born in Nanjing in China he was awarded a PhD from the University of California in 1953, and from 1967-1994 was Professor of Experimental Geology at the Swiss Federal Institute of Technology, Zurich, and 'he was the convener of the First International Conference on Paleoceanography, and was the founder of the journal Paleoceanography'.

"We have had enough of the Darwinian fallacy. It is time that we cry: 'The emperor has no clothes.' "
(K. Hsu, *Darwin's Three Mistakes* in *Geology*, vol. 14, 1986, p.534.)

Dr **Christian Boehmer Anfinsen** (1916-1995),

awarded a PhD in biochemistry from Harvard Medical School in 1943, won the 1972 Nobel Prize for Chemistry for his work on Ribonuclease – crucial to the question of how DNA, and hence the first life, could have come about –, and was Professor of Biophysical Chemistry at Johns Hopkins 1982-1995.

"I think only an idiot can be an atheist. We must admit that there exists an incomprehensible power or force with limitless foresight and knowledge that started the whole universe going in the first place."
(Henry Margenau and Roy Abraham Varghese, ed., *Cosmos, Bios, and Theos* (La Salle, 1992), p.139.)

Professor **Stephen William Hawking** (1942-),

Lucasian Professor of Mathematics at Cambridge University 1979-2009 and the very well known author of books on the origin of the universe, concedes an interesting point here although he isn't a theist.

"The laws of science, as we know them at present, contain many fundamental numbers, like the size of the electric charge of the electron and the ratio of the masses of the proton and the electron....The remarkable fact is that the values of these numbers seem to have been very finely adjusted to make possible the development of life.

...

The universe and the Laws of Physics seem to have been specifically designed for us. If any one of about 40 physical qualities had more than slightly different values, life as we know it could not exist: Either atoms would not be stable, or they wouldn't combine into molecules, or the stars wouldn't form heavier elements, or the universe would collapse before life could develop, and so on..."

(Stephen Hawking, *A Brief History of Time* (New York, 1998), p.129, and the second quote is from an article entitled: '*Hawking brings 'Universe' on PBS down to earth*', in the Austin American-Statesmen, October 19th, 1997.)

Dr **Jonathan Wells** (1942-),

in 1994 was awarded a PhD in Molecular and Cell Biology from Berkeley and is one of the best known figures articulating the Intelligent Design perspective in biology.

"I think in fifty years, Darwinian evolution will be gone from the science curriculum...I think people will look back on it and ask how anyone could, in their right mind, have believed this, because it's so implausible when you look at the evidence."

(I don't know where the quote itself comes from but you can see a good video by him here which corroborate the above opinions: http://www.youtube.com/watch?v=raW6BQscwh4 .)

Dr **Jonathan Tennebaum,**

received his doctorate in mathematics from the University of California at San Diego in 1973, he was a Postdoctoral fellow at Cambridge (1974), Assistant Professor of Mathematics at the University of Copenhagen (1975-1979) etc etc (his languages by the way are: English, German, French, Russian, Danish, Chinese (Mandarin), some Spanish) and has this to say on evolution.

"Now, it is easy to show that Darwinism, one of the pillars of modern biology, is nothing but a kind of cult, a cult religion. I am not exaggerating. It has no scientific validity whatsoever. Darwin's so-called theory of evolution is based on absurdly irrational propositions, which did not come from scientific observations, but were artificially introduced from the outside, for political-ideological reasons."

(http://www.bibliotecapleyades.net/ciencia/ciencia_scientificd ictatorship.htm . Incidentally he gave a presentation to the Russian Duma predicting the current global financial crash, available:
http://www.schillerinstitute.org/duma/duma_tenenbaum.html .)

Professor **John Polkinghorne** KBE,

Professor of Mathematical Physics at Cambridge 1968-79, and President of Queens' College Cambridge 1988-1996, who, as you can see, had a distinguished career as a physicist at Cambridge University before becoming an Anglican priest in 1982.

"When you realize that the laws of nature must be incredibly finely tuned to produce the universe we see...that conspires to plant the idea that the universe did not just happen, but that there must be a purpose behind it."
(*Newsweek* 20th July 1998 available at
http://www.washingtonpost.com/wp-srv/newsweek/science_of_god/scienceofgod.htm .)

Professor **Charles Hard Townes** (1915-),

was Provost and Professor of Physics at MIT, a 1964 Nobel Laureate, and later a Professor at Berkeley (he, and his students, actually coined for the first time the word 'laser').

"Many have a feeling that somehow intelligence must have been involved in the laws of the universe.

Here writing in 2001:

Religion, with its theological reflection, builds on faith. Science too builds on faith. How? For successful science of the type we know, we must have faith that the universe is governed by reliable laws and, further, that these laws can be discovered by human inquiry. The logic of human inquiry is trustworthy only if nature is itself logical. Science operates with the faith that human logic can in the long run understand nature's laws and that they are dependable. This is the faith of reason.

We scientists work on the basis of a fundamental assumption regarding reason in nature and reason in the human mind, an assumption that is held as a cardinal principle of faith. Yet this faith is so automatically and generally accepted that we hardly recognize it as an essential basis for science.

Another quote from that scientist speaking in 2005:

Intelligent design, as one sees it from a scientific point of view, seems to be quite real. This is a very special universe: it's remarkable that it came out just this way. If the laws of physics weren't just the way they are, we couldn't be here at all. The sun couldn't be there, the laws of gravity and nuclear laws and magnetic theory, quantum mechanics, and so on have to be just the way they are for us to be here.

Some scientists argue that "well, there's an enormous number of universes and each one is a little different. This one just happened to turn out right." Well, that's a postulate, and it's a pretty fantastic postulate – it assumes there really are an enormous number of universes and that the laws could be different for each of them. The other possibility is that ours was planned, and that's why it has come out so specially."

(*Newsweek* 20th July 1998, available at http://new.schoolnotes.com/files/bachynsky/Science%20Finds%20God.pdf , the second quote is from Charles Hard Townes, "Logic and Uncertainties in Science and Religion," in *Science and the Future of Mankind: Science for Man and Man for Science* (Vatican, 2001), p.300, and the last quote is from http://berkeley.edu/news/media/releases/2005/06/17_townes.shtml.)

Professor **Paul Davies** (1946-),

of Arizona State University, previously of the University of Cambridge and Professor of Physics at Imperial College, London, the 2002 winner of the Faraday Prize by the Royal Society etc etc, writing here in the New York Times in 2007.

"All science proceeds on the assumption that nature is ordered in a rational and intelligible way. You couldn't be a scientist if you thought the universe was a meaningless jumble of odds and ends haphazardly juxtaposed. When physicists probe to a deeper level of subatomic structure, or astronomers extend the reach of their instruments, they expect to encounter additional elegant mathematical order. And so far this faith has been justified.

The most refined expression of the rational intelligibility of the cosmos is found in the laws of physics, the fundamental rules on which nature runs. The laws of gravitation and electromagnetism, the laws that regulate the world within the atom, the laws of motion — all are expressed as tidy mathematical relationships. But where do these laws come from? And why do they have the form that they do?

When I was a student, the laws of physics were regarded as completely off limits. The job of the scientist, we were told, is to discover the laws and apply them, not inquire into their provenance. The laws were treated as "given" — imprinted on the universe like a maker's mark at the moment of cosmic birth — and fixed forevermore. Therefore, to be a scientist, you had to have faith that the universe is governed by dependable, immutable, absolute, universal, mathematical laws of an unspecified origin. You've got to believe that these laws won't fail, that we won't wake up tomorrow to find heat flowing from cold to hot, or the speed of light changing by the hour.

Over the years I have often asked my physicist colleagues why the laws of physics are what they are. The answers vary from "that's not a scientific question" to "nobody knows." The favorite reply is, "There is no reason they are what they are — they just are." The idea that the laws exist reasonlessly is deeply anti-rational. After all, the very essence of a scientific explanation of some phenomenon is that the world is ordered logically and that there are reasons things are as they are. If one traces these reasons all the way down to the bedrock of reality — the laws of physics — only to find that reason then deserts us, it makes a mockery of science."

And elsewhere the same author notes that:

"Atheists claim that the laws [of physics] exist reasonlessly and that the universe is ultimately absurd. As a scientist, I find this hard to accept. There must be an unchanging rational ground in which the logical, orderly nature of the universe was rooted."

(*New York Times* of the 24th of February 2007, available at: http://www.nytimes.com/2007/11/24/opinion/24davies.html , and the second quote from Paul Davies, *What happened before the Big Bang*, an essay in Russell Standard, *God for the 21st Century* (London, 2000), p.12, available at: http://books.google.com/books?id=C7g2WSzd6IcC&pg=PA10 .)

Professor **William Daniel Phillips** (1948-),

received his PhD in physics from MIT in 1976, was awarded the Nobel Prize in physics in 1997 for his work on lasers, and later installed as the Professor of Physics at the University of Maryland.

"I believe in God. In fact, I believe in a personal God who acts in and interacts with the creation. I believe that the observations about the orderliness of the physical universe, and the apparently exceptional fine-tuning of the conditions of the universe for the development of life suggest that an intelligent Creator is responsible.

Then in response to the question "Dr. Phillips, why does the universe obey any laws at all?" asked of him during a debate at the Whitehouse in 1998 he replied.

"Well, that's a really good question. It's the kind of question that has intrigued and vexed scientists and, I suppose, philosophers and theologians for a long time. It's really quite remarkable.

All of the wonderful things Professor Hawking talked about can actually be described in a very small number of relatively simple equations and then a lot of complicated mathematics. Why is it that the universe is so simple? Why is it that it follows mathematical laws?

Well, people have speculated about this, and one possible answer is that if the universe had been any different from what it is, we wouldn't be here. That is, if the laws of the universe hadn't been what they are or if there were no laws at all, it would have been impossible for life to have evolved. It would have been impossible for us to have evolved to the point that we could ask that question. So that's sometimes called the 'anthropic principle.' Not perhaps to put too much emphasis on people, but it probably applies to amoebas as well, that they wouldn't have been able to evolve either.

On the other hand, there is another answer, which isn't actually that far from that answer, and if you're a person with religious faith, as I am, you could answer that the reason we have a universe that follows laws is because God decided to make the universe in that way, because God wanted us to develop the way we have and to evolve in the way that we have; and that this is, of course, a philosophical and theological answer and it has more to do with one's faith than one's scientific conclusions, but it's an answer that I like very much and that I don't find very different from the first one."

(The first quote is from a 2002 letter to the author T Dimitrov: http://nobelist.tripod.com/sitebuildercontent/sitebuilderfiles/50-nobelists.pdf,
and the second from http://archives.clintonpresidentialcenter.org/?u=030698-speech-by-president-at-millennium-lecture-series.htm .)

Index

3
30 years war......................................66

A
Abiogeneis, Law of..........................58
Ager, Dr David Victor......................61
Albiunus (Procurator)......................10
Alexandria (Egypt).........7, 10, 43, 186
Ampere, Andre Marie....................261
Ananius (High Priest)......................10
Anaxagoras............159, 160, 180, 219
Anfinsen, Dr Christian Boehmer..326
Anicius, Cerialis...............................12
Anselm, St......................................208
Antioch (Syria).............................132
Aquinas O.P., St Thomas...18, 19, 25, 26, 29, 53, 54, 94, 113, 115, 116, 129, 209
Arbour Hill................................81, 82
Arbuthnot, Dr John......141, 152, 153, 156, 239, 240
Archbold OFM (Cap.), Fr Nicholas 68
Archer, Gleason..........................7, 93
Archimedes..............................47, 189
Aristodemus...........................161, 163
Aristotle 19, 20, 22-26, 46, 50, 51, 53, 57, 95, 97, 102, 103, 115, 129, 151, 155, 174, 177, 182, 185
Assisi (Italy).....................................27
Atlanta (USA)............................79, 82
Augustine (of Hippo), St. 46, 116, 119
Augustus (Emperor)....................9, 93
Avicenna..26

B
Babbage, Charles...................267, 271
Bacon, Sir Francis.....35, 95, 201, 204
Bacteria, antibiotic resistant..........138
Ballyogan (Co. Clare).....................70
Bellings, Richard.............................66
Bentley, Richard............................233
Beria, Lavrentit........................90, 100
Berkeley, George...........242, 243, 272
Berlinski, Dr David.........................58

Bible...
  New Testament.......7, 10, 15, 117, 122, 123, 125, 131, 133
  New Testament............................
    First Letter to the Corinthians
   16
    Gospel of St John...........6, 132
  Old Testament. .93, 122, 123, 125, 130, 186
    1 Kings..................................5
    2 Kings..................................5
    Deuteronomy........................6
    Genesis.....53-55, 57, 219, 270
    Isaiah..................6, 7, 124, 125
    Joshua...................................6
    Numbers................................5
    Psalms........................123, 124
    Wisdom......................186, 187
Big Bang Theory 25, 51-53, 120, 154, 319, 322, 323, 334
Blume, Ted......................................79
Bodin, Jean....................................205
Bohemia....................................66, 74
Bollandists.......................................65
Boole, Dr George..........................264
Borel, Dr Emile..........................45, 96
Bou, Madeleine le...........................78
Boyle, Robert..37, 159, 160, 218, 221
Braun, Wernher von......................303
Brisbane (Australia)......................146
Britain......................................47, 189
Bruodin OFM, Fr Anthony.............70
Burke, Edmund.......................89, 100

C
Caesarea (Israel)..........................9, 94
Callahan, Dr Philip.........................79
Caltech (Pasadena, California, USA)
....53, 291
Canada..............................80, 96, 314
Capuchins (an order of Franciscans)
....68, 69
Carthage (Tunisia).........................94

Castanon Gomez, Dr Ricardo.........78
Chain, Prof Ernst...................317, 318
China............135, 144, 243, 249, 325
Chinese Academy of Social Sciences
....91
Cicero, Marcus Tullius.....37, 46, 188, 203, 225, 279
Clare...................................70-73, 99
Cleinias.................................167-171
Clement of Rome, St.....................132
Clongowes Wood College...............84
Colmcille, St..................................64
Cologne (Germany)..................68, 69
Commentarius Rinuccinianus...68, 98
Compton, Prof Arthur....................289
Conant, Dr James Bryant..............302
Confederation of Kilkenny.............66
Conyers (Georgia, USA).................79
Corinth (Greece)....................16, 196
Craddock OFM, Fr Roger.............135
Crick, Sir Francis.....................44, 96
Cyrenius (procurator)......................94

D

Daly OP, Fr Daniel...................69, 98
Darwin, Charles..55, 58-62, 140, 148, 274, 298-300, 307, 318, 325, 329
Darwinism.55, 97, 299, 315, 316, 329
Davies, Prof Paul...................333, 334
Dawkins, Prof Richard......48, 61, 120
Dead Sea Scrolls...........6, 7, 125, 131
Denton, Dr Michael.......................60
Descartes, Rene. 32, 57, 95, 103, 208-211
Dhiban...5
Dillon, Sir Robert...........................66
Dimitrov, Tihomir.........318, 320, 336
DNA....39, 43-45, 48, 55, 59-61, 137, 154, 156, 282, 326
Donaghmore (Co. Dublin)..............66
Dooley, Dr James.....................69, 70
Dublin Castle.................................66
Dublin Review...............................31
Duff, Adam..................................135
Dundalk (Co. Louth).......................81
Dwight, Dr Thomas......................288
Dysert (Co. Westmeath).................67

E

Eccles, Sir John...............51, 308, 309
Ecuador...............................74, 75, 77
Edison, Thomas Alva....................281
Edwards, Anthony William Fairbank
....149
Einstein, Albert 52, 53, 129, 242, 285, 286
Emmerich, Anne Catherine.......74, 77, 102
Ephesus (Turkey)................16, 77, 99
Erdmann, Erika............................309
Euclid.............................43, 224, 236
Evening Herald..............................81
Evil, existence of..........................103
Evodius, St...................................132
Evolution....30, 55, 56, 59-62, 78, 96-98, 135-138, 140, 148-150, 153, 156, 158, 274, 278, 282, 284, 291, 292, 299-301, 307, 310, 314-316, 318, 323, 328, 329
Evolution.....................................329
Exorcism.......................................80

F

Faith, and Reason.........................109
Farabi, Al-.....................................26
Faraday, Prof Michael...265, 266, 333
Fatima (Portugal)...........................65
Festus (Procurator).........................10
Fisher, Ronald A...................141, 148
Fitzgerald, James FitzMaurice........66
Fitzsimon S.J., Fr Henry............66, 98
Flew, Professor Antony.47, 48, 53, 97
Fossil Record......................59, 60, 97
Fowler, Nancy................................79
France.....46, 64, 68, 78, 89, 211, 214, 252
France..244
Friedmann Alexander.....................52

G

Galgani, St Gemma........................77
Germany........68, 74, 78, 89, 302, 317
Germany......................................277
Gibson, Mel...................................77
Gould, Dr Stephen J.......................60

Grant, Dr Valerie J.................150, 156
Greece...........................110, 160, 166
Grey, Arthur (Viceroy of Ireland)...66
Guibert of Nogent.....................64, 98

H
Hadrian (Emperor)..........................12
Haldane, Dr John Scott.........282, 283
Hamilton, Sir William Rowan.....272, 273
Harshbarger, Jeff.............................80
Harvey, William......................57, 207
Hawking, Prof Stephen William...327
Heisenberg, Dr Werner.................295
Helmont, Jan Baptist von.................57
Herschel, Sir John.........................278
Hewish, Prof Antony.....................319
Hippo (Greek philosopher)............182
Hippocrates...................................166
Hogben, Dr George.........................79
Homer..162
Hoyle, Sir Fred....43, 62, 98, 321, 323
Hsu, Dr Kenneth J.........................325
Hume, David........................254, 255

I
Ignatius of Antoioch, St................132
Immaculate Conception..................77
Interest, church prohibition on charging (loans).............................115
Ireland..28, 64, 66, 68, 70, 72, 73, 81, 83, 89, 134, 135, 155, 242
Irenaeus, St...................................132
Irvine, Doreen.................................80

J
James, St (Apostle)..........................10
James, William H..................150, 157
Janet, Dr Pierre...............................78
Jesus Torres, Mother Mariana de....74
John (of Damascus), St...................46
John the Apostle, St......................132
John, St (the Baptist)...............11, 292
Jordan...5
Josephus, Flavius............................10
Joule, James Prescott....................275
Judaea....................................8, 9, 11
Justin the Martyr, St........................93

K
Kant, Immanuel............258, 259, 273
Kelly OC, Fr Ralph.......................135
Kelvin, Lord (Sir William Thompson) 278-280
Kenyon, Dr Dean H......................324
Kenyon, Sir Frederick G...................7
Kepler, Johannes.....96, 205, 206, 269
Kildare (Co. Kildare)....82, 84, 85, 87
Kilmihil Holy Well (Co. Clare).......71
Kobe (Japan)................................146
Kos (Greece)................................166
Kyteler, Alice...............................135

L
Laws of physics...42, 48, 55, 96, 126, 127, 312, 321, 327, 332-334
Laws of physics....................272, 291
Leibniz, Gottfried Wilhelm .173, 209, 231
Lemaitre S.J., Fr Georges.........52, 97
Leslie, John....................................96
Lewis, Clive Staples. .31, 35, 36, 155, 293
Limerick....................................69, 70
Linnaeus, Carl.......................256, 257
Lismore (Co. Waterford).......155, 218
Locke, John..........................222, 230
Lourdes (France)....................65, 113
Louvain (Belgium)..........................52
Lovtrup, Soren..............................316
Lynch, Fr John..........................67, 98

M
MacBrody family.....................70, 99
MacManus, Gerard.........................81
MacManus, Terence.......................81
Maimonides....................................26
Marconi, Guglielmo.....................287
Masonry..74
Mathews, Dean Shailer................292
Matthews, Dr Leonard Harrison...307
Matthews, Robert...........................61
Melanippides................................162
Mesha Stele......................................5
Michael, St (the Archangel).......70-73
Mill, John Stuart...........................262

Millikan, Dr Robert A............291, 292
Moivre, Abraham de 41, 96, 152, 238, 241
Moloney, Margaret...........................70
More, Prof Louis Trenchard..........284
Moreno, Gabriel Garcia...................74
Morneau, Roger................................80
Morowitz, Dr Harold.................43, 96
Muggeridge, Malcolm...................314

N

Nablus (Palestine)............................93
Nanotechnology.......................59, 310
Natural Law....................................114
Natural selection........55, 61, 135-138, 140, 141, 148, 150, 153, 278, 282, 298, 299, 315, 316
Needham, John Turberville........56, 57
Neophytes College...........................70
Nero (Emperor)..........................11, 12
Neumann, St Theresa.......................77
New York (USA)..48, 79, 96, 97, 198, 215, 263, 281, 288, 292, 295, 327, 333, 334
Newman, Cardinal John Henry........31
Newton, Sir Isaac...57, 112, 231, 232, 234, 235, 238, 245, 248, 269, 301
Nicea, Council of...................114, 116
Nigram, Fr Patrick...........................66
Nugent OFM (Cap.), Fr Lavallin....67

O

O'Carroll, Gerry........................81, 82
O'Connell OFM (Cap.), Fr Robert..68
O'Gorman, Thomas..........................70
O'Queely PP, Fr Dermot..................72
Orrery (a model of the solar system) 47, 189, 190

P

P52 (fragment of St John's Gospel). 6, 132
Padre Pio (Franceso Forgione, St Pio of Pietrelcina).............................65, 77
Palestine....................................93, 94
Paley, Revd William........................37
Pasadena (California, USA)...53, 291, 310

Pascal, Blaise. .46, 211, 214, 215, 314
Pasteur, Dr Louis...............57, 58, 276
Patrick, St..64
Paul, St................................16, 196, 226
Penzias, Dr Arno Allan........54, 55, 97
Peppered moths...............................61
Peter, St...132
Petronella de Meath......................135
Phillips, Prof William Daniel........335
Philo..7, 13
Pilate, Pontius.......7, 9, 10, 13, 93, 94, 124
Pitman, Michael George...............315
Pius IX, Pope...................................77
Planck, Prof Max............89, 296, 297
Plato. 28, 46, 102, 161, 167, 173, 174, 199, 202, 245
Pliny the Younger...........................13
Plotinus.....28, 95, 103, 155, 199, 200
Plutarch, Lucius Mestrius.............197
Polkinghorne, Prof John...............330
Polycarp, St...........................132, 155
Polycletus......................................162
Portugal...69
Posidonius...............................47, 189
Prague (Czech Republic)..........70, 99
Prandy, Scott...................................79
Prigogine, Viscount Ilya.................46
Promissory materialism. 51, 151, 308, 309
Proofs of God's Existence..................
    Causation, Proof from...............22
    Degrees of Perfection, Proof from 28
    Fine Tuned Universe Argument 18, 42, 55, 96
    Intelligent Design (Teleology). 36, 39, 42, 45, 51, 55, 56, 126, 173, 216, 254, 278, 304, 310, 322, 332
    Motion, Proof from...................18
    Necessary Being, Proof from the 25
    Ontological Argument.............208
    Sex ratio. .141, 144-151, 153, 154, 156, 157
Puerto Rico......................................79

Q
Quinolone (antibiotic)..........139, 156
R
Raup, Dr David.........................60, 97
Ray, John...............................216, 217
Resurrection......16, 94, 125, 132, 133
Rokeby, Thomas de......................135
Romsey (England).......................145
Rousseau, Jean-Jacques........252, 253
Rudy, Dr Lloyd..............................80
Russia..........................52, 90, 91, 135
Russia...311
S
Salts Textile factory (Tullamore, Co. Offaly)...85
Sanchez, Dr Ramon........................79
Sanders, Fr Nicholas......................66
Sanhedrin (Jewish Council)....10, 122
Sartre, Jean Paul...........................313
Schnoebelen, Bill...........................80
Scotus, Dr John Duns.....................27
Scythia..................................47, 188
Seneca...............32, 95, 192, 194, 195
Siemens, Ernst Werner von...........277
Signs of God (documentary)...........79
Smalley, Prof Richard..................310
Socrates32, 46, 95, 110, 161-165, 174
Solzhenitsyn, Alexander. 90, 100, 311
Spain.........................26, 135, 144
Spallanzani, Abbe Lazzaro........56, 57
Stellar, William..............................79
Stigmata................65, 77-79, 99, 113
Strasbourg (France).................37, 220
Suetonius........................11-13, 16, 93
Sullivan SJ, Fr John..................84-88
Summa Theologica...................18, 95
Sussmilch, Johann Peter...............143
Sweden................................149, 316
Swift, Dr Jonathan 141, 186, 236, 237

Syria..94
T
Tacitus, Cornelius..........11-13, 16, 93
Tahmisian, Dr Theodore Newton..301
Tennebaum, Dr Jonathan..............329
Tertullian..94
Tesoriero, Ron................................79
Thales....................................182, 219
Thompson, Dr William Robin......298
Thompson, Sir Joseph J................290
Tiberius (Emperor)......8, 9, 11, 16, 94
Townes, Prof Charles Hard...331, 332
Trajan (Emperor)....................13, 132
Trent, Council of...................114, 116
Turkey......................................16, 77
U
UNESCO..45
Uzbekistan......................................26
V
Vatican II..............................122, 123
Velasquez, Umberto.......................79
Vespasian (Emperor)......................12
Volta, Alessandro.........................260
Voltaire (Francois-Marie Arouet)...37, 89, 244, 251, 252
W
Wald, Dr George......................56, 97
Wells, Dr Jonathan.......................328
Willesee, Mike.........................35, 78
Wittgenstein, Dr Ludwig......293, 294
World Health Organisation..........317
Wuerzburg OFM (Cap.), Fr Bonaventura von............................68
X
Xenophon.......................46, 161, 165
Z
Zeuxis..162
....51

www.ingramcontent.com/pod-product-compliance
Lightning Source LLC
Chambersburg PA
CBHW030228170426
43201CB00006B/144